"The Church as the Image of the Trinity"

W.E.S.T Theological Monograph Series

Wales Evangelical School of Theology (WEST) has produced a stream of successful PhD candidates over the years, whose work has consistently challenged the boundaries of traditional understanding in both systematic and biblical theology. Now, for the first time, this series makes significant examples of this ground-breaking research accessible to a wider readership.

"The Church as the Image of the Trinity"

A Critical Evaluation of Miroslav Volf's Ecclesial Model

Kevin J. Bidwell

Foreword by Robert Letham

WIPF & STOCK · Eugene, Oregon

"THE CHURCH AS THE IMAGE OF THE TRINITY"
A Critical Evaluation of Miroslav Volf's Ecclesial Model

Copyright © 2011 Kevin J. Bidwell. All rights reserved. Except for brief quotations in critical publications or reviews, no part of this book may be reproduced in any manner without prior written permission from the publisher. Write: Permissions, Wipf and Stock Publishers, 199 W. 8th Ave., Suite 3, Eugene, OR 97401.

Wipf & Stock
An Imprint of Wipf and Stock Publishers
199 W. 8th Ave., Suite 3
Eugene, OR 97401

www.wipfandstock.com

ISBN 13: 978-1-61097-373-1

Manufactured in the U.S.A.

Contents

Foreword / vii

List of Abbreviations / ix

1. Introduction / 1
2. The Influence of Jürgen Moltmann upon Volf's Theological Paradigm in *After Our Likeness* / 11
3. Other Theological Influences upon Volf in Relation to *After Our Likeness* / 24
4. Volf's Trinitarian and Ecclesial Paradigm / 41
5. Free Church Ecclesiology: John Smyth as Volf's Chosen Ecclesial Representative / 57
6. Volf's Dialogue with Joseph Ratzinger / 89
7. A Critical Evaluation of Volf's Dialogue with Ratzinger / 114
8. Volf's Dialogue with John Zizioulas / 123
9. A Critical Evaluation of Volf's Dialogue with Zizioulas / 143
10. A Critical Evaluation of "The Ecclesiality of the Church" / 162
11. A Critical Evaluation of "Faith, Person, and Church" / 184
12. A Critical Evaluation of "Trinity and Church" / 192
13. A Critical Evaluation of "Structures of the Church" / 213
14. A Critical Evaluation of "The Catholicity of the Church" / 229
15. Conclusion / 235

Appendix: Suggested Reading / 241
Bibliography / 245
Scripture Index / 265
Index of Names / 267

Foreword

IT IS MY PLEASURE to commend this book by Kevin Bidwell, the substance of his thesis for the PhD degree awarded by the University of Wales, Trinity Saint David, in 2010. As his supervisor, I had the privilege of many fruitful and stimulating discussions on his work, and it is a delight to see it now in print.

The importance of Dr. Bidwell's subject can hardly be overestimated. Miroslav Volf needs no introduction to anyone even vaguely familiar with the current theological landscape. His distinguished career has taken him from Croatia to Yale, via Fuller Theological Seminary and the University of Tübingen. His many writings have had a strong focus on a social doctrine of the Trinity, a liberationist theology, and an egalitarian ecclesiology.

Dr. Bidwell's research into Volf's Trinitarianism is both thorough and critical. Social Trinitarianism has gained great vogue in recent decades. In many ways it is a reaction against a perceived tendency to modalism in the Western church. Its stress on three Persons in "relationships" of mutuality has engendered criticisms of tritheistic tendencies. The doctrine of perichoresis, in which the Fathers recognized that the three Trinitarian persons mutually and indivisibly indwell one another, has been updated by many feminist social Trinitarians to speak of an eternal "dance" in which the three revolve around each other in pure mutuality, without privileges and power. In Volf's hands, this reshaped doctrine of perichoresis undergirds his egalitarianism in ecclesial and social terms, in which the church is a society of equals, understood in a wide ecumenical context.

Dr. Bidwell explores Volf's use of his acknowledged sources at some length. Jürgen Moltmann, Volf's own research supervisor, has strongly influenced him, and many of Moltmann's interests are also evident in his work. Readers may also be interested in Volf's use of the writings of the Separatist leader, John Smyth, which Dr. Bidwell subjects to enlightening scrutiny. One of the clear weaknesses in Moltmann is his use of sources, picking extracts from a range of writers out of context, without discussing their purpose, and deploying them in virtual proof-text fashion for his own unconnected agenda. Dr. Bidwell asks how far Volf follows in this tradition.

Dr. Bidwell's analysis of Volf's writing is incisive, highly critical, and at times provocative. In particular, he points to a lack of coherent biblical exegesis underlying Volf's project. He subjects his social Trinitarianism to an extensive and penetrating critique.

This book is a significant contribution to debate on Volf, social Trinitarianism, the doctrine of the Trinity, and the application to the life of the church. It is a contribution that cannot be ignored.

Robert Letham
Senior Lecturer in Systematic and Historical Theology
Wales Evangelical School of Theology

Abbreviations

ANF	*Ante-Nicene Fathers*
AOL	*After Our Likeness*, by Miroslav Volf
BAC	*Being as Communion*, by John Zizioulas
BEM	*Baptism, Eucharist and Ministry*
CAO	*Communion and Otherness*, by John Zizioulas
CCC	*Catechism of the Catholic Church*
EE	*Exclusion and Embrace*, by Miroslav Volf
ITC	*Introduction to Christianity*, by Joseph Ratzinger
LXX	Septuagint
NCC	Niceno-Constantinopolitan Creed (381)
NPNF	*Nicene and Post-Nicene Fathers*
NT	New Testament
OC	Orthodox Church
OT	Old Testament
RCC	Roman Catholic Church
WCF	Westminster Confession of Faith (1646)

THE TRANSLATION OF ELIZABETHAN ENGLISH

Where Elizabethan English is used in source materials that are quoted, these references are inserted using modern English. For example, in the writings of John Smyth or John Robinson, their works in their original form contain the use of many dated words, which some readers may find difficult. It is hoped that this move does not detract from the accuracy of the works cited but rather attains an enhanced readability and comprehension of their theologies.

BIBLE TRANSLATION USED

English Standard Version (ESV), London: Harper Collins, 2002.

DATES OF THEOLOGIANS AND CHURCH FATHERS

The birth–death dates that are inserted into this book are mainly taken from *The Concise Oxford Dictionary of the Christian Church*, ed. E. A. Livingstone (Oxford: OUP, 2000).

1

Introduction

A RESURGENCE OF INTEREST IN THE DOCTRINE OF THE TRINITY

"PERHAPS NO AREA OF Christian theology has received such intense and fruitful work in the last century as our understanding of the Trinity,"[1] according to Miroslav Volf and Michael Welker. Indeed, the latter half of the twentieth century has experienced a significant theological renaissance concerning the doctrine of the Trinity and Karl Barth (1886–1968) is credited by many as having being influential upon this resurgence of Trinitarian interest.[2] R. W. Jenson believes that it is "from Barth that twentieth-century theology has learned that the doctrine of the Trinity has explanatory and interpretative use for the whole of theology; it is by him that the current vigorous revival of Trinitarian reflection was enabled."[3] In 1967, Karl Rahner mournfully remarked that "should the doctrine of the Trinity have to be dropped as false, the major part of religious literature could well remain virtually unchanged."[4] Almost all Christian theological traditions have since joined this chorus of support for a renewed emphasis upon the Trinity.

One of the features of this development has been an understanding that the doctrine of God is the doctrine of the Trinity and vice versa. An

---
1. Volf and Welker, *God's Life in Trinity*, xiii.
2. Barth, *Church Dogmatics*, 1975.
3. Jenson, "Karl Barth," 1:42.
4. Rahner, *Trinity*, 10–11.

excellent example of this is Thomas F. Torrance in *The Christian Doctrine of God: One Being Three Persons*, and he introduces his work by stating:

> This monograph is devoted to clarifying understanding of the most profound article of the Christian Faith, the doctrine of the Holy Trinity. This exposition takes place within the frame of the biblical and Nicene tradition of the One Holy Catholic and Apostolic Church. It is heavily influenced by Greek Patristic and Reformed theology with particular acknowledgments of debt to Athanasius the Great . . . and Karl Barth.[5]

There is a noticeable recovery of patristic studies within contemporary Trinitarian theologies, and this often leads to a fresh marriage of both Eastern and Western schools of thought. Additionally, studies have widened their theological horizons to allow the doctrine of the Trinity to inform their whole frame of theological understanding.

Colin E. Gunton exemplifies these new thought patterns by incorporating Eastern Trinitarian theologies into his research and writings. The key influences for him are most notably the Cappadocian fathers (Gregory of Nazianzus, Basil of Caesarea, and Gregory of Nyssa), John of Damascus, and Gunton's contemporary, John D. Zizioulas. This leads Gunton to explore the differences between *Eastern* and *Western* Trinities and to critically analyze what he perceives to be deficiencies within Western theological thought, a supposed result of Augustine of Hippo's work on the Holy Trinity.[6]

Perhaps one of the most significant ecumenical links that is commonly made between the doctrine of the Trinity and the doctrine of the church is the theme of *koinōnia*, or more simply, communion. Zizioulas makes a significant contribution in *Being as Communion: Studies in Personhood and the Church* to the development of a Trinitarian ecclesiology, and both he and Gunton reach the same conclusion in answer to the enquiry as to what the church, as part of God's creation, should reflect; the answer is apparently found in the word *koinōnia*.[7] Together they believe that this word is best translated as "community or perhaps

---

5. Torrance, *Christian Doctrine of God*, ix.

6. Gunton, "Eastern and Western Trinities," in *Father, Son and Holy Spirit*, 43–44; Gunton, *Promise of Trinitarian Theology*, 31–57; Gunton, "The Church," in *Theology*.

7. Gunton, *Promise of Trinitarian Theology*, 71–73; Zizioulas, *Being as Communion*, 134–35.

sociality."⁸ Zizioulas sets out to demonstrate that the "church is the image of the Triune God" and "not simply an institution, but a mode of existence, a way of being."⁹ Thus the being of God is clearly understood to be bound up with ecclesiology, while his view on ecclesial personhood sees humans created as *imago Trinitatis*.¹⁰

New lines of fruitful enquiry have also begun to emerge, and this has led to new questions for theological reflection concerning the practical outworking of this fresh appreciation of the Triune God. The notion that the church is the image of the Trinity is gathering momentum in the evangelical and Western world and is no longer a concept embraced solely by the Eastern Orthodox Church. Velli-Matti Kärkkäinen recognizes the growing significance of *koinōnia* for many ecclesiologists; Volf wholeheartedly endorses a Trinitarian motif; Robert Letham, Donald Macleod, and Torrance likewise echo the need for Reformed churches to be reenvisioned with a perspective rooted in the triune life of God.¹¹

Volf specifically catches sight of the potential for the recovery of the doctrine of the Trinity to enrich and inform all aspects of ecclesiology. With this in mind, he has developed a dynamic thesis that grasps this theological challenge, proverbially speaking, with both hands. His proposal *After Our Likeness: The Church as the Image of the Trinity* (*AOL*) attempts to ensure that a Trinitarian framework informs the relationship between persons and community for Christian theology. It is this thesis that is to be the prime focus of this theological research, which also includes a critical appreciation and evaluation of all aspects of his proposal.

In reflecting on these large-scale theological advances, though, there is little room for complacency, because, as Letham points out, "in the West, the Trinity has in practice been relegated to such an extent that most Christians are little more than practical modalists."¹² He further adds that many people regard an appreciation of the Trinity to be "of no real consequence for daily living."¹³ Could a fresh focus on the Trinity

8. Gunton, *Promise of Trinitarian Theology*, 73.

9. Zizioulas, *Being as Communion*, 15, 19.

10. Zizioulas, *Communion and Otherness*, 249.

11. Kärkkäinen, *Introduction to Ecclesiology*, 160; Volf, *After Our Likeness*; Letham, *Through Western Eyes*; Macleod, *Shared Life*; Torrance, *Trinitarian Faith*.

12. Letham, *Holy Trinity*, 407.

13. Letham, *Through Western Eyes*, 271–72.

reinvigorate our theology and ecclesiology? Volf seems to think so, as he writes:

> It is obvious but not trite to state that the Triune God stands at the beginning and at the end of the Christian pilgrimage and, therefore, at the centre of Christian faith. Christians are born as they come out of the baptismal waters into which they were submerged in the name of the Holy Three. After crossing the ultimate threshold of the resurrection and the final judgment where their pilgrimage ends, "in the deep and bright essence" of the exalted divine being, they will behold and recognise, in the words of Dante's *Divine Comedy*, three spinning circles of "different colours" but of "the same dimensions."[14]

AN OVERVIEW OF MIROSLAV VOLF'S *AFTER OUR LIKENESS: THE CHURCH AS THE IMAGE OF THE TRINITY*

Professor Volf is a distinguished scholar. He is the Henry B. Wright Professor of Systematic Theology at Yale Divinity School, and he is the director of the Yale Center for Faith and Culture. His theological trajectory includes being the son of a Pentecostal pastor in Novi Sad (former Yugoslavia) during the communist regime of Marshall Tito; he gained a bachelor of arts degree at the Evangelical–Theological Faculty in Zagreb, Croatia; a masters at Fuller Theological Seminary; and doctorate of theology at the University of Tübingen, Germany.

Volf (1956–) has completed two doctoral theses at the University of Tübingen, with Professor Jürgen Moltmann (1926–) supervising both of them. The first thesis was completed in 1986 with the title "The Marxist Understanding of Work: A Theological Evaluation."[15] *AOL* was originally a manuscript that was "submitted as a *Habilitationsschrift*—a dissertation required for a post-doctoral degree—at the Evangelical Theological faculty" in 1994.[16] Volf explains that he revised the original manuscript for publication and made it a little bit more user-friendly.[17] It would be logical, therefore, to deduce that something of the influence of the theology of Moltmann should be found upon Volf's own work for

---

14. Volf, *God's Life in Trinity*, 3; Alighieri, *Divine Comedy: Paradiso*, canto xxxiii, 540.

15. Volf, "Response to Robert Goudzwaard," 61.

16. Volf, *AOL*, xi.

17. Ibid.

"the church as the image of the Trinity." However, before we set out an overview of this specific proposal, let us hear an endorsement that Volf bestows upon his very able supervisor.

In honor of Moltmann's seventieth birthday, on April 8, 1996, a group of international thinkers and theologians compiled a collection of writings to form a book, *The Future of Theology: Essays in Honour of Jürgen Moltmann*.[18] Volf writes in the introduction:

> Perhaps no single other theologian of the second half of our century has shaped theology so profoundly as has Moltmann. He appeared on the world scene with his *Theology of Hope* (1964) and took most of its capitals by storm. Not only were his subsequent performances "sold out," but the power of his vision and the originality of his method helped inspire a host of new directors—above all, the originators of various theologies of liberation—who modified his approach and put it to creative uses.[19]

If we were to describe in two words the theological influence of Moltmann upon the thinking of Volf, and his thesis under discussion, perhaps they would be *liberation* and *Trinity*. These two significant impulses emanate from Volf's attempt to outline connections between the Trinity and ecclesiology. *AOL* could be labeled as a new critical theory that calls for a listening ear and one that endorses a reworking of the Trinity and a reworking for our understanding of the church. So, how does Volf structure his argument in the book?

AOL commences with a relatively brief introduction that then divides the thesis into two parts. Part 1 engages two dialogue partners separately: the first is Joseph Ratzinger (now Pope Benedict XVI), with a subheading "Communion and the Whole," and the second is Metropolitan John Zizioulas, "Communion, One, and the Many." Part 2 then presents five chapters for a reenvisioning of the church in the image of the Trinity.[20]

In introducing his book, Volf uses the deliberate language of bold liberation as he encourages his readers to embark on a journey with him. He calls for a "cry of protest" and motivates people to "storm the ecclesial walls with the cry 'We are the Church!'"[21] This particular slogan,

18. Volf, Krieg, and Kucharz, *Future of Theology*.
19. Ibid., ix.
20. Volf, *AOL*, v–vii.
21. Ibid., 9.

he believes, was the "protest out of which the Free Churches emerged historically," and he identifies himself with the English Separatist movement and two of its leaders, John Smyth (?1570–1612) and Henry Ainsworth (1571–1622).[22] He interprets this movement by echoing the words of Peter Lake, who understands it as a "populist revolt against any sort of ministerial élite." Volf adds his own commentary on the situation by stating that it was a "populist revolt against the hierarchical structure of the church."[23] Furthermore, Volf contends that there is an unmistakable "red thread running through all their writings" and that is "the antimonarchical and generally antihierarchical political implications of this basic, anticlerical ecclesiological decision."[24]

The primary concern of *AOL* is to rediscover this "cry of protest of the Free Churches ('We are the church!')" and place it into a Trinitarian framework, while laying down an ecclesiological program for change.[25] This pursuit engages in continuous dialogue, or rather criticism, of Catholic and Orthodox ecclesiologies. Volf expresses a yearning for the recovery of community, a term he perceives to be "concrete relationships within the social edifice that is the [local] church," and he inquires how these relationships "ought to look like if they are to correspond to the community of the Triune God."[26] Ultimately he concludes that "the ecclesiological dispute concerning the church as community is therefore simultaneously a missiological dispute concerning the correct way in which the communal form of Christian faith today is to be lived authentically and transmitted effectively."[27] This missiological thrust combined with a strategy for church reform sets the tone for much of what Volf envisages, in what could be termed *ecclesiological revisionism*. But, what are the changes that he thinks are required for this rediscovery of the church?

---

22. Ibid., 9–10.

23. Ibid., 10; Lake, *Moderate Puritans*, 89. Stephen Brachlow offers a different reading of the situation; he asserts that the issue of ministerial authority was one that was fluid and diverse in opinion among the English Separatists. Brachlow, *Communion of the Saints*, 174–75.

24. Volf, *AOL*, 10.

25. Ibid., 11.

26. Ibid., 11n7.

27. Ibid., 11.

"Christianity has become a religion of the so-called Two-Thirds World," according to Volf, and he perceives that there is a global shift from traditional hierarchical models to participative models of church configuration.[28] He endorses Russell Chandler's opinion that we are presently witnessing a "process of congregationalization" of all Christianity, and Volf insists that this process demands more lay participation in the life of the church.[29] Volf perceives that the Free Churches are the church of the future.

A final thread of Volf's thesis is the attempt to keep *AOL* as an ecumenical endeavor. In keeping with this notion he aims to avoid the pitfalls of the Episcopal and the original Free Church models that sought "one correct ecclesiology"; in contrast, he acknowledges the validity for a plurality of models.[30] John Smyth is his chosen representative from the Free Church tradition, and he even goes as far as stating that "he is the voice"[31] of that tradition. In developing his own contribution to the debate, Volf is not afraid to dialogue critically with Catholic and Orthodox ecclesiology but also to counteract individualistic tendencies in the Free Churches to keep all of these "models in motion."[32]

Part 1 of *AOL* can be described as a critical analysis of Ratzinger's and Zizioulas's theology of community, but this inevitably leads to the consideration of other theological themes such as Christology, soteriology, anthropology, revelation, and their doctrine of the Trinity. As is expected, all theological strands overlap at some point. In part 2, the aim is not one of criticism but rather construction. This begins with a chapter on "The Ecclesiality of the Church" that seeks to define what makes the church the church, and this is followed by a study in the next chapter, "Faith, Person, and Church," that pursues a communal view of personhood. Following on from this comes what may be understood as the heart of Volf's ecclesial construction, a chapter on the relationship between the "Trinity and the Church." This in turn leads him to propose a revision of the "Structures of the Church" before a final perspective is presented on "The Catholicity of the Church."[33] Professor Volf sums

28. Ibid, 11–12.
29. Ibid., 13–18; Chandler, *Racing toward 2001*, 210–11.
30. Volf, *AOL*, 21.
31. Ibid., 23.
32. Ibid., 19–24.
33. Ibid., 24–25.

up: "I focus on the local church itself in this ecumenical study of the ecclesial community as an icon of the Trinitarian community."[34]

AN OUTLINE OF THIS RESEARCH AND THE METHODOLOGY

Our research seeks not only to critically evaluate *AOL* but also endeavors to engage with the key theological influences that inform Volf's presuppositions in relation to his proposal. The chosen starting point is an investigation, in chapter 2, 3, and 4 of this monograph, of Volf's theological paradigm; our methodology examines the work of Moltmann and other theological influences that include Wolfhart Pannenberg, Catherine Mowry LaCugna, and Judith Gundry-Volf. Most often a theologian's paradigm is like an iceberg, with only a fragment of a person's assumptions exposed in open view. Similarly, any credible exploration of uncharted territory demands a thorough three-dimensional profile of the unmapped terrain. This research attempts to trace out the contours of Volf's theology, and this involves looking at some of the less obvious sources that have informed and influenced his proposal.

Hopefully this approach paves the way for a more detailed sketch of the profile of Volf's Trinitarian and ecclesial paradigm while obviously interacting with a whole range of writings by the author himself. Chapter 5 examines the context of Volf's proposal, one that sits within the Free Church tradition, and therefore it includes a much needed analysis of the English Separatists and Volf's chosen ecclesial representative, John Smyth. The ecclesial movements in the sixteenth and seventeenth centuries are quite difficult for any researcher because of the ever-changing church landscapes, combined with a high degree of theological fluidity among its leaders. It is for this reason that much more than a brief survey of Smyth has been offered in order to assess whether Volf has read and used his chosen Separatist leader accurately. This matter aside, the issues that these Separatist leaders faced has much weight to add to any attempt to construct a doctrine of the church. For this reason alone, an ecclesial survey of that timeframe yields much helpful material for the church in our generation.

Our critical evaluation continues in chapters 6 to 9 where part 1 (chapters 1 and 2 of *AOL*) of Volf's monograph dialogues critically with Ratzinger and Zizioulas. Volf's own examination draws out his

---

34. Ibid., 25.

understanding of these two representative theologians to provide meaningful insight into the theologies of the Eastern and Western churches, namely Catholic and Orthodox. Our line of enquiry is primarily concerned with their doctrine of God and the church in an attempt to establish if there are any deliberate links made between the two. This study also demonstrates how and why Volf, armed with his theological epistemology, then attempts to mount a challenge upon the hierarchical doctrines and practice of these two wings of the Christian Church, each of which represent formidable theological bulwarks contrary to his own conclusions.

Any new means of interpretation logically drives an agenda not only to deconstruct its opponents but also to put forward alternative theories. Liberation theologians like to call their quest, according to Volf, what Jon Sobrino describes as "Marx's epistemological revolution."[35] Arguably, *AOL* presents an epistemological revolution for theology and the church. Chapters 10 to 14 of this monograph place Volf's second part of his venture under the microscope, which are his five proposals for the doctrine of the church (chapters 3 to 7 of *AOL*). The growing influence of a nonhierarchical doctrine of the Trinity demands a critical evaluation because the implication from this new school of thought fuels a significant reshaping of church life.

An example of the advancements that are being made by the theological assumptions held by Volf, Moltmann, and others is found in *The Cyprus Agreed Statement of the International Commission for Anglican–Orthodox Theological Dialogue, 2006*.[36] This dialogue takes place under the heading *The Church of the Triune God*, thus indicating the desire of both parties to connect the divine and ecclesial communities together. It is this same concern that motivates Volf in his noble task; however, a critical question remains: what is the doctrine of the Trinity that the church is expected to reflect? Volf proposes changes to the historic DNA of the doctrine of God held by theologians across the centuries in the Eastern and Western churches. This discussion is no longer under the radar but is fast becoming a platform for a lot of contemporary debate.

Much of the drive toward the ordination of women into the presbyterate and episcopate derives its momentum from a nonhierarchical

---

35. Sobrino, *Christology at the Crossroads*, 35; Volf, "Doing and Interpreting," 14.
36. Anglican Consultative Council, *Church of the Triune God*.

doctrine of the Trinity.[37] This proposal by Volf likewise interacts with many other theological disciplines such as Christology, soteriology, missiology, and other fields. It is this potential future influence upon the missiological goals of local churches worldwide that motivates this research to scrutinize Volf's theological paradigm. Many of the theological questions that are raised in *AOL* are valid, and they offer rich lines of new theological enquiry; our end goal is similar to that of Volf but with differing conclusions for "the church as the image of the Triune God."

---

37. Ibid., 82.

2

The Influence of Jürgen Moltmann upon Volf's Theological Paradigm in *After Our Likeness*

INTRODUCTION

THIS CHAPTER SEEKS TO understand the foundational assumptions that guide Volf's theological paradigm and to explain why he puts forward his particular idea for the church as the image of the Trinity. Thomas Kuhn (1922–1996) in his ground-breaking work brought the whole issue of paradigm[1] into common view to highlight the significant difference in methodologies among researchers.[2] An excellent definition of a paradigm is "a set of beliefs that guide action."[3] The metaphor of a house illustrates the interlinking of ideas that fit together to form a theological paradigm, the foundation being a mixture of the researcher's ontology and epistemology, the walls constituting methodologies, and the roof, interpretations. Generally speaking, it is not required for a theologian to justify his or her assumptions (ontology and epistemology), and the focus lies on methods applied. However, any study that is able to determine a theologian's assumptions is then more able to understand why certain conclusions are reached and on what basis. So, upon what presuppositions is Volf's theological paradigm built?

---

1. Kuhn, *Structure of Scientific Revolutions*.
2. Schwandt, *Dictionary of Qualitative Inquiry*, 183–84.
3. Denzin and Lincoln, *Handbook of Qualitative Research*, 183.

Two key themes for assessment are his ideas for the doctrine of the Trinity and the doctrine of the church. Once these two models are understood, it is probably easier to see how and why Volf fuses these together to formulate his proposal. Additionally this provides a framework to see how and why he critiques his two dialogue partners (Ratzinger and Zizioulas). The first part of our investigation seeks to understand this social model for Trinitarian and ecclesial relations by examining the theological influences upon Volf's thinking. It is proposed that Jürgen Moltmann (1926–) in both his role as Volf's research supervisor and mentor, as well as his writings, exerts a primary influence that undergirds much of Volf's work. Other influences are investigated, but a priority is placed upon this particular theologian's grasp of the Trinity and especially how Moltmann's theology is applied to the church. We also analyze Volf's own writings that have a direct bearing upon *AOL*, in order to construct an accurate framework of his theology. Our aim is to summarize the assumptions that form the substructure of Volf's doctrine of the Trinity and ecclesiology.

A SOCIAL MODEL OF THE TRINITARIAN AND ECCLESIAL RELATIONS

The dominant theme that underpins Volf's model for the church is a theological construction of social Trinitarian relations that envisages a social being of equality. Our study needs to dissect this understanding of the doctrine of the Trinity, one that is particularly espoused by Moltmann, but also others. There is only a minimal attempt made by Volf to fully explain his understanding of the Trinity in *AOL* and, by his own admission, he "presupposes a complete doctrine of the Trinity" while claiming that a "comprehensive Trinitarian reflection is not possible within the framework of this chapter [chapter 5, 'Trinity and Church']."[4]

Consequently some of Volf's other writings are examined to yield a more complete explanation of his particular brand of a Trinity that is social. These gleanings are not exhaustive because he has not, to date, written a book specifically on the subject of the Trinity anywhere near the same magnitude as Moltmann. Wolfart Pannenberg is also quoted by him at times, as one who holds to a similar theological construct of the Trinity, as is Catherine Mowry LaCugna. For this reason, they are

---

4. Volf, *AOL*, 198.

The Influence of Jürgen Moltmann upon Volf's Theological Paradigm

briefly introduced in the next chapter, but their works are not primary sources for his theological scheme. Any detailed critical analysis of his theological model and their proponents is left until chapter 10 (onwards) of this monograph. The immediate need in this chapter is an enquiry into the epistemological assumptions that guide Volf's social doctrine of the Trinity because that model is supposed to be reflected by the church.

THE INFLUENCE OF JÜRGEN MOLTMANN

Even a cursory study of the writings of Volf reveals the weight of influence that Moltmann exerts upon Volf's theological understanding. Moltmann was his doctoral (1986) and postdoctoral (1994) supervisor at the University of Tübingen, and he has remained a close friend and mentor. Volf holds him in the highest esteem, and he expresses those sentiments as he affectionately pens: "Perhaps no single theologian of the second half of our century has shaped theology so profoundly, as has Moltmann."[5] Reciprocal public endorsement is wholeheartedly supplied by Moltmann for the publishers of Volf's main theses that deal with the relationship of the Trinity to the church.[6] *AOL* was originally a dissertation for a postdoctoral degree supervised by Moltmann.[7] This in no way undermines the reality that Volf is his own theologian, but the social doctrine of the Trinity proposed by Moltmann's *The Trinity and the Kingdom* (1980)[8] is one that he endorses.

Volf states: "I will adopt the general features of the social model of Trinitarian relations as proposed especially by Jürgen Moltmann," and again he writes that "in following Moltmann, I by contrast [to the hierarchical relations within the Trinity and the church as understood by Ratzinger and Zizioulas] take as my premise the symmetrical relations within the Trinity."[9] He concisely states Moltmann's view that there are "connections between the divine and ecclesial communities" and that

---

5. Volf, "Introduction," ix.

6. For example, the prefaces and back pages of Volf's *AOL* and *Exclusion and Embrace* highlight the point. (Further reference to *Exclusion and Embrace* is abbreviated with the use of *EE*). The faculty website for Yale Divinity school contains a full description of Professor Volf's academic achievements and his CV: http://www.yale.edu/divinity/faculty/Fac.MVolf.shtml.

7. Volf, *AOL*, xi.

8. Moltmann, *Trinity and the Kingdom*.

9. Volf, *AOL*, 198, 236.

a pivotal issue for him "sharply focuses on the issue of 'hierarchy' vs. 'equality.' "[10] It is worthy of mention at this early stage that he notes that there is still only a brief sketch of Trinitarian ecclesiology in Moltmann's essay entitled with the subheading "Clerical Monotheism," and that this is less than three pages.[11] However, there are frequent applications of this social Trinitarian model to general kingdom principles throughout Moltmann's writings that seemingly offer a fresh approach to the doctrine of the Trinity to be applied by the church.

Volf's proposal similarly attempts "to develop a non-hierarchical but truly communal ecclesiology based on a non-hierarchical doctrine of the Trinity."[12] In order to understand this influence upon Volf, we need to grasp Moltmann's paradigm, and a good starting point is a trilogy of theological contributions that were written before *The Trinity and the Kingdom*.

A Trilogy of Theological Contributions

All theology has a history and a context from which it is derived. There are three systematic works of Moltmann that he himself considers to be an "unplanned trilogy"[13] and these are: *Theology of Hope* (1964),[14] *The Crucified God* (1970),[15] and *The Church in the Power of the Spirit* (1975).[16] These writings guide and inform Moltmann's whole theological approach; therefore anyone studying his method must appreciate his theological foundation that is revealed in these books. These three works are given in the chronological order in which they were published, and each of them was completed before his social doctrine of the Trinity fully emerged. They most likely paved the way for his doctrine of God, and in some measure his ecclesiology flows from his own theological construct of the Trinity. Our aim at this point is to understand Moltmann's theological paradigm as opposed to critical analysis.

---

10. Ibid., 4; and Moltmann, *Trinity and the Kingdom*, 200–202.

11. Volf, *AOL*, 4. The proposal in view by Moltmann especially concerns the subheading, "Clerical Monotheism" in *Trinity and the Kingdom*, 200–202.

12. Volf, *AOL*, 4.

13. Moltmann, *History and the Triune God*, 168.

14. Moltmann, *Theology of Hope*.

15. Moltmann, *Crucified God*, xvii.

16. Moltmann, *Church in the Power*.

The Influence of Jürgen Moltmann upon Volf's Theological Paradigm

A study of this trilogy of Moltmann's theological contributions significantly aids our pursuit to understand his theological paradigm. All three of these books must be seen as a whole unit of thought because Moltmann himself asserts that they "dovetail into one another and their subject matter overlaps."[17] A common thread throughout each book is arguably a Hegelian dialectic that assumes an evolutionary development for theology and the church. This leads Moltmann and his followers to an eschatological expectation for future hope because evolutionary progress is assumed; therefore this worldview actively encourages wholesale theological revisions.

We conclude that the starting point for Moltmann's doctrine of God is chiefly christological and one that is centered on the crucified Christ. This approach endorses theologies that overthrow traditional understandings of the divine attributes in favor of divine passibility. He refutes the need for an immanent Trinity and the distinction between the two natures of Christ because these doctrines would make the teaching for divine suffering untenable. This posture espoused by Moltmann enables the theory for divine passibility to be made workable because Jesus' passion on the cross is seen to be something that the Father equally experienced.[18] An acceptance of the ontological Trinity or the two natures of Christ (Creed of Chalcedon) makes this assertion virtually impossible because such distinctions often support the idea that there is a difference between what Christ suffered and what the Father experienced.[19]

This critical theory proposed by Moltmann has implications for the church and society, in providing a new hermeneutical lens to demand reform along the lines of what is today seen as classic liberation theological models. This mandate for reform embraces the feminist agenda for the liberation of women from all patriarchal oppression[20] and extends the traditional soteriological boundaries that are normally restricted to forgiveness of sins. This framework feeds into his doctrine of the Trinity, which is one of the main pillars underlying Volf's postulation for the connection between the church and the Trinity.

---

17. Moltmann, *Church in the*, xvi.
18. Moltmann, *Crucified God*, 243–55.
19. Ibid., 235–43, 248.
20. Moltmann, *Secular Society*, 56.

"THE CHURCH AS THE IMAGE OF THE TRINITY"

The Trinity and the Kingdom

An Ecumenical Pursuit

The Trinity and the Kingdom (1980) is part of a series of systematic contributions to theology that follow on from Moltmann's earlier trilogy. Here, he aims to avoid the "coercion of a dogmatic thesis" and "thinking contrary to others but thinking with them and for them."²¹ His outlook asserts that "Christian theology has to be developed in ecumenical fellowship" as one that "takes account of other Christian traditions."²² He directs the reader's thoughts to the inspiring fifteenth-century Russian icon of the Trinity by Andrei Rublev; he writes that "it is only in unity with one another, which springs from the self-giving of the Son 'for many,' that men and women are in conformity with the Triune God."²³ This work by Moltmann is unashamed in its exploration of a social understanding of the doctrine of the Trinity.

Recovering the Trinity in the Western Theological Tradition

Moltmann mourns the neglect of the Trinity in contemporary theology and indeed during the historical development of "conceptions of God which have been developed in Western history."²⁴ He identifies three monotheistic notions of the Christian God: God as supreme substance, God as absolute subject, and God as the Triune God.²⁵ In his analysis, he rejects an excessive stress upon the oneness of God that he perceives to be common in the Western tradition. Moltmann believes that "the unity of the absolute subject" is pushed in the West in such a degree that the "Trinitarian Persons disintegrate into mere aspects of the one subject" and that "this leads unintentionally and inescapably to the reduction of the doctrine of the Trinity to monotheism."²⁶ In dialogue with an Orthodox Jew, Pinchos Lapide, he encourages him to "leave behind the concept of [God's] unity as the smallest indivisible particle,"²⁷ and this

---

21. Moltmann, *Trinity and the Kingdom*, xi, xii, xiv.
22. Ibid., xiv.
23. Ibid., xvi.
24. Ibid., 1–2.
25. Ibid., 2, 10–20.
26. Ibid., 18.
27. Lapide and Moltmann, *Jewish Monotheism*, 64.

statement reinforces his notable aversion of the concept of unity within the doctrine of God.

Contrary to this tradition, he favors a starting point beginning with Jesus the Son, because he says that this moves the church to consider the Trinity of the persons, before finally contemplating their unity.[28] Moltmann's social (related to the way the persons live together) doctrine of the Trinity assumes a different hermeneutic, which "leads us to think in terms of relationships and communities" and the way people relate to God, each other, to humankind as a whole and with the whole of creation.[29] He makes an interesting proposition by suggesting that the disappearance of the social doctrine of the Trinity paved the way for the development of individualism, especially in the West.[30] Panentheistic ideas are embraced with his ecological pursuit, and he weaves this into his Trinitarian vision for praxis, a move that hopefully prevents any doctrine of the Trinity from becoming a sterile or an isolated theological axiom.[31]

The Divine Attributes and the Cross

There are four interconnecting divine attributes that Moltmann puts forward to direct his doctrine of God: passibility, love, freedom, and openness.[32] No contradiction is seen, nor, indeed, is a difference made between the immanent and economic Trinity, because he refuses to accept a contradiction between liberty and necessity in the activity of God.[33] The concept for divine passibility, which supposedly manifests itself through the cross of Christ, becomes for Moltmann the central interpretative lens by which the Trinitarian attributes and relations are understood. This revision of the sufferings of Christ leads to a wholesale redefinition of the relationships that exist among the Trinity with respect to suffering, God's freedom, and God's love.[34] Moltmann believes

---

28. Moltmann, *Trinity and the Kingdom*, 19.

29. Ibid.

30. Ibid., 199.

31. Moltmann, *God in Creation*, 98, 100, 212.

32. Moltmann, *Trinity and the Kingdom*: God's passibility, 21–30, 41–52, 75–83; God's love, 57–60; God's freedom, 52–56; God's openness, 94–97.

33. Ibid., 52–56.

34. Ibid., "The Passion of God"; this chapter sets out the essentials of the doctrine of divine passibility that is developed in more detail in *The Crucified God*.

that Origen is the only Greek or Latin church father to have caught sight of this idea of a suffering and passionate God.[35] Subsequently appeals are made to a strange mix of sources to buttress his argument for theopathy, a theology that he admits is "contrary to the mainstream Christian tradition—starting from God's passion not his apathy."[36] It must be understood that this doctrine of theopathy and God's passibility is fundamental to Moltmann's whole theology.

He explains: "the cross on Golgotha has revealed the eternal heart of the Trinity. That is why we must trace the thread back from the historical, earthly cross to the eternal nature, if we are to perceive the primordial heavenly image."[37] An acceptance of divine passibility produces a radical shift of understanding in the eternal relations between the Father, the Son, and the Holy Spirit. For example, the chapter on "The Passion of God" suggests that "self-sacrifice is God's very nature and essence"; the historical passion of Christ reveals the eternal passion of God where "His whole being is the eternal sacrifice of self-love . . . at the same time perfectly self-less."[38] This means for Moltmann that "God has to give himself completely; and it is only in this way that he is completely God"; "love has to suffer"; "God's eternal bliss is not bliss based on the absence of suffering . . . pain is not avoided"; and also "creative love is ultimately suffering love."[39]

Flowing from this paradigm of divine passion, love is interpreted as "the passionate self-communication of the good"—"love is the goodness that communicates itself from all eternity," and this theology of love "is not patriarchal but rather feministic (for the Shekinah and the

---

35. Moltmann, *Trinity and the Kingdom*, 23–25; Moltmann-Wendel and Moltmann, *God—His and Hers*, 72–73. Origen, "Epistle to the Romans," 92–95. The only verse that Moltmann cites that Origen seemingly expounds as having an insight into the notion for divine suffering is Rom 8:32. Here Origen only makes an oblique reference in commenting on the phrase "spare his Son," and this does not constitute substantive evidence for this doctrine at all.

36. Moltmann, *Trinity and the Kingdom*, 25. The strange mix of sources are: Abraham Heschel and Franz Rosenweig who explain the rabbinic and kabbalistic doctrine of the Shekinah, 25–30; J. K. Mozley and C. E. Rolt's Anglican theologies for the eternal sacrifice of love, 30–36; the Spanish philosopher Miguel de Unamuno's mysticism on the pain of God, 36–42; and the Russian-Orthodox philosopher of religion, N. Berdyaev's notion of tragedy in God, 42–47.

37. Moltmann, *Trinity and the Kingdom*, 31–32n32.

38. Ibid., 32–33.

39. Ibid., 33–34, 60.

The Influence of Jürgen Moltmann upon Volf's Theological Paradigm

Holy Spirit are the feminine principle of the Godhead)."[40] This seemingly solves the theodicy problem in as far as evil and sin are products of freedom, and freedom is intrinsic to the nature of God for Moltmann.[41]

He paints the traditional model of God's freedom based on "God the Lord"—one that embraces sovereignty and power over creation—in a negative light, and he exchanges this for a conception where "freedom belongs to the language of community and fellowship,"[42] whereby God's freedom lies in friendship. Any thesis envisaging a social Trinity inevitably has to tackle the notion of lordship, and Moltmann emphatically refuses to sidestep this issue.

The whole plan of creation and each stage of Christ's redemptive purpose he views through a Trinitarian lens, and he insists that all that God does is "based on God's nature not just on his will."[43] A question that now legitimately arises is, what is the nature of this God? It is hard to pinpoint a single sentence where Moltmann defines the nature of God. However, he does state the importance of the "self-surrender of the Son, a giving up" and that this "activity of the Son in redemption is as a representative, as liberator, as redeemer and as lord"; this means "the kingdom of the Son is the kingdom of brothers and sisters, not a kingdom of the Lord and his servants."[44]

God's openness reemerges in this book, and this continues to be an intriguing notion for Moltmann.[45] He again endorses Christian panentheism and states that the "union of the divine Trinity is open for the uniting of the whole creation with itself and in itself."[46] Alongside this assertion, he describes the history of the kingdom of God with further panentheistic overtones as he writes of an "eschatologically open history now," one that is "open and inviting."[47] He seemingly leans toward open theism when he discusses the kingdom of God by saying it is a "world

---

40. Ibid., 57.
41. Ibid., 47.
42. Ibid., 56.
43. Ibid., 114.
44. Ibid., 80–83, 88; Moltmann deliberately lowercased "lord" in the original.
45. Ibid., 94–96.
46. Ibid., 96, 106–8 explains the notion of Christian panentheism.
47. Ibid., 95.

open to the future," one that is an "open system" where "God keeps the world's true future open."[48]

Trinitarian and Kingdom Relations

Moltmann asserts that the "Trinitarian relationships have their foundation in the nature of the Triune God," and therefore he resolutely claims that "patriarchal religion is not Trinitarian, but monotheistic."[49] The traditional interpretation of the Niceno-Constantinoplitan Creed is upheld concerning the eternal generation of the Son, albeit with a deliberate attempt to overcome the use of sexist language. The generation of the only begotten Son by the Father is construed by him in nonpatriarchal terms, and he even prefers to talk of a "motherly Father" that has "brought forth a son."[50] This correlating of the church to the inner relations of the Trinity allows him again to pursue a vision for the "fellowship of men and women without privilege and subjection, for in fellowship with the firstborn brother, there is no longer male and female, but all are one in Christ, and joint heirs according to the promise (Gal. 3:28)."[51]

An investigation into the inner life and orderliness of the Trinity by Moltmann reveals a unity of the persons that is grounded in the doctrine of perichoresis. Any order is understood to be based only on origin because, he explains, all proceeds from the Father's nature, not his will, where the Father is the source of the Godhead.[52] He accepts the common creedal affirmations of begetting and procession; however, he casts aside the notions of divine monarchy, tritheism, modalism, and subordinationism. He endorses the doctrine of perichoresis as one that apparently handles all the theological pitfalls that have beset historical Trinitarian constructions.[53] He explains that the unity of the persons "does not lie in the one lordship of God," but that it is to be "found in the unity of their tri-unity."[54]

---

48. Ibid., 209–10.
49. Ibid., 153–54, 163, 167.
50. Ibid., 164.
51. Ibid., 164–65.
52. Ibid., 150, 166–67.
53. Ibid., 174–76.
54. Ibid. He asserts that the monarchy only applies to the constitution of the Trinity (176) and claims that the patristic theologians understood perichoresis as the sociality of the three divine persons (198).

In developing this unique proposal, Moltmann comes dangerously close to a wholesale rejection of monotheism, and he appears to downplay the idea that the three persons are *homoousious*.[55] The persons of the Trinity are deemed as nonidentical, equal, and bound by their triunity. This framework for the Trinity is applied to the kingdom of God, one that is espoused to be a kingdom of freedom.

The Kingdom of Freedom

Moltmann's introductory statements set the scene for his conclusions, which rest upon a nonhierarchical Trinity that leads to a nonhierarchical kingdom. Here are some of his bold assertions: "monotheism is monarchism"; "the notion of a divine monarchy in heaven and on earth . . . provides the justification for earthly domination—religious, moral, patriarchal—and it makes a hierarchy, a 'holy rule.'"[56] He critiques all forms of political monotheism, and he devotes several paragraphs to an exposé of "clerical monotheism."[57] Following his rejection of the Roman Catholic Church (hereafter called RCC) and other similar monarchical episcopates that supposedly represent God as Almighty, he recognizes instead that it is "God as love who is represented in the community of believers," and he believes that this more suitably depicts a "community free of dominion."[58] This paradigm shift prefers terms such as *consensus*, *the principle of concord*, *dialogue*, and *harmony*. He affirms the presbyterian and synodal church structures as a valid replacement of hierarchies because here he recognizes the practice of "leadership based on brotherly advice that best corresponds to the doctrine of the social Trinity."[59]

Finally, it is noteworthy that Moltmann resorts to using an obscure source, Joachim of Fiore, to highlight a historical attempt to formulate a Trinitarian doctrine of the kingdom that leans toward a charismatic ecclesiology.[60] This model for a kingdom of freedom unequivocally refutes freedom as lordship, based on a male society, and it favors a community of mutual participation in love and solidarity.[61] Similarly, an absolutist

55. Ibid., 177, 190.
56. Ibid., 191.
57. Ibid., 200–202.
58. Ibid., 202. Clerical monotheism is briefly expounded in 200–202.
59. Ibid.
60. Ibid., 203–9.
61. Moltmann, "Liberating Church," in *Theology and Joy*, 82–87. Here he explores

sovereign God is replaced by Moltmann with a suffering and passionate God who calls men and women to freedom.[62] This statement captures the heartbeat of Moltmann's doctrine of God; freedom is, for him, a most important aspect of this social doctrine of the Trinity, something to be reflected in the kingdom of freedom.[63]

This radical reworking of the doctrine of the Trinity encompasses a framework that handles both the being and attributes of the Triune God, and this theological reconstruction is best summarized by Moltmann's own words:

> I have developed a social doctrine of the Trinity, according to which God is a community of Father, Son and Spirit, whose unity is constituted by mutual indwelling and reciprocal interpenetration. If this is correct, then we find the earthly reflection of this divine sociality, not in the autocracy of a single ruler but in the democratic community of free people, not in lordship of the man over the woman but in their equal mutuality, not in ecclesiastical hierarchy but in a fellowship church.[64]

Moltmann's Theological Paradigm

Now we conclude this section of our study with an attempt to summarize the theological approach of Moltmann, because his influence is so prevalent upon Volf's thesis in *AOL*. Moltmann's theological framework could be explained as involving five movements that proceed in a logical order, before arriving at the last stage, which is a critical theory for theology, the church, and society. Once we understand the hermeneutical principles and methods that he applies, then it becomes possible to plot out where he ends up theologically, and this demonstrates how and why he got there. So, what is Moltmann's hermeneutical lens?

The first movement could be described as "Hegelian openness" in what appears as continuing theological revelation until the final eschatological hope is realized. This hope is indeed positive hope because it is founded upon an assumption that there are progressive evolutionary

---

this notion of freedom.

62. Moltmann, *Trinity and the Kingdom*, 215–18.

63. Ibid., 192. The final chapter of the thesis is called "The Kingdom of Freedom," which most likely reflects his primary desire to see this "freedom" reproduced in the church.

64. Ibid., preface written in 1990, vi–vii.

developments for theology, ecclesiology, and eventually all of a society that it impacts. The second movement could be termed "the eschatological goal" that all of creation is moving forward as a seeming act of the Trinity. This goal in many ways is an expanded view of salvation that embraces liberation and peace for all of creation. The third stage is identified as a "Christological revision of the cross," and this can be placed under the theological umbrella of the doctrine of divine suffering (passibility).

A fourth movement realizes a "social doctrine of the Trinity" with four divine attributes seemingly explaining the outflow of all divine activity. These attributes are God's openness, passibility, love, and freedom. Much of this doctrine of the Trinity appears to be squeezed into the all-controlling concept of perichoresis. The fifth and final movement is a "call to reformation" in what could also be termed "a political theology of liberation." This critical theory of liberation views an evil world through rose-tinted spectacles of liberation, which envisages a social doctrine for the church and society. This vision firmly anticipates liberation from all forms of hierarchical and other oppressions by humankind, in the development of a "kingdom of freedom." This political theology then becomes the mandate by which the church should proactively engage with its world.

Any meaningful assessment of the influence of Moltmann upon Volf must diligently engage in a critical analysis of the theological foundations upon which these five movements are based. Perhaps the best way to conclude this section is by the words of Moltmann in his own personal reflection of his theology:

> If I were to attempt to sum up the outline of my theology in a few key phrases, I would have at the least to say to that I am attempting to reflect on a theology which has: a biblical foundation, an eschatological orientation and a political responsibility. In and under that it is certainly a theology in pain and joy at God himself, a theology of constant wonder.[65]

---

65. Moltmann, *History and the Triune God*, 182.

3

Other Theological Influences upon Volf in Relation to *After Our Likeness*

HAVING LOOKED AT THE relationship between Volf and Moltmann in the previous chapter, we will choose three other theologians for our discussion. Their order of treatment reflects a possible order of priority in terms of their influence upon Volf's thesis. Wolfhart Pannenberg is considered first, due to the fact that he is referenced as a key author whom Volf uses to support his doctrine of the Trinity, which then feeds into his doctrine of the church, as an image of the Trinity. Two feminist theologians are examined briefly, and these are Catherine Mowry LaCugna and Volf's wife, Judith Gundry-Volf. In our summary, two other feminist authors are introduced, Letty M. Russell and Elisabeth Schüssler Fiorenza, not as influences, but as helpful guides to supplement our attempt to understand the theological paradigm of Volf.

WOLFHART PANNENBERG

Wolfhart Pannenberg (1928–) is a retired professor of systematic theology[1] at the University of Munich, where he was also the director of the Ecumenical Institute. He is recognized by Letham as a theologian who "exhibits prodigious scholarship and great care,"[2] and his main work in view is his *Systematic Theology*, which comprises three volumes. This work is one that Volf particularly references for his conception of the

---

1. Pannenberg, "The Need for Systematic Theology," in *Introduction to Systematic Theology*. This book outlines his commitment to the field of systematic theology.

2. Letham, *Holy Trinity*, 312.

Other Theological Influences upon Volf in Relation to After Our Likeness

Trinity. It is necessary to consider how Volf uses Pannenberg to support his own thesis, summarize Pannenberg's view of the Trinity and church structures, and give an overview of the differences between Pannenberg and Moltmann.

How Does Volf Reference Pannenberg?

Perhaps the clearest statement that Volf makes to explain the foundational presuppositions that support his doctrine of the Trinity is in chapter 5 of *AOL*, "Trinity and Church." Here he explains:

> A comprehensive Trinitarian reflection . . . is not possible within the framework of this chapter. Instead, I will adopt the general features of the social model of Trinitarian relations as proposed especially by Moltmann (though also by Pannenberg), developing only certain aspects of this model, especially where required by consideration of the correspondence between the Trinity and the church.³

He does not give us specifics as to which of Pannenberg's doctrine of the Trinity is most pertinent to him, but he cross-references the relevant Trinitarian sections from volume 1 of Pannenberg's *Systematic Theology*.⁴ Volf does not explicitly state that Pannenberg is not a primary source upon his own thesis, but it is probably safe to assume that his influence is secondary to Moltmann, due to the bracketed reference.

There are only three other references to Pannenberg's writings within the main body of *AOL* (and a further four footnote references), which would also seem to support the suggestion that he is not a primary theological influence. The first quotation refers to the structure of Trinitarian and ecclesial relations ("Trinity and Church," chapter 5) to support Volf's own opinion. Volf's doctrinal conception accepts that the Trinitarian persons and their relations are complementary and that the Father, Son, and Holy Spirit are "perichoretic subjects."⁵ He endorses and quotes Pannenberg's idea that the persons of the Triune God are "living realisations of separate centres of action."⁶ The second reference is from chapter 6, "Structures of the Church," and Pannenberg's

---

3. Volf, *AOL*, 198.
4. Ibid., 198n38; Pannenberg, *Systematic Theology*, 1:259–336 and 422–32.
5. Volf, *AOL*, 215 and 215n105.
6. Ibid., 215; Pannenberg, *Systematic Theology*, 1:319.

thought is introduced, in a reflection on the particular task of officeholders, where they jointly agree that they are "publicly responsible for the concerns common to all Christians."[7] The third reference relates to "The Catholicity of the Church" (chapter 7), and Pannenberg is affirmed in his claim that "only in the glory of the eschatological consummation . . . will the church of Christ be realised fully and completely as catholic."[8]

The footnote references offer further material for consideration. In chapter 4, "Faith, Person, and Church," Pannenberg is cited to buttress Volf's understanding that a "human being's personhood as constituted by God . . . results in a person . . . being able to encounter both society and nature in freedom."[9] In "Trinity and Church," Pannenberg is understood to be a theologian who sees "all of theology as an explication of the doctrine of the Trinity."[10] In the same chapter, Volf then lays down a significant point of departure from Pannenberg's theological paradigm for the Trinity; this relates to the monarchy of the Father. Pannenberg states that the "monarchy of the Father is . . . the result of the common operation of the three Persons. It is thus the seal of their unity,"[11] and Volf rejects this assertion and insists, in direct contradiction, that the "divine unity . . . does not need the monarchy of the Father as its seal."[12] Furthermore, Volf commends the critiques by Henry Jansen and John O'Donnell of Pannenberg's view of the inner-Trinitarian relations.[13]

The traditional Protestant doctrine of the universal priesthood of all believers is upheld by Volf, while he simultaneously rejects the RCC distinction between the general and particular priesthood expounded in *Lumen Gentium*.[14] Volf utilizes Pannenberg to support his position because he supposedly "takes a similar view" to "reaffirm and underscore non-hierarchical church relations."[15] Before we proceed further, we need to examine the theology of Pannenberg with particular reference to his

---

7. Volf, *AOL*, 247, 247n111; Pannenberg, "Okumenisches Amtsverständnis," 278.

8. Volf, *AOL*, 268 and 268n32; Pannenberg, "Die Bedeutung der Eschatologie," 105.

9. Volf, *AOL*, 184, 184n126; Pannenberg, *Anthropology in Theological Perspective*, 234.

10. Volf, *AOL*, 193n12.

11. Pannenberg, *Systematic Theology*, 1:325.

12. Volf, *AOL*, 216n106.

13. Volf, *AOL*, 216n106: Jansen, "Relationality"; O'Donnell, "Pannenberg's Doctrine of God," 96.

14. Volf, *AOL*, 246n10; Abbott, "Dogmatic Constitution of the Church," 9–106.

15. Volf, *AOL*, 246n108; Pannenberg, "Okumenisches Amtsverständnis," 272.

understanding of the Trinity, and also his doctrine of the church in relation to church structures.

What Is Pannenberg's Conception of the Trinity and the Subsequent Structures of the Church?

The Conception of the Trinity

In our consideration as to how Volf references Pannenberg, we observed that he highlights two sections from the first volume of Pannenberg's *Systematic Theology* as primary sources. These are the whole of chapter 5, "The Trinitarian God" and a small section on "Love and the Trinity" and from chapter 6, "The Unity and Attributes of the Divine Essence."[16] In Pannenberg's conception of the being of God, there are four aspects worthy of mention: the monarchy of the Father, the Father's lordship and divine rule, the relations that exist among the three persons based upon mutual self-distinction, and the endorsement of monotheism.

The monarchy of the Father is a consistent thread that is interwoven into the whole of Pannenberg's Trinitarian paradigm,[17] and this theme entwines the idea for the Father's divine rule.[18] The opening subtitle, "The God of Jesus and the Beginnings of the Trinity" in large measure marks out where this chapter is heading. He clearly expresses his concept of divine monarchy with a number of deliberate statements:

> The kingdom or monarchy of the Father is established in creation. . . . The Father does not have his kingdom or monarchy without the Son and the Spirit, but only through them. . . . The Son is not subordinate to the Father in the sense of ontological inferiority, but he subjects himself to the Father. In this regard he is himself in eternity the locus of the monarchy. . . . The monarchy of the Father . . . is the seal of their [the three Persons] unity. . . . In his monarchy the Father is the one God.[19]

These affirmative statements are no mere excursus, but they embody the conclusion of sixty-four previous pages, which includes careful referencing of biblical texts, along with appeals to the Eastern theological fathers such as Origen and especially the Cappadocians. Pannenberg

---

16. Volf, *AOL*, 198n38; Pannenberg, *Systematic Theology*, 1:259–336 and 422–32.
17. Pannenberg, *Systematic Theology*, 1:274–80, 324–25, 334, 385, 421, 432.
18. Ibid., 259–73.
19. Ibid., 324–26.

credits Origen as providing an "adequate biblical basis" for the doctrine concerning the eternal begetting of the Son that supposedly led to the emergence of the concept for an "eternal trinity in God."[20] This leads Pannenberg to appeal for the "reciprocal self-distinction of the Persons as the concrete form of Trinitarian relations"[21] that draws on the works of the Cappadocians. He concludes that the *filioque* clause adopted by the Western church is to be withdrawn, because he believes that this formulation mistakenly thinks of the relations of the persons in terms of their origin.[22]

Pannenberg prefers a double theological thrust that comprises an insistence on the monarchy of the Father that relies on terminology associated with origin (one that goes beyond a traditional understanding) and a push toward a definitive distinction of the three persons (that also goes beyond traditional theological boundaries). He writes on the matter of relations based on origin:

> Relations among the three Persons that are defined as mutual self-distinction cannot be reduced to relations of origin in the traditional sense. The Father does not merely beget the Son. He also hands over his kingdom to him and receives it back from him. The Son is not merely begotten of the Father. He is also obedient to him and he thereby glorifies him as the one God. The Spirit is not just breathed. He also fills the Son and glorifies him in his obedience to the Father, thereby glorifying the Father himself. In so doing he leads into all truth (John 16:13) and searches out the deep things of Godhead (1 Cor. 2:10–11).[23]

Pannenberg seems to imply that the Father only is *autotheos*, and there is an explicit demonstration in his theology of a subjection of the Son and the Holy Spirit to the Father's monarchy,[24] even though he denies subordinationism or Sabellianism.[25]

---

20. Ibid., 306 and 275; Origen, "De Principiis," in *Ante-Nicene Fathers* (hereafter called *ANF*), 1.2, 4, 7, 10, 242–67.

21. Pannenberg, *Systematic Theology*, 1:278–80; Basil of Caesarea, "Ep. 38. 7," in *Nicene and Post-Nicene Fathers* (hereafter called *NPNF*); Gregory of Nyssa, "Against Eunomius," *NPNF*, 146–47; Gregory of Nazianzus, "Orations," *NPNF*, 40, 43.

22. Pannenberg, *Systematic Theology*, 1:318–19.

23. Ibid., 320.

24. Ibid., 324–36.

25. Ibid., 334.

Other Theological Influences upon Volf in Relation to After Our Likeness

This view of the Trinitarian relations is, by Pannenberg's own admission, one that goes beyond Dumitru Staniloae, Moltmann, and R. W. Jenson,[26] and yet Volf still quotes him to buttress his own argument in *AOL*. Pannenberg states:

> If the Trinitarian relations among Father, Son and Spirit have the form of mutual self-distinction, they must be understood not merely as different modes of being of the one divine subject but as living realisations of separate centres of action. Whether we must also view these centres of action as centres of consciousness depends on whether and in what sense we can apply the idea of consciousness, which derives from human experience, to the divine life. We must say with Kasper, and against Rahner, that a divine consciousness subsists in threefold mode.[27]

As a result of these and other bold statements, Letham interprets him as having a clear "tritheistic tendency."[28] However, Pannenberg still holds a firm grip upon monotheism by asserting that "the doctrine of the Trinity is in fact concrete monotheism."[29]

The theological connection between the Trinity and love come into our view as the remaining focus of this section. Pannenberg gives this subject specific treatment, and he positively undergirds his doctrine of the Trinity with the attribute of divine love. He agrees with Eberhard Jüngel, Heinrich Scholz, and Josef Pieper in asserting that "the mutual love of the Trinitarian Persons" is more than just related to their activities; instead, "love is a power which shows itself in those who love and in their turning to one another, glowing through them like fire."[30] We conclude that for Pannenberg, love is the fountainhead from which everything flows, but the monarchy of the Father is never lost in his Trinitarian framework. Hence he concludes:

---

26. Ibid., 319n183; Staniloae, *Orthodox Dogmatic Theology*, 267; Moltmann, *Trinity and the Kingdom*, 175; Jenson, *Triune Identity*, 108.

27. Pannenberg, *Systematic Theology*, 1:319; Volf, *AOL*, 215.

28. Letham, *Holy Trinity*, 320.

29. Pannenberg, *Systematic Theology*, 1:335. This also raises many other unanswered questions beyond the scope of this study, for example the deity of Christ. This theme is handled in Pannenberg, *Jesus: God and Man* and Pannenberg, *Systematic Theology*, 2:379–89. His Christology is strongly critiqued by Letham, *Holy Trinity*, 312–14.

30. Pannenberg, *Systematic Theology*, 1:426; Jüngel, *God as the Mystery*, 321; Scholz, *Eros and Caritas*, 67; Pieper, *Über die Liebe*, 182.

> Divine love constitutes the concrete unity of the divine life in the distinction of its personal manifestations and relations. The personal distinctions among Father, Son and Spirit cannot be derived on an abstract concept of love. We may know them only in the historical revelation of God in Jesus Christ. But on this basis they and their unity in the divine essence make sense as the concrete reality of the divine love which pulses through all things and which consummates the monarchy of the Father through the Son in the Holy Spirit.[31]

It can be already anticipated in some measure as to how this theological plan for the doctrine of God and the Trinity will be played out in the structures of the church. With such a strong emphasis on the distinction of the persons combined with the monarchy of the Father we would expect a reduced emphasis upon an egalitarian structure in the church. This would follow logically if Pannenberg consistently applies his doctrine of the Trinity to his doctrine of the church, and we now turn to his *Systematic Theology* volume 3 to find our answer to this speculation.

The Structures of the Church

The whole subject of ministerial hierarchy is by no means dismissed or ignored in Pannenberg's ecclesiological thought, and he handles this subject in connection with the unity of the church. He clarifies his support for Luther's view that the "divinely instituted pastor must rule a congregation with preaching and the sacraments"[32] and that "at its core, the church's ministry of leadership is thus a teaching ministry."[33] Following on from this ecclesial understanding, his opinions reveal a positive attitude towards episcopacy, and he writes: "In the church's life there is [the] need not only of a local ministry of leadership on the part of the pastor who is called to teach the gospel but also of a regional ministry of leadership and supervision such as bishops took up in the medieval church."[34] Furthermore he believes that the "centrality of the eucharist in the life of the church" needs to be restored with a fresh emphasis on the communal element that lies behind the symbolism of the Lord's Supper.[35]

---

31. Pannenberg, *Systematic Theology* 1:432.
32. Pannenberg, *Systematic Theology*, 3:415n964; Luther, *Works of Luther*, vol. 6, 441, 24–25.
33. Pannenberg, *Systematic Theology*, 3:415.
34. Ibid., 3:419.
35. Pannenberg, *Christian Spirituality*, 40–49.

Other Theological Influences upon Volf in Relation to After Our Likeness

This seeming affirmation for a hierarchical and episcopal church ministry seems to gain further momentum, as he claims that "if any Christian bishop can speak for the whole church in situations when this may be needed, it will be primarily the bishop of Rome."[36] Furthermore he elaborates by suggesting that "we ought freely to admit the fact of the primacy of the Roman Church and its bishop in Christianity."[37] However, Pannenberg does engage in critical analysis of the universal claim of the Roman papacy itself and its supposed infallible teaching office. He also sides with an interpretation of Matt 16:16–18 that thinks of Peter as being the main person in Christ's teaching here. He states that "today theological exegesis of the New Testament, including Roman Catholic Church exegesis, has reached widespread consent that these New Testament sayings about Peter, no matter how else we might assess them, refer only to Peter, not to any successors in his office."[38] While he is comfortable with the office of bishop, as with the Eastern Orthodox Church, he does distance himself from the claim of the RCC that the bishop of Rome has preeminence over the other bishops.

In contemplating the task that Christian theology plays in a secular culture, he delicately handles some examples of "excessive assimilation" of contemporary culture, one of which he believes is "feminism in theology."[39] While he does not see any "dogmatic reason which would prohibit the ordination of women" or reason to exclude them from the "priestly ministry of the church," he rejects any attempts that are made to change the traditional forms of God-language and the usage of the term "Father" on feminist grounds.[40] In our examination of the theology of Pannenberg, it is quite plain that there are a number of similarities but also marked differences in the theological conception of the Trinity and the church with Moltmann. To this subject we now turn.

---

36. Pannenberg, *Systematic Theology*, 3:420.

37. Ibid., 421; Pannenberg, "Teaching Office." Here he expounds within a confessional and mainly Lutheran context the value of "supra-local" ministries for the good of the church, to prevent the deterioration of "Christian doctrine" (231) and other matters. He affirms the role of the pope as a mouthpiece for Christendom as a potential good for all of Christendom (232).

38. Pannenberg, *Systematic Theology*, 3:429 and 429n1010. His whole discussion is under the subheading, "Ministry to the Unity of Christianity as a Whole," 420–31.

39. Pannenberg, *Christianity in a Secularized World*, 53.

40. Ibid., 54.

Do Pannenberg and Moltmann Differ from Each Other?

There has been sustained critical dialogue between these two men on their differing conceptions of the Trinity, even though they occupy similar ground in a number of areas. In Moltmann's words, the main difference between Pannenberg and himself is that the latter "has developed his doctrine of the Trinity from the idea of the 'reciprocal self-distinction of Father, Son and Spirit as the concrete form of Trinitarian relations.'"[41] Also that "because he maintains the monarchy of the Father, he dispenses with the idea of communion or fellowship in the divine perichoresis and, instead of this, takes up the monarchy into the relationships within the Trinity"; Moltmann cannot understand why Pannenberg has to maintain the idea of monarchy.[42]

Pannenberg reciprocates his differences with Moltmann with a series of what must be seen as fundamental theological matters. He rejects Moltmann's claim to uphold the *filioque* clause and the "proposed formula that the Spirit proceeds from the Father and the Son and [that the Spirit] receives form from the Father and the Son"; this he "perceives is no better than the Augustinian tradition."[43] Pannenberg does not adopt direct language that speaks of a social doctrine of the Trinity, and he emphasizes that Moltmann only comes close to his own idea (of mutual self-distinction of the three persons), but he differs from Moltmann in that he prefers instead "to see the three Persons as three individuals that then enter into relations with one another."[44] In contradiction to Moltmann, the monarchy of the Father plays an important role in Pannenberg's doctrine, and he states:

> In the immanent Trinity, then, we are not to distinguish as Moltmann does (*The Trinity and the Kingdom*, 183) between a constitutional level and a relational level, between on the one side the constitution of the Trinity (162f) from the Father, the non-originated origin of deity, by the generation of the Son and procession of the Spirit (165), and on the other side the pericho-

---

41. Moltmann, *History and the Triune God*, xviii; Pannenberg, *Systematic Theology*, 1:335.

42. Moltmann, *History and the Triune God*, xix; cf., Pannenberg, *Systematic Theology*, 1:283, 335, and 347.

43. Pannenberg, *Systematic Theology*, 1:318–19n181; Moltmann, *Trinity and the Kingdom*, 180, 187.

44. Pannenberg, *Systematic Theology*, 1:319n183; Moltmann, *Trinity and the Kingdom*, 175.

retic mutuality of the personal relations in the life of the Trinity (171f). Instead the monarchy of the Father is itself mediated by the Trinitarian relations. How could we protect the unity in the eternal cycle of the divine life and the perichoretic unity of the three Persons if the monarchy of the Father were not accepted as the source of deity (175)?[45]

Furthermore, Pannenberg resolutely defends Christian monotheism, and he dissents with Moltmann's seeming polemic against it; he also points out that Moltmann's constitution of the Trinity exposes him to criticism concerning the unity of the Trinitarian God.[46] An assessment of the similarities and differences in the doctrine of God between these two theologians is taken up by Roger Olson and Letham;[47] however, both have downplayed some of the significant structural dissimilarities between these two theologians.

The impact of these dissimilarities is particularly seen in their doctrine of the church and their proposals for church structures, which are markedly unlike each other. Moltmann fiercely puts forward a notion for nonhierarchical church structures, which reflects his egalitarian model of the Trinity. Contrary to this, Pannenberg espouses theological support for an episcopal church, which fits his notion for the monarchy of the Father. This simple test alone seems to fit our hypothesis that the church is an image of the Trinity and in particular an image of a particular theologian's doctrine of the Trinity. As the doctrine of the Trinity is revealed, so the doctrine of the church unfolds, and the two doctrines appear either consciously or subconsciously, inextricably linked.

Pannenberg walks "hand in hand" with Moltmann concerning the ordination of women in the ministry, but the former walks a much more conservative path concerning the development of new theological God-language to buttress a feminist argument. Similarly regarding a theology of liberation, Pannenberg supports Moltmann, but, again, he pursues a more conservative approach with theological provisos, to guard against potential cultural assimilation. Concerning the matter of soteriology in the context of liberation, Pannenberg understands this to be focused on freedom from "the powers of sin and death" that comes "only by the death of Christ and faith in God" and the need for oppressors to be

---

45. Pannenberg, *Systematic Theology*, 1:325.
46. Ibid., 1:335–36, 335n217.
47. Olson, "Trinity and Eschatology," 213–27; Letham, *Holy Trinity*, 298–321.

freed from the power of sin.[48] This soteriology is much narrower than Moltmann's, and it is probably fair to say that he handles this subject in a way that is more responsible and grounded much more in the biblical documents and historic church creeds.[49] Moltmann freely acknowledges that there are differences and conflicts between them both, especially in the arena of political theology.[50]

Is There a Theological Difference between Pannenberg and Volf?

Volf seems to side with Moltmann on all the issues of difference that have just been explained in the previous subsection, but there are two other specific matters that require our attention. In writing on the doctrine of the Trinity, Volf uses Pannenberg to buttress his own argument but this leaves him open for scrutiny. A cornerstone premise by Pannenberg is the notion that the persons of the Triune God are "living realisations of separate centres of action,"[51] which Volf uses to support his idea that they are "perichoretic subjects."[52] However, as has been outlined, this notion of perichoresis is not the main thrust of Pannenberg's thesis. This raises the question as to whether Volf is reading Pannenberg carefully enough at this crucial juncture. While Volf and Moltmann firmly uphold perichoretic union for their social doctrine of the Trinity, Pannenberg does not appear to give it the same importance.[53]

With respect to the structures of the church, Volf not only departs from Pannenberg but also wrongfully uses him by stating "Pannenberg takes a similar view."[54] Volf asserts that his own proposal is for an ecclesial framework that is egalitarian and polycentric, one that is "emphatically [a] nonmonocentric-bipolar understanding of the church."[55] This latter phrase is extremely convoluted theological language that means

---

48. Pannenberg, *Christianity in a Secularized World*, 55.

49. Pannenberg, *Apostles' Creed*. The chapter on "The Forgiveness of Sins" (160–69) particularly highlights his conservative views concerning soteriological matters.

50. Moltmann, *Secular Society*, 57.

51. Pannenberg, *Systematic Theology*, 1:319.

52. Volf, *AOL*, 215 and 215n105.

53. Pannenberg, "Subjectivity and Society," in *Anthropology in Theological Perspective*. Even here he does not touch on a social doctrine of the Trinity or the church or indeed neither does he employ that language. However, he handles the concept of sociality in relation to individualism and society.

54. Volf, *AOL*, 246n108.

55. Ibid.

a nonhierarchical structure, which Volf pursues, but this places him in opposition to Pannenberg's episcopal forms of church government that are monocentric and bipolar (priest and laity). This discussion brings the influence of Pannenberg into view, and this is an important aspect of our critical evaluation of Volf and *AOL*. This analysis is continued and summarized in chapter 12 of this monograph, but our next step is to assess two other theological contributions that influence Volf's theology in relation to *AOL*, the first of which is LaCugna.

CATHERINE MOWRY LACUGNA

The Catholic and feminist theologian Catherine Mowray LaCugna (1952–1997) does not exert so much of a direct influence upon Volf's thinking, but he endorses her Trinitarian paradigm as being similar to his own. Therefore a brief excursus to summarize her theological scheme helps us to clarify Volf's. Ted Peters observes that she follows "Rahner's rule, where the economic Trinity is the immanent Trinity and vice versa," and he states that the "LaCugna corollary is this; theology is inseparable from soteriology and vice versa."[56] This highlights the significant connection that often exists between soteriology and a theologian's doctrine of the Trinity. (We have seen from Moltmann that his doctrine of divine passibility is soteriological, and this impacts his view of the divine attributes.)

LaCugna's main thesis presents itself in *God for Us*, and Volf believes that this proposal makes "significant programmatic marks about the relation between the Trinity and the church."[57] Volf highlights her section in the book that considers the theme of ecclesial life and her support for the church as an "icon of the Trinity, a visible image that represents in concrete form the ineffable and invisible mystery of the Triune life."[58] The question that always arises following such an assertion is, which model of the Trinity should the church be an icon of?

LaCugna holds a very similar conception of the Trinity to Volf, and she explains that church members are an icon of the Trinity when they "exist together 'perichoretically,' in mutual giving and receiving, without

---

56. Peters, *God as Trinity*, 124 and quoted from LaCugna, *God for Us*, 211.
57. Volf, *AOL*, 4.
58. LaCugna, "Ecclesial Life," in *God for Us*, 401–3.

separateness, or subordination, or division."[59] She outlines an ideal that joins hands with the feminist and Latin American liberation theologies. The human community according to LaCugna, is to mirror the "divine community of three coequal Persons, by equating divine substance with perichoretic inter-relatedness."[60] Volf shares the same view as LaCugna concerning the significance of perichoretic communion for the doctrine of the Trinity, and they equally reject all forms of inner-Trinitarian subordination and the monarchy of the Father, as espoused by many Eastern theologians. This has obvious implications for the shaping of family and church authority structures, and this Christian revision by LaCugna forms a blueprint for eschatological hope.[61] She plainly asserts that her goal is theological feminism, one that is in opposition to patriarchy, all androcentric biases in theology and complementarian theologies.[62] This may seem surprising when we remember that she writes as a Roman Catholic.[63]

Furthermore, in explaining matters relating to the Trinity and the church, Volf quotes an article jointly written by LaCugna and Killan McDonnell[64] that outlines the limits that exist in using the Trinity as a model for the church. Their helpful guidelines are a constant reminder to safeguard our theology against over-stretching the correlation between the Trinity and the church; however their own caution does not cause them to draw back in asserting a nonhierarchical model of community to be applied to the church and the world. In this respect Volf follows in the same ecclesiological footsteps as Moltmann, LaCugna, McDonnell, and others.

JUDITH GUNDRY-VOLF

Judith Gundry-Volf is a research fellow and associate professor (adjunct) of New Testament at Yale Divinity School and belongs to the same faculty as her husband. Her biographical profile shows that her theological path has involved teaching posts at the same academic institutions as her husband, and similarly, as with Elisabeth Moltmann-Wendel, she is also

---

59. LaCugna, *God for Us*, 402.
60. Ibid., 278.
61. Ibid., 266–78.
62. Ibid., 267–70.
63. LaCugna, "God in Communion." This chapter gives a more expanded feminist critique of traditional notions of the Trinity.
64. LaCugna and McDonnell, "'The Far Country,'" 202–5.

a theologian in her own standing. She has coauthored a book with her husband, *A Spacious Heart*,[65] and she has authored a number of her own articles, some of which are quoted in *Exclusion and Embrace* (hereafter called *EE*), but not in *AOL*. Therefore, a grasp of her theological position allows a fuller picture of this theological influence upon her husband.

The articles that are referenced by Volf in *EE* are worthwhile to summarize because these provide a window into Gundry-Volf's theological paradigm. In the chapter in the book on "Gender Identity," Volf explains: "the problem of gender identity and difference remains a significant one. Clearly, when half of the human race (women) is consistently deemed inferior and frequently mistreated, we have a problem of major proportions."[66] With this apparent problem in view, he expresses that the Trinitarian relations should be a key to solving the problematic relationship between the genders, and he enquires into the significance that the debate concerning the gender of God language may have.[67]

In the midst of this gender identity discussion in the same book, Volf affirms the rejection of any subordination between male and female persons and their relations, as he uses a dual interpretive lens of his social doctrine of the Trinity and his exegesis of Gal 3:28.[68] He uses Gundry-Volf to buttress this argument and to reinterpret Gen 1 and 2 regarding the roles of male and female, in asserting that "what has been erased in Christ is not the sexed body, but some important culturally coded norms attached to sexed bodies."[69] Secondly, this same discussion follows on to consider 1 Cor 11, where he "underscores the equality of genders" without "erasing the differences in genders"[70] in line with an essay by Gundry-Volf.

Volf adopts the position of Gundry-Volf in her essay on "Spirit, Mercy and the Other" as he attempts to explore this line of thought. She seeks to reinterpret certain NT narratives concerning Jesus, for

---

65. Gundry-Volf, *Spacious Heart*.
66. Volf, *EE*, 167.
67. Ibid., 169.
68. Ibid., 182–83.
69. Ibid., 184; Gundry-Volf, "Male and Female in Creation and New Creation: Interpretations of Galatians 3:28c in 1 Corinthians 7," in *To Tell the Mystery*, 102. Robert H. Gundry is her father, and she comments: "This essay is officially dedicated to Robert Gundry, both a mentor and father to me," 121.
70. Volf, *EE*, 186; Gundry-Volf, "Gender and Creation," 151–71.

example the meeting between the Samaritan woman at Jacob's well who encounters Christ. This encounter is understood by Gundry-Volf to provide a platform to overcome "ethnic and religious exclusivism" because she believes that faith in Jesus should lead to the "creation of inclusive fellowship."[71]

An article in the *New York Times* concerning discussion on the fifth chapter of Ephesians and the principles of headship and submission perhaps serves us well in informing us of Gundry-Volf's paradigm. Peter Steinfels summarizes her assertion:

> [The] New Testament passages like the one in Ephesians were Christian adaptations of the "household codes" that Greco-Roman moralists had developed to instruct the heads of families in running their affairs. She suggested that these adapted codes—which also addressed the relations between parents and children, slaves and masters, people and government—could be seen as a retreat from an earlier, more egalitarian ethos among Jesus' followers. Paul had earlier declared that "there is no longer male and female; for all of you are one in Christ Jesus" (Galatians 3:28), and had also referred to female leaders in the early church. This retreat was a response to suspicions that Christians were upsetting a social order based on patriarchal authority.[72]

Her predominant hermeneutic is an egalitarian belief system that reinterprets biblical passages on the basis that any contradiction to her own worldview must therefore be flawed. This is typified in an article where she expounds this approach and states that "Galatians 3:28 served as a theological basis for the egalitarian practice in the early church."[73] Other NT passages that seemingly teach differently she sweeps aside with claims that "these texts [1 Cor 11:3–14, 14:34–35; Eph 5:22–33; Col 3:18–19; 1 Tim 2:11–15; 1 Pet 3:1–6] are struggling to take seriously the social and cultural contexts of the Christian women and men in patriarchal settings."[74]

The key hermeneutical lens for Gundry-Volf appears to be her reading of Gal 3:28, which portrays relationships "between man and

---

71. Gundry-Volf, *Spacious Heart*, 18.
72. Steinfels, "Beliefs."
73. Gundry-Volf, "Gender Distinctives," 46.
74. Ibid.

Other Theological Influences upon Volf in Relation to After Our Likeness

woman in the Lord in a non-hierarchical way,"[75] and she views the whole of the NT in such light. Therefore we can deduce that she rejects the infallibility of Scripture on the basis that she assumes that all of its authors wrote from a culturally conditioned, patriarchal world. These theological presuppositions similarly undergird all of Volf's writings, and while it would be speculative to assume that Gundry-Volf has been the one to influence him in this direction,[76] it has been nonetheless helpful to examine her theology.

SUMMARY

The specific aim so far is to appreciate the theological paradigm of Volf, in relation to his proposal in *AOL*. The methodology we employ is a detailed understanding of the sources that have most influenced him, and we have sought to outline some of the secondary theological influences upon Volf's theology. Despite the secondary nature of these sources, it does not diminish their importance to his thesis, and it underlines the feminist hermeneutic at work in his theology. This hermeneutic lens anticipates a critical reworking of the doctrine of God, the church, and society.

In a personal email, Volf commented that Letty M. Russell and Elisabeth Schüssler-Fiorenza are not theological influences upon his proposal.[77] At first, this writer thought this was the case because both authors are cited in the introduction to the American edition. However in *AOL* he upholds their desire to "dismantle the model of the church as a 'household ruled by a patriarch' and replace it with the model of 'a household where everyone gathers around the common table to break bread and share table talk and hospitality.'"[78] Their feminist reenvisioning of the church has not been a direct influence upon *AOL*, but they reach similar conclusions for an egalitarian and nonhierarchical ecclesiology. Volf takes the discussion a step further, in that he enriches this

---

75. Ibid., 48.

76. Volf, "Church as a Prophetic Community," 30n84. Here Volf writes: "I want to thank Dr Judith Gundry-Volf for her critical reading of this paper and the valuable suggestions." This would seem to indicate that she has had a firm influence upon his theological perspectives.

77. Volf, email to author, February 2008.

78. Volf, *AOL*, 2; Schüssler-Fiorenza, *Bread Not Stone*; Schüssler-Fiorenza, *Jesus*, 190; Russell, *Church in the Round*, 42.

feminist hermeneutic with a Trinitarian proposal for the church as the image of the Trinity. This seems to have been overlooked by Moltmann-Wendel, Gundry-Volf, Schüssler-Fiorenza, and Russell, and only worked out in part by LaCugna.

Our discussion in this chapter concerning Pannenberg involves significantly different matters, namely the doctrine of God and the Trinity and its relation to the church. A critical observation is put forward, one that questions whether Volf is reading Pannenberg with sufficient accuracy. This revolves around the theological differences between Moltmann and also Volf's social doctrine of the Trinity that differs on key points with Pannenberg's repeated stress on the monarchy of the Father. Yet despite this, Pannenberg's doctrine of the Trinity is used by Volf to buttress his own proposal in *AOL*. Pannenberg envisages a markedly different doctrine of the church to Moltmann and Volf. Our concluding impression following our separate and comparative studies of Pannenberg's and Moltmann's doctrine of the Trinity and the church is that this validates the opinion that a theologian's doctrine of the Trinity indeed molds his or her doctrine of the church.

4

Volf's Trinitarian and Ecclesial Paradigm

AFTER OUR LIKENESS: THE CHURCH AS THE IMAGE OF THE TRINITY

IN THE INTRODUCTION TO chapter 2, it is put forward that if we discern the assumptions undergirding theologians' paradigms, then we can better understand how and why they reach certain conclusions. Volf is no exception to this rule: he holds eight beliefs that become apparent in *AOL*, and these need to be placed under the magnifying glass. Volf rarely qualifies or justifies the theological validity of his own assumptions, and conversely he takes it for granted that contrary positions are flawed.

The ultimate goal of *AOL* is an "ecumenical ecclesiology" that "spells out a vision of the church as an image of the Triune God"; this engages with the predominant themes of the "relation between the Trinity and community" and a "promising model of the relationship between person and community."[1] Community is considered in relation to the local church, with the Free Church model especially in mind. Volf's Trinitarian paradigm needs to be grasped before it is possible to comprehend the unfolding of his ecclesiology.

The first of these eight assumptions that are visible in *AOL* is a non-hierarchical doctrine of the Trinity. He explains that this is more fully expounded in one of his articles, "The Trinity Is Our Social Program." He elucidates in *AOL* that he tries "to develop a non-hierarchical but

---

1. Volf, *AOL*, x–xi, 2.

truly communal ecclesiology based on a non-hierarchical doctrine of the Trinity."[2]

Secondly, he assumes a communal ecclesiology that is egalitarian because he believes that this is the only way forward for the church, and he takes for granted his third premise—an unquestioned, direct relationship between the Trinity and the church, as the image of the Trinity. He puts forward that the doctrine of the Trinity has explanatory significance for ecclesiology, and he assumes without justification that the ecclesial metaphor of the church as an "icon of the Trinitarian community"[3] is unquestionably valid.

His fourth premise concludes that "ecclesial individualism and old-style hierarchical holism"[4] are defective and that he prefers an ecclesial sociality. Volf consistently attempts to knock down his twin opponents of individualism and authoritarianism because he considers these to be responsible for many ecclesial ills. Apparently "we must learn to think of free and equal persons as communal beings from the outset, rather than construing belonging as a result simply of their 'free decisions.'"[5]

A fifth supposition is the endorsement of feminist theologies and women's ordination. Again he does not explicitly justify why he believes this, but he asserts: "I do not specifically address the ordination of women; I simply assume it."[6] Sixthly, Volf accepts that an ecumenical ecclesiology[7] is what is required, and his seventh assumption concerns the seeming crucial importance that he places on the whole issue of the "transmission of faith"[8] and with that missiology, so that churches can most accurately reflect, in Volf's view, the Triune God's being and attributes.

The eighth and final tenet of his theology is an eschatological theme[9] that he especially applies to his concept for the catholicity of the church. There is undoubtedly overlap between these different presuppositions,

---

2. Volf, *AOL*, 4.
3. Ibid., 25.
4. Ibid., 3
5. Ibid.
6. Ibid., 2.
7. Ibid., 19–25.
8. Ibid., 1, 4–5; Walls, *Missionary Movement*.
9. Volf, *AOL*, 128–29, 264–70, 281–82.

and no doubt more assumptions could be highlighted, but this summary maps out the contours of Volf's theology.

Direct reference is made by Volf in *AOL* to some of his other writings, and these offer more explanation of these postulates. These five articles are: "The Church as a Prophetic Community," "Worship as Adoration and Action," "Soft Difference," "When Gospel and Culture Intersect," and "The Trinity Is Our Social Program." It is our intention here to firstly discern the theological influences and conjectures for Volf's line of argument before we engage in a detailed, chapter by chapter critical analysis of his book. We will firstly examine these five articles and then in the following subsection consider his other writings that are pertinent to our study.

FIVE RELATED ARTICLES WRITTEN BY VOLF

Volf directs the readers of *AOL* to five of his articles that specifically highlight his thought on ecclesiological themes.[10] The best approach we can take is to deal with these articles in their chronological order. "The Church as a Prophetic Community and a Sign of Hope" (1993) shows that the "church is a sign" and that "church means the various churches, especially at the local level."[11] Furthermore, Volf stresses that churches are "prophetic communities and signs of hope," and he states: "theologically I believe that the primary locus of ecclesiality is the local church."[12]

He perceives a sign character of the church that in turn gives a missiological thrust to this statement. This means that a church is a "sign of hope" because the church's prophets make the "Christian message speak to the great issues of the day," and the church symbolizes this message in "its structures and its life."[13] The church should be focused on the Trinity according to his view, and its members are to pray for the work of the Holy Spirit. He also asserts that "the efforts of the church to communicate and to signify will be futile if it does not listen to the voice of the Spirit and strive to be renewed into the likeness of the Triune God."[14]

---

10. Volf, *AOL*, 7.
11. Volf, "Church as a Prophetic Community," 9.
12. Ibid., 14.
13. Ibid., 25.
14. Ibid.

"Worship as Adoration and Action" (1993) is essentially a Christian theology of work, and Volf seeks to remove what Luther supposedly considered to be a "false dichotomy between the sacred and the secular."[15] There is an eschatological theme that is linked to the Trinity, and he explains: "Through their [Christians'] adoration they anticipate the enjoyment of God in the new creation where they will communally dwell in the Triune God and the Triune God will dwell among them (Rev. 21–22)."[16] This message seeks to widen traditional thought patterns regarding the role of Christians in society.[17]

In "Soft Difference" (1994) he pursues a contemporary application from 1 Peter for a Christian's understanding of identity with, and difference from, the societies that they find themselves in.[18] This exploration builds on the ideas of Max Weber and Ernst Troeltsch, who perceive that "one cannot separate theology from sociology."[19] Volf's study concludes that the life of a Christian should be lived out on the stage of a non-Christian environment. He puts forward the need for a soft difference between Christians and their surrounding culture, in a way that maintains a Christian identity, necessary for the church.[20] Volf's article "When Gospel and Culture Intersect" (1998) follows a similar vein, where he proposes the need for "difference not accommodation."[21]

The most illuminating article relating to our research is "The Trinity Is Our Social Program: The Doctrine of the Trinity and the Shape of Social Engagement" (1998). The initial question addressed in this essay by Volf is, "Can we copy God?" He appeals to his own eschatological vision and to a host of other writers in making connections between the Trinity and the church,[22] and he writes:

---

15. Volf, "Worship as Adoration," 203.
16. Ibid., 208.
17. Volf, *Work in the Spirit*. Here Volf expands his thought that is outlined in the article "Worship as Adoration and Action," and he particularly critiques Luther's theology for Christian work (105); Volf, "On Loving with Hope," 28–31.
18. Volf, "Soft Difference," 2.
19. Ibid., 1; Weber, "Die protestantischen Sekten"; Troeltsch, *Social Teaching*, 2:994.
20. Volf, "Soft Difference," 14.
21. Volf, "Gospel and Culture Intersect," 205.
22. Volf, "Trinity Is Our Social Program," 403n2. There is an appeal to some rather obscure theological sources such as John Donne and F. D. Maurice, and the footnote reads: "Proposals about a correspondence between the Trinity and society, and less eschatologically intoxicated ones for that matter, can be traced back further than the

> More than just the good news of what God has done, the gospel is a social project [that] humanity needs to accomplish. Because the resurrection of Christ is immanent to all human beings, the participation in the Triune life of God is not just an eschatological promise, but a present reality and therefore also a historical program.[23]

Quite correctly Volf agrees with Peters that "we as creatures cannot copy God in all respects."[24] Instead, he pursues a goal of "copying God in some respects," and his model for human community considers "to what extent it should do so."[25] However it should be noted that Volf attempts here to construct a political theology for society as opposed to a model restricted only to ecclesiology, and he defines his vision for social change thus: "instead of concentrating on the structures of social arrangements I will concentrate on the character of social agents and their arrangements, an issue no less 'political' than the issue of social structures."[26]

The question that constantly comes to mind as one engages in making any connection between the Trinity and something else, whether it is the church or social structures, is, what is the theological model for the doctrine of the Trinity that is being adopted? Volf lays down some clear boundary markers in this essay that provide a window into the "soul" of his theology for the Trinity. This article reveals the structural components for Volf's doctrine of the Trinity, and this will now be considered with two subheadings entitled: "The Being of God" and "The Divine Attributes of the Trinity."

The Being of God

The theological starting point for the Trinity often influences the end point, and Volf begins his pursuit for a doctrine of the Trinity by setting out his objective to explore two issues. He clarifies that "one issue is 'identity', a relative newcomer in Trinitarian thinking, and the other is

---

19th century, for instance in the thought of John Donne in the 17th century and are to be found in other 17th century thinkers, such as F. D. Maurice." See Nicholls, "Divinity Analogy," 570–80; Nichols, "Political Theology," 45–66; Christenson, *F. D. Maurice's Theology*; Ranson, "Trinity and Society," 64–74.

23. Volf, "Trinity Is Our Social Program," 403.
24. Ibid., 404; Peters, *God as Trinity*, 186.
25. Volf, "Trinity Is Our Social Program," 405.
26. Ibid., 406.

'self-donation.'"[27] The idea of self-donation he relates to the divine attributes of the Trinity as something to be copied by the church, but this can be laid aside for a moment. Our immediate concern is his hypothesis that identity should be the starting point for the doctrine of God because this is central to his treatise. He is "interested in what may be described as the 'Trinitarian construction of identity'—in the formal features of the identity of a divine person in relation to other Persons."[28] There are three structural features to this social doctrine for the Trinity.

An Egalitarian Understanding of the Trinity

Much of Volf's ambition is to dispose of negative hierarchical connotations for the doctrine of God, and he posits what he believes are two mutually exclusive doctrines of equality and hierarchy. "Though the debate between the advocates of hierarchy and equality in the Trinity is of great significance," he insists, "for how the doctrine of the Trinity should shape social vision," he then continues "I will not pursue it here further," but concludes that he has "sided with the egalitarians."[29] This is a bewildering proposition because in this article, as in *AOL*, he fails to carefully explain how and why he has come to this conviction, in what is, by his own admission, a matter of "great significance."[30] Furthermore he does not accommodate other theological stances on the same issue, such as a Reformed construction of the Trinity in the way that Letham expounds to combine equality and order together. Letham's position argues for the "equal ultimacy" of the persons of the Trinity while maintaining an ordered constitution between the Father, the Son, and the Holy Spirit.[31]

Volf claims that "recently voices have emerged contesting hierarchical constructions of the doctrine of the Trinity," ones who are "advocating Trinitarian egalitarianism" but his footnote only mentions

---

27. Volf, "Trinity Is Our Social Program," 408 and 408n21; Jenson, *Triune Identity*, 105–11; he suggests that "identity" replaces the ancient notion for hypostasis. Volf, however, is "more interested in what may be described as the 'trinitarian construction of identity'—in the formal features of the identity of a divine person in relation to other persons" (Volf, "Trinity Is Our Social Program," 403n21).

28. Volf, "Trinity Is Our Social Program," 408n21; Volf, "Christian Identity and Difference."

29. Volf, "Trinity Is Our Social Program," 408.

30. Ibid.

31. Letham, *Holy Trinity*, 463 and 179n29.

one theologian, namely Moltmann.³² He declares without qualification, that "in a community of perfect love between Persons who share all divine attributes, a notion of hierarchy is unintelligible"; he also accuses those who hold hierarchical constructions of the Trinity as being "projections of the fascination with earthly hierarchies onto the heavenly community."³³ This argument may be valid, but it applies equally to his own theology because it could similarly be asserted that he also projects his earthly fascination for egalitarianism onto the being of God.

A Doctrine of the Trinity that Excludes Monotheism

Volf examines the value of the traditional model of monotheism for Christian theology that has been held for centuries by churches from both East and West, and he again takes his quest for social identity as his starting point.³⁴ He argues that "in recent decades the issue of identity has risen to the forefront of discussion in social philosophy" and that the "major concerns of the nineties seem to be about identity."³⁵ He gives the impression that he is a theologian who is primarily interested in the anthropological questions for human identity before he addresses matters that pertain to theology. He defines identity as being "about the recognition of persons who differ in gender, skin colour or culture."³⁶ In the light of this perceived need to recover the issue of human identity, he makes a rather dramatic move that essentially rejects Christian monotheism.

He appeals to Regina M. Schwartz's exploration of the relation between identity and monotheism in *The Curse of Cain: The Violent Legacy of Monotheism*. Volf believes that she "rightly claims that any understanding of divinity centering on the singleness of an omnipotent subject will tend to forge 'hard' identities and foster violence."³⁷ Monotheism, he alleges, has "deleterious effects on the processes of identity formation," and he suggests the alternative is found "enshrined in the doctrine of the Trinity."³⁸ It may come as a surprise, but his quantum theological leap

32. Volf, "Trinity Is Our Social Program," 407 and 407n19.
33. Ibid.
34. Ibid., 408.
35. Ibid., 408 and 408n22; here he appeals to Menand, "Culture Wars," 18, and Taylor, "Politics of Recognition," 25–73.
36. Volf, "Trinity Is Our Social Program," 408.
37. Schwartz, *Curse of Cain*, x, 16, 38, 63, 69, 88.
38. Volf, "Trinity Is Our Social Program," 408.

that essentially denies monotheism is only supported in his argument by reference to one author, Schwartz.

Perichoresis is the Central Trinitarian Notion

This proposal by Volf for human and Trinitarian identities is built on what he considers to be the central Trinitarian notion, perichoresis.[39] He understands the doctrine of perichoresis to be the mutual indwelling of the three divine persons, and he grounds this idea in the historic and traditional understanding of this concept. He establishes his doctrinal notion through appeals to John of Damascus, Gunton, Zizioulas, and the Johannine Jesus (John 10:38, 14:10, 17:21).[40] Here as elsewhere he freshly explores his chosen slant to determine what implications there may be for identity.

The proposals he makes for his social vision of the Trinity in relation to identity, he labels as "non-reducible" and "not self-enclosed."[41] This upholds his distinction for the identity of a person while he maintains fluid boundaries between each person. Volf grounds his teaching on human personhood by connecting his doctrine for the being of God with his axiom for the foremost attribute of the Trinity—namely the divine self-donation of the cross.[42]

The Divine Attributes of the Trinity

Trinitarian self-donation is seen as the image for human communities to model themselves upon, according to Volf, in a world of oppression, injustice, and deceit. He appeals to Matt 5:48 where Jesus encourages his hearers to "be perfect, as your heavenly Father is perfect." He contends that we are to imitate the divine love of the Trinity through the "greatest gifts of the Crucifed: grace and forgiveness."[43] A brief exposition of Rom 13:8–14 is offered in support of his thesis, and he points out that "when Paul turns to address the relationship between the 'strong' and the 'weak' (Romans 14:1—15:13), he repeatedly appeals to the self-giving of Christ

---

39. Ibid., 412.

40. Ibid., 409–12; John of Damascus, "De Fide Orthodoxa" [Exposition of the Orthodox Faith], *NPNF*, 1.8, 5–6; Gunton, *The One, the Three*, 214; Zizioulas, *Being as Communion*.

41. Volf, "Trinity Is Our Social Program," 410.

42. Ibid., 411–12.

43. Ibid., 413–14.

as the model to emulate."⁴⁴ This social Trinitarian vision based on the cross he understands to be a repetition of the divine love that involves the "Triune God's engagement with the world in order to transform the unjust, deceitful, and violent kingdoms of this world into the just, truthful, and peaceful 'kingdom of our Lord and of his messiah' (Revelation 11:15)."⁴⁵

A good deal of his argument is expounded further in *EE* in connection with Paul's exhortation for the church to "welcome one another as Christ has welcomed you" (Rom 15:7). He inserts a commentary on this verse by Rowan Williams to buttress this social model for justice. Williams writes:

> Generosity, mercy and welcome are imperatives for the Christian because they are a participation in the divine activity; but they are also imperative because they show God's glory and invite or attract human beings to "give glory" to God—that is, to reflect back to God what God is.⁴⁶

Perhaps the best way to summarize this perception of self-donation and its application is to hear Volf himself as he concludes his ideal in this article, where he pronounces that he is looking for:

> A People whose social vision and social practices image the Triune God's coming down in self-emptying passion in order to take human beings into the perfect cycle of exchanges in which they give themselves to each other and receive themselves back ever anew in love.⁴⁷

OTHER WRITINGS BY VOLF

One essay that sheds further light on Volf's doctrine of the Trinity is "Being as God Is: Trinity and Generosity" (2006).⁴⁸ Here he explores some of the divine Trinitarian attributes, namely "creativity, generosity, reconciliation and identity"⁴⁹ with a particular focus on generosity. This

---

44. Ibid., 415.
45. Ibid.
46. Williams, "Interiority and Epiphany," 29–51. This is also quoted in a later publication: Williams, *On Christian Theology*, 255.
47. Volf, "Trinity Is Our Social Program," 418–19.
48. Volf, "Being as God Is."
49. Ibid., 7.

article presents a more detailed exposition of the act of self-donation (a term seemingly coined by Volf, as one that embraces the more commonly applied idea of divine self-giving), which is something he actively encourages the church to imitate as the "content of *imitatio trinitatis*."[50] *Free of Charge: Giving and Forgiving in a Culture Stripped of Grace* (2005) seeks a similar agenda in a popular format, and he emphasizes "God the Giver" and "God the Forgiver" as something to be replicated by God's disciples.[51]

Concerning ecclesiology, there are two essays that characterize Volf's thinking, even though they were written four years later than *AOL*. In one essay he describes the Lord's Supper as an "eschatological table," as something that is "very much a summary of the whole of Christian life, at whose heart lies the self-giving of God for sinful humanity"; and this he believes is the "sum of Christian hopes for communion between the Triune God and God's glorified people."[52] Anyone who studies Volf cannot fail to be impressed with his passion for the church to reflect Christ. He condenses this idea in a different article where he writes that "the only thing that truly matters is that the church be a reflection of Christ's own light, in that it continues his mission anointed by the Spirit."[53]

An important thread that runs through Volf's worldview is his repeated concern for liberation and political theology.[54] He writes in 1983 that "liberation theology puts practice—in particular, the practice of liberation—in the centre of theological work."[55] *AOL* is a critical theory, and Volf hopes to lead his readers toward revolutionary changes for the church, founded on his egalitarian doctrine of God. Volf asserts that "liberation theologians have rendered important service to theology in forcefully drawing fresh attention to the fact that theology must always be orientated to practice."[56] *AOL* forcefully pursues a liberation theme by drawing fresh attention to a nonhierarchical model to be practiced by

50. Ibid.

51. Volf, *Free of Charge*. Another two books again develop this theme: Volf, *End of Memory*, and Volf and Katerberg, *Future of Hope*; the latter follows the theme of retrieving hope, for a contemporary culture that appears to be losing hope.

52. Volf, "Theology for a Way."

53. Volf, "Nature of the Church," 75.

54. Volf, "Unclean Spirit Leaves," 13–24.

55. Volf, "Doing and Interpreting," 11. Other articles by Volf that expand on this political theology that includes liberation are "Response to Robert Goudzwaard," "Church, State and Society," "Responses to Democracy," and "Meaning of Reconciliation."

56. Volf, "Doing, and Interpreting."

theology and the church. Volf "advocates the weakness of the Crucified as a new form of power," and he "seeks to bring the reign of the Triune God to bear on all domains of life."[57]

This quest for liberation explains the dynamic thrust behind his writings that seem to anticipate a theology with "hands and feet" to effect real change. His vision for a public theology probably has roots in his doctoral dissertation (1986), researched at the University of Tübingen on "the Marxist understanding of Work, a theological evaluation."[58]

One final article for comment that was probably a forerunner to *AOL* is "Catholicity of 'Two or Three': Free Church Reflections on the Catholicity of the Local Church" (1992). This writing combines many strands of thought from a Free Church perspective that find their fuller expression in his later works. This essay includes dialogue with Catholic and Orthodox ecclesiology, a reflection on catholicity that is eschatological, the employment of John Smyth to represent the Free Church tradition and his use of the principle of "two or three" from Matt 18:15–20, and a concern for an ecumenically informed ecclesiology.[59]

SUMMARY

Social Trinitarianism is a relative newcomer in the theological world, and Volf is one of a number of prominent authors who advocate this reconstruction for the doctrine of God. The validity of this proposal and the strength of its foundational premises are examined in chapters 10, 11, 12, 13, and 14 of this monograph. Volf's model deliberately attempts to recover the much-neglected doctrine of the Trinity and its application for the church. His theological construct promotes an egalitarian, anti-monotheistic vision of the Triune God, where perichoresis is the central thread that holds together a reenvisioned identity for humanity. Volf's notion for human identity comprises total equality, with unashamed social implications that provides support for the cause against all forms of apparent hierarchy.

Volf's whole theology makes steps in the right direction by handling the divine attributes in a way that connects them to a Trinitarian view of God. Self-donation is seemingly the prime attribute he hopes to

---

57. Volf, "Theology, Meaning and Power," 113.
58. Volf, "Response to Robert Goudzwaard," 61.
59. Volf, "Catholicity of 'Two or Three.'"

see reflected by the church both now and in the future. Volf's theology knows no bounds in aiding a social vision that is expected to overflow into a world of injustice to effect a change. There is one more book that requires some treatment, before we can complete our exploration of the theological paradigm of Volf in relation to his treatise *AOL*, and to this we now turn.

EXCLUSION AND EMBRACE: A THEOLOGICAL EXPLORATION OF IDENTITY, OTHERNESS AND RECONCILIATION

Volf regards this book as a "necessary companion" to his thesis on the Trinity and the church, and he spells out that "the vision of the Triune God provides the foundation there as here [*AOL*]"[60] even though a different question is asked. He clarifies that:

> Instead of asking what the doctrine of the Trinity implies for the formal relations between person and community, I ask how the vision of the Triune God's coming into the world of sin ought to inform the way in which we live in a world suffused with deception, injustice and violence.[61]

This explains a fundamentally different purpose for writing this book in 1996 compared to *AOL* in 1998, but the same doctrine of the Trinity and of the church is held in both books. His ecclesiology is not fully worked out until *AOL* is published two years later. There are two motifs that Volf picks up in *EE* that are pertinent to our study: these are gender identity and the attributes of the Trinity.

Gender Identity: A Social Understanding of a Nonhierarchical Trinity

One of the eight presuppositions that Volf assumes in *AOL* is the ordination of women, a stance that is simply assumed without qualification. However in *EE* he lays down clear reasons as to why he endorses such a view with connections to his nonhierarchical doctrine of the Trinity. *EE* is a highly developed piece of writing that fleshes out his assumption concerning the inner-Trinitarian relations, and because these ideas are not reiterated by him in *AOL*, insight into this book is extremely valuable.

---

60. Volf, *AOL*, 7.
61. Ibid.

He argues that the "content of gender identity is rooted in the sexed body and negotiated within a given cultural context" so that the "portrayals of God in no way provide models in what it means to be male or female."[62] The significance of gender-language in relation to God is assessed by Volf including a brief dialogue with feminist theologians such as Elizabeth A. Johnson, Mary Daly, and Mary Stewart Van Leeuwen.[63] Daly's blunt statement that "if God is male, then male is God"[64] is affirmed by Volf, who then asserts that "God does not model gender identity."[65] While the sexed body is acknowledged to be the basis for gender difference, his model encompasses the fluidity of gender identities. He then explains his thought "by exploring the nature of the Trinitarian identities and their implications for gender identities and relations."[66]

He endorses the notion proposed by Serene Jones, one that connects gender identity to the Trinity; Jones writes that "God's very reality is radically multiple, radically relational and infinitely active."[67] Volf then, quite briefly investigates Ratzinger's doctrine of the Trinity in *Introduction to Christianity*,[68] and he firmly rejects what he believes to be Ratzinger's "most radical kind of hierarchy within the Trinity."[69]

Appeals are made instead to Moltmann's *The Trinity and the Kingdom*, especially where Moltmann "refuses to dissolve Persons into relations and seeks to affirm their equality."[70] Volf upholds Moltmann's distinctions between the "level of constitution" and the "level of life" among the persons of the Trinity and the view in *The Spirit of Life* that interprets the Father as "no longer the First, but One among the others."[71] Volf paves the way for himself so that he is able to easily propose that "the Father therefore constitutes the mutual relations between the Persons as

---

62. Volf, *EE*, 181.
63. Johnson, *She Who Is*; Daly, *Beyond God the Father*; Van Leeuwen, *Gender and Grace*.
64. Daly, *Beyond God the Father*, 19.
65. Volf, *EE*, 172.
66. Ibid., 175–76.
67. Jones, "God Which Is Not One," 109–141, quoted in Volf, *EE*, 176–77.
68. Ratzinger, *Introduction to Christianity*, 131–36.
69. Volf, *EE*, 179.
70. Ibid.; Moltmann, *Trinity and the Kingdom*, 171–73.
71. Volf, *EE*, 180; Moltmann, *Spirit of Life*, 308.

egalitarian rather than hierarchical."[72] He concludes that identity "rests on the twin notions of self-giving and mutual indwelling," and he draws on the theological influence of John of Damascus and Amy Plantinga Pauw in establishing his perichoretic thinking of identity.[73]

The whole thread of Volf's argument concerns gender identity in *EE*, and this eventually leads him to make one of his most clear statements to throw light on his hermeneutic for theology. He writes:

> I will proceed by reflecting theologically on three key biblical statements on gender. All three appear implicitly or explicitly in subordinationist passages (Genesis 1 and 2; 1 Corinthians 11:2–16; Ephesians 5:21–33). I will simply disregard the subordinationism as culturally conditioned and interpret the statements from within the framework of an egalitarian understanding of the Trinitarian relations and from the perspective of the egalitarian thrust of such central biblical assertions as the one found in Galatians 3:28: "There is neither male nor female; for you are all one in Christ Jesus."[74]

There are two dimensions of Volf's doctrine of the Triune God's being and attributes for his proposal in *EE* worthy of mention: perichoresis (also called mutual interiority), and self-giving (donation). Galatians 3:28 could be justly described as Volf's all-controlling passage through which the rest of the Bible is then reinterpreted.

The Doctrine of the Cross: An Explanation of the Divine Trinitarian Attributes

In various expositions Moltmann seeks to formulate the implication of the cross for the world, most especially in one of his later works, *The Spirit of Life*, which gives prominence to the idea of solidarity with the victims.[75] Volf takes up this theme and explains that solidarity has a "liberationist thrust," and he pursues Moltmann's definition that the cross is the "divine atonement for sin, for injustice and violence on earth."[76] Volf

---

72. Volf, *EE*, 180.

73. Ibid., 181; John of Damascus, "Exposition of the Orthodox Faith," 1.8; Plantinga Pauw, "Personhood, Divine and Human," 2, 14, in Volf, *EE*, 181.

74. Volf, *EE*, 182–83.

75. Moltmann, *Crucified God*; *Trinity and the Kingdom*; *Way of Jesus Christ*; *Spirit of Life*, 130–38.

76. Moltmann, *Spirit of Life*, 136; Volf, *EE*, 22–23.

supports Sobrino's claim that "Christ died for the ungodly" (Rom 5:6) and then writes in *EE* of "divine self-donation for sinful humanity and human self-giving for one another."[77] *EE* is in many ways the outworking of Volf's liberation theology that focuses on the single divine attribute—divine self-donation.

Building on Gustavo Gutiérrez's and Moltmann's liberation theologies, Volf moves beyond Moltmann's vision for a "kingdom of freedom,"[78] and he insists on the "primacy of love over freedom" where he places the "project of liberation into a larger framework" called a "theology of embrace."[79] This provides a safeguard against the potential perpetuation of oppression against the oppressors that could be fostered in some liberation ideologies. Volf's central motif for his theology of embrace is an anticipation of forgiveness and reconciliation for the oppressed and the oppressors, as exemplified by the crucified Christ. He echoes the model of reciprocal Trinitarian relationships for reciprocal reconciliation because of the passion of God on the cross.[80] As Williams puts it:

> The inconceivable self-emptying of God in the events of Good Friday and Holy Saturday is no arbitrary expression of the nature of God: this is what the life of the Trinity is, translated into the world.[81]

There is a perpetual flowing of ideas between Volf's theologies for the cross and for the Trinity, and these two recurring themes are interwoven to form a theological paradigm for a nonhierarchical, perichoretic Trinity of self-giving action, a model to be mirrored by the church and the world.

A SUMMARY OF VOLF'S TRINITARIAN AND ECCLESIAL PARADIGM

While Volf's theology draws upon an eclectic mix of sources, his references to the works of Moltmann are voluminous, and this influence is felt upon almost every aspect of his theological thought. Moltmann and

---

77. Sobrino, *Jesus the Liberator*, 231; Volf, *EE*, 24.

78. Moltmann, *Trinity and the Kingdom*, 56, 191–222; Gutiérrez, *Theology of Liberation*.

79. Volf, *EE*, 105; Volf, "Christliche Identität und Differenz," 3, 356–74.

80. Volf, *EE*, 125–31.

81. Williams, "Barth on the Triune God," 147–93.

Volf are associated with process theology; therefore their paradigms are far from static; in fact they exude dynamism, and this compares favorably with some traditional theologies. Progressive growth and evolving thought is expected in order that their work continues to be relevant to a contemporary world.

Volf demonstrates a persistent concern for a contextual ecclesiology that is relevant to the Free Church tradition, one that is ecumenical, with an eschatological expectation, nonhierarchical, and with a major concern for gender identities. His revision of the Trinity is a social model where the being of God is rooted in equality between the persons of the Trinity; he downplays monotheism and promotes perichoresis to be the central notion for identity and relations. Alongside this framework for the being of God, he highlights a single Trinitarian attribute, from God's passion on the cross; this is labeled as self-donation, but it is more commonly understood to be the concept of divine self-giving.

Volf's doctrine of the Trinity molds his doctrine of the Free Church, which is effectually a radical theology for liberation from all forms of individualism and hierarchy. He embraces many aspects of the feminist agenda, and he departs from historical theology as he makes his anthropological concern for identity the starting point for his reflections on the Trinity. He argues that Free Churches need to be reshaped into the image of his reconstituted doctrine of the Trinity.

We conclude that Volf's theological paradigm embraces a hermeneutic that views all theology, including a doctrine of God, the church and society, through an egalitarian window. His egalitarian interpretation of Gal 3:28 is the framework through which he dismantles all hints of subordination to bring about a perceived agenda for liberation. He rejects any relational subordination between male and female or among races and cultural groups to bring about the formation of his dual interpretive theological lens comprising his social doctrine of the Trinity and his exegesis of Gal 3:28.

5

Free Church Ecclesiology: John Smyth as Volf's Chosen Ecclesial Representative

JOHN SMYTH: AN INTRODUCTION

JOHN SMYTH (?1570–1612) STANDS at the end of a line of dissent, in a movement labeled by B. R. White as the "English Separatist Tradition" (1555–1648).[1] White asserts that this tradition "reached its climax"[2] through Smyth's doctrinal developments. An excellent synopsis of Smyth's theological career is given by Jason K. Lee:

> John Smyth is one of the most intriguing figures in Baptist history. Though most renowned as a pioneer of the General Baptists, Smyth was actually a Baptist for less than two years. His pilgrimage of faith included stages as a Puritan, a Separatist, a Baptist, and a Mennonite. These changes took place in a period of about a decade.[3] (The term "Puritan" refers to those of a Reformed theology, who remained within the Church of England; "Separatists" are those who held a similar theology as the Puritans, but saw the corruption of the Church of England as being irreparable. Therefore they founded independent congregations outside of the authority of that church; "Baptist" is used for those groups or

---

1. White, *English Separatist Tradition*, 1–19. The time span given is from the Marian martyrs, when in 1555, men like Nicholas Ridley and Hugh Latimer were executed, among many others, until the arrival of Governor Bradford in the New World and his production of a record of the *Mayflower* survivors, in 1648.
2. White, *Doctrine of the Church*, i.
3. Lee, *Theology of John Smyth*, xi.

individuals (mainly English) who accept the practice of believers' baptism but maintain a distinct existence from Continental "Anabaptists"; "Mennonite" refers to the Anabaptists of the Dutch tradition).[4]

Volf rests much of his proposal upon this theological pioneer and freely admits that his "point of departure is the thought of the first Baptist, John Smyth, and his notion of the church as the 'gathered community.'"[5] It is not explicitly stated from where the point of departure is from, but we can safely assume that this refers to not only Catholic and Orthodox ecclesiology but also the mainstream Protestant movements that arose from the Reformation. He engages in continual dialogue and critical assessment with his chosen representatives of those traditions: Ratzinger (Catholic) and Zizioulas (Orthodox). Again he states even more emphatically: "In the broad dialogue I carry on with Ratzinger and Zizioulas, I am often inclined to lend an ear to the voice of the first Baptist—'Se-Baptist'—John Smyth," and then he echoes Henry Martyn Dexter's view that he was "one of the most gifted, and, with all of his faults, one of the best of the great company who have borne that name."[6]

"He is the voice of the Free Church Tradition," states Volf without qualification; he then asserts that Smyth's "theological maturation and ecumenical presentability I hope to contribute here."[7] However, it must be underlined that while Smyth has free access to "whisper into his ear" as one who "began a tradition," Volf in no way intends to repeat Smyth simply with "new words and new arguments," but instead, he aims to "enrich that tradition with ecumenical dialogue with other traditions."[8]

The term "Free Churches" has generally been seen as a section of Protestantism, but the defining boundaries have historically been somewhat fluid; therefore a measure of caution should be exercised in any strict usage of this expression. Nonetheless, Volf qualifies his usage of this terminology by affirming two primary meanings: those churches that are congregational in constitution as well as those that consistently maintain the need for a separation between church and state.[9] The works

---

4. Ibid., xi n1.
5. Volf, *AOL*, 2.
6. Ibid., 23; Dexter, *Congregationalism*, 323.
7. Volf, *AOL*, 23.
8. Ibid., 23–24.
9. Ibid., 9n2.

John Smyth as Volf's Chosen Ecclesial Representative 59

of Smyth unashamedly inform the proposal in *AOL*, and quotations by him form a consistent thread throughout.

In Smyth's day there were a number of ecclesial movements that emerged among the English church leaders, and many of his contemporaries became identified with different understandings of authority. A key text for discussion was Matt 18:15–20. During this time of ferment, Smyth developed a number of distinguishing features in his doctrine of the church that set him apart from the tradition he had long held, and this paved the way for developments among the future English Baptists. However our eyes are not particularly fixed on a historical study of Smyth but on a theological goal; that is an understanding of his notion of the church and any demonstrable links he makes with the Trinity.

Where Is the Seat of Church Authority (Matt 18:15–20)?

One of the consequences of the Separatist movement that somewhat polarized positions was the evolutionary development of idea as to the exact seat of church authority. During this pursuit of a pure church two ideals or admonitions emerged: some Anglicans and Presbyterians understood that for practical purposes, that authority rested with the ministers and elders; whereas many of the Independents and Separatists favored the view that this was to reside within the congregation.[10] It must be recognized though, that during this time of flux that there was much variance in the Puritan ideals, and hard and fast boundaries do not always work well in assessing this time period. However, many of its leaders did struggle with the question of church authority, and it is perhaps helpful to understand in some measure how these two positions developed.

From the outset, any church that looked to John Calvin and Geneva as its theological fountainhead invariably included church discipline as a nonnegotiable ingredient for a truly Reformed church. In 1539, during a time of temporary exile in Strasbourg, the pastor from the church, Calvin, clearly defended the Reformed doctrine of the church in a letter to Cardinal Sadolet. He writes that "there are three things on which the safety of the church is founded, namely, doctrine, discipline and

---

10. The historical context of English church reform during the late sixteenth and early seventeenth century is a much-discussed topic. See the appendix for suggested reading.

the sacraments"[11] and also that "the body of the church, to cohere well, must be bound together by discipline as with sinews."[12] This concern for a well-ordered church highlights discipline as an important strand of Calvinistic ecclesiology.

The majority of the Puritan movement, and especially the Separatists up until 1608 at least, were "convinced Calvinists"[13] according to White, besides which the application of outward discipline would most likely have been more pressing with the use of church covenants to bind believers together. How else could the ideal of a pure church be realized and maintained other than through rigorous discipline? Regarding Presbyterians who advocated a different pattern for Anglican government while remaining within the church, White clarifies that in the "1570–80s they looked to Calvinistic Geneva as the ideal church" and that they were seeking "the one apostolic pattern revealed in Scripture, the Presbyterian pattern."[14] This discloses a recurring issue that has remained to our day concerning the reformation of church polity and practice. Whether or not there is a single NT pattern and blueprint to be copied has remained a topic for much debate, and this matter cannot be side-stepped concerning any vision that may pursue a connection between the Trinity and the church.

The *locus classicus* for the subject was Matt 18:15–20, and the precise meaning of the phrase "tell it to the church" (18:17) was hotly contested. Did this mean "tell the elders" or "tell the congregation"? White has probably irreversibly established that there was a developed Separatist tradition, and he devotes almost one whole chapter to these matters concerning Matt 18:17. In an analysis of the apparent changing views of the English Separatist pastor in Amsterdam, Francis Johnson (1562–1618), White discerns: "In the interpretation of the key text, Matthew 18:17, 'tell the church' he [Johnson] now understood 'the church' to be 'the elders', and not, as the English Separatists had all held until then, 'the whole congregation.'"[15]

---

11. Calvin, "Reply by John Calvin to the Letter by Cardinal Sadolet to the Senate and the People of Geneva," in *John Calvin: Tracts and Letters*, 38. Hereafter called *Calvin's Tracts*.
12. Calvin, *Calvin's Tracts*, 55.
13. White, *English Baptists*, 18.
14. White, *Doctrine of the Church*, i–iii.
15. White, *English Separatist Tradition*, 142.

The way this passage was expounded often impacted what was a delicate balancing act between the spiritual authority of the elders and the congregation. This was frequently a reaction to the clerical control of parishes where members had little input in church governance. Church discipline may have been the starting point for discussion, but this led to other matters relating to the locus of authority for the calling of ministers and congregational decision making. White maintains that a vital principle throughout Separatism (at least up until the end of Smyth's ministry) was the conviction that Anglican ministry in its entirety was to be rejected as impure and apostate.[16]

The shifting of church authority from the hands of the ordained ministers into the midst of the gathered believers led to an irreversible distancing from the Church of England. This left no room for the episcopal authority of bishops while simultaneously rejecting Calvin's presbyterianism. Perhaps this issue of authority also opened the door for many other unexpected wholesale changes that emerged, such as the validity of Anglican baptism and Calvinistic soteriology.[17] Hopefully this sketch of the background to the times in which Smyth ministered is helpful, prior to our more detailed investigation of his theology.

Ecclesiology in the Mix: The English Separatist Movement

"The suppressed reformation"[18] is how Alexander Mackennal aptly describes this movement, and Meic Pearse encapsulates the impatience of some of its leaders by describing it as a "reformation without tarrying for any."[19] There are two major strands of thought concerning the Separatist tradition and its relationship with the broader dissenting tradition.

In the first place, many are deeply indebted to White's lucid assessment that there was indeed a clearly defined Separatist tradition that developed. He writes of "those hasty Puritans" whose view of the reformation was "played out on a stage . . . as a tale of two cities, London and Amsterdam, with Geneva, Middleburg, Edinburgh, and

---

16. Ibid., 158.

17. Lee, "Sixteenth- and Seventeenth-Century Background," in *Theology of John Smyth*. This offers some helpful background of the historical context of John Smyth. This book also maps Smyth's theological changes concerning baptism and soteriology, which ran parallel to Smyth's changing views on authority.

18. Mackennal, *Story of the English Separatists*, 1–27.

19. Pearse, *Great Restoration*, 167–74.

Leyden providing the background."[20] White has proposed a clearly marked-out timeframe for this tradition that extends from the Marian martyrs to the pilgrim fathers, with Smyth perceived to be the culmination and the end of the line of this tradition. He asserts that it particularly spanned from "Robert Browne, who first published books defining the notion of the separatist doctrine of the church, to Smyth in whom the Separatist tradition reached its climax"[21] and also that it was "here that the separatist tradition reached its ultimate conclusion" and that following Smyth's death there was "no further dynamic development of Separatist tradition."[22]

In contrast, Stephen Brachlow contends that White is too narrow in his treatment of this tradition and laments that he only makes "a very cursory discussion of Robinson and the ecclesiology of [Henry] Jacob" and that the ecclesial differences between the radical Puritans and Separatists was not as great as he has proposed.[23] Patrick Collinson echoes Brachlow's contention that significant diversity manifested itself in these practical ecclesiologists, and he argues that too often ecclesiastical historiographies have been "a concern for identity."[24] In the words of one observer, Robert S. Paul, "the original contribution of the English Reformation . . . was the doctrine of the church."[25] This all-consuming passion to understand the constitution of a true gospel church was the daily concern of many of these church leaders, irrespective of where the boundary lines are placed between Separatists, Independents, Presbyterians, and Anglican Puritans.

Historical research is, however, often messy. Contrary to Paul's view, Jeffrey K. Jue reports that "more recent studies demonstrate the multi-variegated theological landscape of early Stuart England."[26] Anthony Milton similarly claims that "there was a broad spectrum of views" between 1600–40 "running from crypto-popish 'Arminian' zealots on the one hand, through to die-hard Puritan nonconformists

---

20. White, *English Separatist Tradition*, xiv.
21. White, *Doctrine of the Church*, i.
22. Ibid., 371, 418.
23. Brachlow, *Communion of Saints*, 4.
24. Collinson, "Early Dissenting Tradition," 527–66, 550.
25. Paul, "Way to Wyn Them," 93.
26. Jue, "Active Obedience of Christ," 103.

on the other."²⁷ This diversity seems to be confirmed by Chad Van Dixhoorn's understanding of the purpose of the Westminster Assembly, in that he believes the assembly's concern was mainly for religious unity so that England and Scotland could be Reformed in "doctrine, worship, discipline and government."²⁸ Therefore historical theology should treat the first half of the seventeenth century with great care because it appears that a rainbow of theology and ecclesiology existed among the Puritan preachers.

IS JOHN SMYTH "THE VOICE OF THE FREE CHURCH TRADITION"?

We have highlighted Volf's assumption that Smyth is "the voice of the Free Church tradition" and that his definition of that church tradition encompasses a congregational constitution that affirms a separation between the church and state.²⁹ These assertions, while being neat and tidy, throw up many unanswered questions for today's church. The outline given for a Free Church may be applicable for Smyth's day, but does it fit ours? "Is this notion for a Free Church too simple for the twenty-first century," in what can be an open-ended and ever-changing ecclesial landscape? As far as Smyth being "the voice" to represent this fluid contemporary movement, we can conclude that this is too boldly asserted by Volf for any practical purpose.

White confidently asserts that Smyth is "the climax of the Separatist tradition": a tradition understood to mean those church leaders at the time who believed in a model that pursued a complete separation between the church and state and also between "gathered believers" and the state church. A good deal of this theology, however, was not worked out ultimately on English soil but in the political safe haven of the Netherlands and later exported back into England. The desire here is not to reproduce the material supplied by the excellent biographies of Smyth such as those produced by W. T. Whitely, W. H. Burgess, H. M. Dexter, White, Brachlow, and Lee; instead we seek to be rather single-minded in focusing on Smyth's ecclesiology. In sum, the time frame of

---

27. Milton, *Catholic and Reformed*, 5.
28. Van Dixhoorn, "Westminster Larger Catechism," 2.
29. Volf, *AOL*, 23 and 9n2.

crucial interest is from 1606 to 1612; according to Whitely's chronological table[30] there are some key events worth highlighting.

In 1606, as an ordained Anglican preacher, Smyth seceded to pastor the Gainsborough Separate Church, which was twinned with a congregation in nearby Scrooby, where he became acquainted with the famed leaders John Robinson, William Bradford (who later became the governor of the Plymouth Plantation), and William Brewster. The year 1608 was probably when Smyth and his congregation emigrated to Amsterdam, 1609 the time when believers' baptism was introduced, and 1612 marks his death and the forming of the first Baptist Church in Spitalfields, London, by his former associate Thomas Helwys, who incidentally had previously seceded from the disbanded congregation led by Smyth in Amsterdam.[31]

The two most significant works by Smyth that relate to his developing ecclesiology are "Principles and Inferences Concerning the Visible Church" (1607) and "The Differences of the Churches of the Separation: Containing a Description of the Liturgy and Ministry of the Visible Church" (1608).[32] Additionally Volf introduces a handful of quotes from his other writings (which will be noted later), but these two works form the source material of most of the quotations upon which his thesis develops. It is the final outworking of this theology in Amsterdam prior to the dissolution of the church that he founded that must be summarized as his ecclesial legacy and final position for analysis.

Continuity with the Separatist Tradition

In order to ascertain the ecclesiology of Smyth, we can perhaps best tackle it by considering the ways in which he maintained continuity with the tradition from which he came and also the significant ways that he established his own doctrine of the church and, in doing so, demonstrated marked discontinuity with his fellow Separatist pastors in the Netherlands. These four points of continuity illustrate the main thrust of Smyth's ecclesial links with the Separatists.

---

30. Whitely, *Works of John Smyth*, xv.

31. Ibid., xv; Brachlow, "Robinson and the Separatist Tradition," 6–22.

32. Smyth, "Principles and Inferences," and "Differences of the Churches," in *Works of John Smyth*. It must be noted that all quotations by Smyth are done so with the use of the modern English language for the sake of clarity. Volf, however, maintains the use of Smyth's Elizabethan English when quoting him.

The Use of Church Covenants as the Basis for the Membership of a Gathered Church

The story of personal and church covenants is most likely a study all of its own, and Gwyn Davies, in writing on this subject, affirms that Smyth's church at Gainsborough (1605–1606) had a covenant. In doing so he explains that this was the common practice of gathered congregations, and the idea was also adopted previously by Robert Browne at Norwich around 1580/81 and John Greenwood's congregation in London in the late 1580s.[33]

Robinson similarly held this view for defining a basis for the membership of a true church. He states his position that "two or three, separated from the world . . . and gathered into the name of Christ by a covenant made to walk in all the ways of God known unto them, is a church, and so has all the power of Christ."[34] Whitely observes that Bradford of Austerfield held the same conviction, whose memorable words for a covenant are: "They shook off the yoke of antichristian bondage and as the Lord's free people, joined themselves (by a covenant of the Lord) into a church estate, in fellowship of the gospel, to walk in all his ways, made known, or to be made known unto them, according to their best endeavours, whatsoever it should cost them, the Lord assisting them."[35] Smyth took as the essential point, writes Whitely, that "as he found it in Scripture, to walk in all God's ways"; he and his friends were pioneering to "conform to what should become known."[36]

Smyth's own writings frame his view succinctly: "A visible communion of saints is of two, three, or more saints joined together by covenant with God and themselves, freely to use all the holy things of God, according to the Word for their mutual edification and God's glory (Matt. 18:20, Deut. 29:12, Ps. 147:19 and 149:6–9, Rev. 1:6.)."[37] He explains that this covenant has two parts: "1. respecting God and the faithful, 2. respecting the faithful mutually (Matt. 18:20)." It is a covenant "that contains all the duties of love whatsoever."[38] In these two pages of his

---

33. Davies, *Covenanting with God*, 39–40.
34. Robinson, *Works of John Robinson*, 132; George, *John Robinson*.
35. Whitely, *Works*, lxii.
36. Ibid.
37. Ibid., 252.
38. Ibid., 254.

writings (252, 254) he undergirds this definition by quoting Matt 18:20 no less than eight times and Matt 18:17, three times.

The Locus of Congregational Authority for Censures and Ministry Based on Matthew 18:15–17

This matter apparently solved the dilemma regarding apostolic and ministerial succession and the ordination of men into office, conferred upon them by other ministers. White explains that Robinson's and other Separatist leaders adherence to the principle of congregational authority meant a rejection of the ecclesiology of the Reformed church who held the "tell the elders" view for Matt 18:17. Additionally, White believes that Smyth was the "strongest advocate" for the interpretation that the final seat of church authority was the congregation and also that no one before him had "so clearly or unambiguously" stated this "ultimate conclusion."[39]

Not only were church censures ultimately subjected to the final word pronounced by the gathered church, but this naturally involved the subordination of the ministry to the congregation also. This latter point was also agreed upon similarly, according to Burgess, by "Robinson, Ainsworth and Jacob,"[40] to name but three. Smyth expounds in his usual plain language that the "churches' power of casting out is twofold: first officers out of office and second of members out of communion."[41] This became the basis for a Separatist understanding of a true church and a true ministry.

The Rejection of Assumed Episcopal Authority

Although the rejection of assumed episcopal authority has indirectly, already been proposed, this vital link in the Separatist chain is worthy of being given separate mention. Smyth denied all succession of ministers "except in the truth."[42] The rejection of episcopal claims of authority is something that will be seen later in this monograph as a crucial assumption for Volf's ecclesiology.

---

39. White, *Doctrine of the Church*, 137, 159, 371.
40. Burgess, *John Smyth the Se-Baptist*, 137–39.
41. Smyth, *Works*, 263–64.
42. Smyth, *Works*, 758; White, *English Separatist Tradition*, 139.

The Immediacy of the Presence of the Risen Christ in the Congregation

Matthew 18:20 became the primary appeal for the importance of the presence and authority of the risen Christ in the midst of the gathered believers meeting on the basis of the aforementioned definition. Indeed the foundation for a congregational polity was the authority and mediation of the mind and will of Christ transmitted through the assembled congregation. White expounds that for Smyth, the congregation was "subordinated to the presence of the risen Christ in their midst" and that he probably went further than Browne in this area, which perhaps led him to freely cast off all forms of inherited traditions.[43] Simon Doney similarly argues that the "essence of Separatism is the Lordship of Christ" where "members of the redeemed community . . . were expected to obey his [Christ's] will as revealed in the Bible."[44] With this definition, then, Smyth would have found himself to have been in the mainstream of Separatism.

Discontinuity with the Separatist Tradition

The changes Smyth made probably stem from his covenantal commitment and the essential point, "to walk in all of God's ways." This notion that revelation was progressive led to an almost accidental phenomenon of "always progressing" rather than "always reforming." Whitely perceptively comments that this idea held by Smyth that "revelation is progressive" was the feature "that most surprised and annoyed other people; within six years they saw Smyth move rapidly from one position to another; no sooner was one book in their hands than it was superseded by another with fresh points broached; things once advocated were dismissed as unimportant; or with Augustine's frankness were retracted as mistakes."[45]

Both White and Whitely advocate that he was clearly seeking a "single pattern"[46] supposedly laid down in Scripture "to which every church should conform," and this provided a twin motivation and justification for his actions, despite the shifting sands of his ecclesiology. Champlin Burrage echoes these sentiments and summarizes that he aimed "to

---

43. White, "Doctrine of the Church," 366, 422; White, *English Separatist Tradition*, 137; Coggins, "Theological Positions of John Smyth," 246; and the reply: Shantz, "Place of the Resurrected Christ," 199–203.

44. Doney, *Lordship of Christ*, 368.

45. Whitely, *Works*, lxii.

46. White, *English Baptists*, 12; Whitely, *Works*, lxix.

restore the church to its primitive condition" and that "on the strength of that [Gainsborough–Scrooby] covenant he justifies his many changes of mind."[47] Once the shackles of previously held traditions were thrown off, Smyth seemed to vigorously pursue his vision for local churches, but arguably he only succeeded in forming yet another "new tradition." This discontinuity with the Separatist leaders of his day and the Genevan blueprint can be summarized under three headings: church government and liturgy, baptism, and theology.

Church Government and Liturgy

A clear break from the other Separatists and the Genevan church model was evident when a triform church government of pastor, elder, and teacher was replaced with a uniform ministry of pastor as the only recognized leadership function. The collapse of the three offices into the one was according to White "a contradiction of the Barrowist practice" and perhaps the greatest "non-hierarchical move" among his predecessors and contemporaries.[48] This must have seemed to be a logical outworking of a congregational polity in Smyth's mind. He writes in 1608 that a church even without an eldership has the "power to preach, pray, sing psalms, administer the seals of the covenant: also to admonish, convince, excommunicate, absolve and all other actions either of the kingdom or the priesthood."[49]

Furthermore his democratic view is reinforced as he lays down that the "presbytery has no power but what the church has and gives unto it" and that the "church has some power which the presbytery has not, namely elections, communication and consequently all other sentences."[50] This move to bring the ministry under full subjection to the mind and will of the congregation is unequivocally stated, and Burgess proposes that he "gave clear expression to this vital idea of one rank of

---

47. Burrage, *Early English Dissenters*, 234. Burrage refers to Smyth's covenant in "The Differences of the Churches of the Seperation" where he states his Gainsborough–Scrooby covenant as: "For it is our covenant made with our God to forsake every evil way whether in opinion, practice that shall be manifested unto us at any time and therefore let no man plead now, as some have formerly done, these men are inconsistent." Smyth, *Works*, 271.

48. White, *English Separatist Tradition*, 127.

49. Smyth, *Works*, 315.

50. Ibid.

minister and church government."⁵¹ This determines that the authority of an eldership is one that is conferred by the congregation.

The liturgy also came under his scrutiny and revision with what appears a radical discontinuity and most probably an overreaction in forging new paths. Dexter notes these differences⁵² that included the prohibition of the use of all books in the exercise of public worship, prophesying (preaching), and Psalm singing,⁵³ and Burgess illustrates this extremity in that "even the reading of Scripture was cast out of public worship."⁵⁴ Public ministry was to be conducted "from the heart," and this did not negate the view that a church should have "prophets and private persons," observes Burgess, but he notes that Smyth's "overemphasis on prophesying . . . points to a weakness of the church order."⁵⁵

Baptism

Dexter infers that it was the influence of the Anabaptists in Amsterdam that led Smyth to his "reform and reorganisation on the basis of a new baptism."⁵⁶ With the rejection of the authority of the Church of England, its ordinances and practices, baptism would inevitably have come into view, and this included the validity of infant baptism. Smyth took the somewhat brave step toward believers' baptism, but this decisive event was embroiled in controversy because Smyth first baptized himself, and the congregation he was in charge of were then baptized by Smyth.⁵⁷ Burgess comments that this particular move toward baptism explains the name of "Se-Baptist" that has remained to this day, but that it was originally a slur term that combined the word Baptist and Separatist into a single title of disparagement.⁵⁸

This mode of baptism was altogether new for the English Separatists even though the continental Anabaptists had a long history of adult baptism.⁵⁹ For this reason Burrage comments that "regarding baptism

---

51. Burgess, *John Smyth the Se-Baptist*, 140.
52. Dexter, *Congregationalism*, 6–7.
53. Smyth, *Works*, 273, 306.
54. Burgess, *John Smyth the Se-Baptist*, 95.
55. Ibid., 101, 106.
56. Dexter, *Congregationalism*, 17.
57. Whitely, *Works of John Smyth*, xciii–iv.
58. Burgess, *John Smyth the Se-Baptist*, 155–66.
59. Klaassen, *Anabaptism in Outline*, 162–89. This section covers the Anabaptist

Smyth was neither the first, not the only Se-Baptist, therefore he is not such a unique figure in church history as Dexter would have us believe."[60] However it does appear that he was the first among the English leaders to introduce this practice; "it was Smyth among the Separatists," writes Brachlow, "who first challenged and rejected the practice of infant baptism."[61] This move represented a climactic stage in Smyth's theology and Separatist ecclesiology, and this Anabaptist advancement had significant implications for succeeding generations.

Even though Smyth embraced antipaedobaptist convictions, Keith Sprunger's historical observations record that there is little evidence to support that this development "inevitably followed from radical puritanism or separatism."[62] Brachlow perceives that Smyth's new baptism registered an irreversible theological disruption with the other Separatist pastors, and he writes:

> In the Reformed tradition generally, the Separatists defended infant baptism on the basis of the Old Testament rite of circumcision. Baptism was the sign or seal of God's promise and "everlasting covenant of grace made with the faithful and their seed, and of righteousness which is by faith in Jesus Christ."[63] While the weight of this argument rested heavily on the unconditional covenant of grace, radical Puritan and Separatist soteriology and ecclesiology, as we have seen, laid considerable stress on the conditional covenant relationship and the importance of visible obedience.[64]

It is inferred in this last sentence by Brachlow that the widely held stress on conditional church covenants probably opened the door for Smyth's baptism that testified to the believers' gospel obedience.[65] This discontinuity dramatically surfaced when Smyth refuted his colleague Richard Clifton on the issue of infant baptism. Clifton argued for the inclusion

---

view on baptism, and 187–89 handles the influence of Menno Simons, the founder of the Mennonites.

60. Burrage, *Early English Dissenters*, 239. Grenz, "Isaac Backus," 221–31. This article gives insight into the development of the Baptist tradition in New England in the eighteenth century.

61. Brachlow, *Communion of Saints*, 152.

62. Sprunger, "English Puritans and Anabaptists," 46, 128.

63. Ainsworth and Johnson, "Apology or Defence," 151.

64. Brachlow, *Communion of Saints*, 151.

65. Ibid., 151–52.

of the children of believing parents into church membership through the rite of baptism, and this he based on the covenant promises given to Abraham's seed in Gen 17:10–12 and to the Christians in Acts 2:39: "for you and for your children and for all who are far off, everyone whom the Lord our God calls to himself."[66] Smyth broke with his colleagues and insisted that "the ancient practice of paedobaptistry in ancient anti-Christian churches is no more to be respected than the ancient practice of prelacy."[67]

The title of Smyth's treatise that sought to overthrow Clifton's traditional mode of baptism was highly provocative; it was called *The Character of the Beast; or, The False Constitution of the Church*.[68] It was this kind of behavior and polemic that undoubtedly led Robinson (1576?–1625) to defend the consistent Separatist position on baptism against Smyth's new doctrine. Smyth was now accusing his fellow English pastors of justifying a falsely constituted church because they refused to follow him at this point. Robinson wrote that our "adversaries claim that infant baptism is a popish washing" performed by a "popish priesthood," and this indirect reference to Smyth and his disciples served notice on their alleged erroneous sacrament.[69] The reform of this ordinance was historic but also a double departure by Smyth from his peers because Lee, Davies, Burgess, White, and Whitely unanimously testify that this "baptism now replaced the church covenant."[70] However the use of the Trinitarian baptismal formulation was upheld.[71]

Theology

Smyth arrived in Amsterdam during a time of theological ferment concerning the theology of Jacobus Arminius (1560–1609), and this was prior to the settlement of the matter at the Synod of Dort (1618–19).

---

66. Ibid., 151.

67. Smyth, *Works*, 577–79.

68. Ibid., 563. The full title is "The Character of the Beast; or, The False Constitution of the Church Discovered in Certain Passages Between Mr R. Clifton and John Smyth: Concerning true Christian baptism of new creatures or new born babes in Christ; and false baptism of infants born after the flesh."

69. Robinson, *Works*, 452 and 416–71.

70. Lee, *Theology of John Smyth*, 165; Davies, *Covenanting with God*, 51; Burgess, *John Smyth the Se-Baptist*, 155–56; White, *Doctrine of the Church*, vii; Whitely, *Works*, xciii.

71. Whitely, *Works*, 565. See also "Character of the Beast."

Burgess records that he evidently abandoned Calvinistic soteriology that included election, particular redemption, predestination, and the whole Reformed system of theology in favor of Arminian proposals for a partial depravity, conditional election, and universal atonement.[72] Prior to this development, the 1598 confession was a standard rule of faith for his fellow preachers, but Smyth's newly drafted 1610/11 confession of faith shows that his faith now embodied Arminian theology.[73]

White boldly asserts that all the other Separatists, and the future independents it may be added, were all "clear cut Calvinists";[74] however this statement is perhaps too global.[75] Lee also notes, along similar lines to White, that Smyth's "rejection of Reformed views put him at odds with the Separatist tradition from which he came," and Burgess recognizes that he even toyed with strange ideas concerning the incarnation, and Smyth supported groups who even questioned the validity of the usage of the term "the Trinity."[76] Lee observes that there were five further significant changes that Smyth made to his Christology, once he became a Mennonite.[77]

Whatever one's thoughts are concerning the debate and the issues at stake, this shift upon the content of the gospel impacted the transmission of faith. The church he led collapsed as a result of his divisive principles, practices, and theology, and his longtime friend Helwys seceded and exported these new measures back to England. With such dramatic discontinuity with those who had gone before him, it remains questionable as to the validity of what White, who himself is a Baptist Historian, calls "John Smyth's re-modelled Separatism."[78] Robinson remained constant to his views and perhaps the question remains open: is Smyth the beginning of the Baptist tradition and Robinson the climax of the Separatist tradition?

---

72. Burgess, *John Smyth the Se-Baptist*, 175–76.

73. Smyth, *Works*, 733–50.

74. White, *English Baptists of the Seventeenth Century*, 18.

75. Coffey, *John Goodwin*. Chapter 7 is called " 'The Great Spreader of Arminianism,' 1647–53." Certainly Coffey indicates that Goodwin's later independent congregation was Arminian, much to the chagrin of other Independents and leading Puritans.

76. White, *English Baptists*, 8; Lee, *Theology of John Smyth*, 208; Burgess, *John Smyth the Se-Baptist*, 177.

77. Lee, *Theology of John Smyth*, 242–43.

78. White, *English Baptists*.

How Has Volf Used the Works of Smyth in His Proposal?

Volf's theological concern in *AOL* is for the future well-being of the Free Churches, a movement that perceives to particularly extend into the so-called Two-Thirds World. The definition he puts forward for "Free Churches" is loosely framed as those with a "congregationalist church constitution which also affirm a constant separation between church and state."[79] Running alongside this vision, Volf joins theological hands with Smyth to endorse a high view of the church, the nonnegotiable value of membership to a local church and the ecclesiality of salvation. He quotes Smyth's writings to support this: "They that are not members of the visible church are no subjects of Christ's kingdom" and "every man is bound in conscience to be a member of some visible church established into this true order."[80] It is necessary to explain here that the churches that conform to this supposed "true order" certainly implies a narrow field of catholicity.

As we examine the ways that Volf uses Smyth, we will be able to see with greater clarity the ecclesial model that he envisages and whether he represents Smyth fairly. Let us firstly look at his definition of a Free Church, followed by his question, "where is the church?" and then enquire into Volf's links with the Trinity, church structures, and finally the principles he proposes for ecumenical catholicity.

The Definition of a Free Church

There appears to be an aversion by Volf in using Smyth's terminology for the communion of the saints because this phraseology regarding "a true visible church" is potentially divisive. Instead (chapter 3 of *AOL*) Volf favors the somewhat oblique term, a "concrete church."[81] One of Smyth's most well-known statements is quoted as the "starting point" for Volf's discussion: the church is "a visible communion of saints . . . two, three, or more saints joined together by covenant with God and themselves, freely to use the holy things of God, according to the Word, and for their mutual edification and God's glory."[82] Volf observes that the two elements of this definition that are of significance to his proposal are "joining together" and "covenant"; the latter conception of a covenant is

---

79. Volf, *AOL*, 9n2, 11–18.
80. Ibid., 172; Smyth, *Works*, 267, 256.
81. Volf, *AOL*, 175–81.
82. Ibid., 175; Smyth, *Works*, 252.

explained in Smyth's words to be a "vow, promise or oath," and this covenant between believers consists of "all the duties of love whatsoever."[83]

In an attempt to get to the heart of Smyth's theological thought, Volf highlights Smyth's use of a mutualistic idea of a covenant that he interprets as the "decisive element of these two ideas [joining together and covenant]"; and he describes that "human activity was so predominant in Smyth's thinking."[84] Volf develops this thought further and suggests that "a constitutive element of the being of the church" is "the human will to come together and to abide together as a concrete church"; furthermore the role that the human will plays in belonging to a concrete church is seen as an "indispensable element" of Free Church ecclesiology.[85]

There appears to be little justice done by Volf as to the content of the covenant that Smyth used as a basis upon which a church is founded, and little effort is made to clarify the intent of Smyth in writing "The Differences of the Churches of the Separation." The introduction to this epistle sets before the reader's eyes a clear aim to distinguish between a true and false church, and between one that adheres to the primitive and apostolic pattern and one that does not. Similarly Smyth states that "it is our covenant made with our God to forsake every evil way, whether in opinion or practice"; and by this term "forsake every evil way" he means a separation from the Church of England into the formation of what he understood to be "true churches of the Separation."[86] Therefore the "decisive element" does not appear to be the involvement of the "human will" or "human activity" but something altogether different; namely the joining together to form a true and pure church. The concept of a so-called concrete church in the way that Volf describes as a "fellowship of siblings who are friends, and the fellowship of friends who are siblings,"[87] appears to lead the discussion in an altogether different direction to Smyth.

Where Is the Church?

Chapter 3 of *AOL* explores the ecclesiality of the church to answer the question, what does it mean for the church to call itself a church in the

---

83. Volf, *AOL*, 175; Smyth, *Works*, 254.
84. Volf, *AOL*, 175; Smyth, *Works*, 254.
85. Volf, *AOL*, 177.
86. Smyth, "The Differences of the Churches of the Separation," *Works*, 270–72.
87. Volf, *AOL*, 181.

first place? Volf's discussion quickly moves to consider, "where is the church?" and he assumes that it is "the presence of the Spirit of Christ that makes a church a church"; this could roughly parallel the thoughts of the Separatists on the immediacy of the risen Christ in the congregation.[88]

The Reformation concept of the marks of a true church (preaching pure doctrine, the right administration of the sacraments, and discipline) is omitted, and instead Volf claims that "the early Free Church tradition emphasised two other conditions [in addition to the Word, sacraments, and the presence of the people] regarding the constitutive presence of the Spirit of Christ in a church."[89] These conditions are "obedience to Christ's commandments" and the "biblical organisation of the church."

An unwarranted generalization is made when he asserts that Smyth, the English Separatists, and the early Free Church tradition are all synonymous terms.[90] Obedience was pursued by the Separatists, and in this respect Smyth is quoted to endorse the theological principle that the members of a true church "are men separated from all known sin, practicing the whole will of God known unto them."[91] The phrases that are extracted from Smyth's writings regarding biblical organization are all perfectly valid to support a congregational view in contrast to episcopacy. In other words a true church must be organized, so that, in Volf's words, "Christ's dominion is realized through the entire congregation."[92] Smyth is quoted to summarize this: "we say the church or two or three faithful people separated from the world and joined together in a true covenant and promises and the ministerial power of Christ given to them."[93]

Following his perceptive summation of the Separatist ideals, Volf, in three dramatic moves arrives at an entirely new construction of the ecclesiality of the church. The first move is to dismantle the commonly held ecclesiology of Smyth for the constitution of a true visible church and to take instead "Matthew 18:20 as the sole principle and foundation for what a church is and how it manifests itself." Smyth's conviction that denied ecclesiality to Episcopal churches is swept aside as "an expression

88. Ibid., 130; see 1.3, A, iv.
89. Volf, *AOL*, 131.
90. Ibid., 131–32.
91. Ibid., 131; Smyth, *Works*, 253.
92. Volf, *AOL*, 132; Smyth, *Works*, 252, 267, 274, 403.
93. Ibid, 132; Smyth, *Works*, 403.

of sectarian narrow-mindedness and arrogance."[94] Despite this aspersion he then quotes Smyth's famed definition of the church and singularly highlights Matt 18:20 ("For where two or three are gathered in my name, there am I among them") as the basis that "shaped the entire Free Church tradition."

In breaking down Smyth's description, it is evident that the central thrust of his ecclesiology rested on the two dynamic principles of covenantal obedience and congregational church authority. The latter flows from the much-discussed interpretation concerning Matt 18:17 ("tell the church"), which assumed that the seat of church authority was among the congregation. When this is rightly understood, then even a minimum of two or three people gathering on these principles will then constitute a true visible church.

The second move, or even arguably a second point of departure from Smyth, is to add a congregational confession of faith in Christ as Savior, with baptism and the Lord's Supper as two additional constitutional ingredients to identify the presence of the church. The being of the church is reenvisioned and so are the importance of baptism and the Lord's Supper: Volf writes that "through baptism a person becomes a Christian, and through the Lord's Supper a person lives as a Christian" and that without these two sacraments, admittedly linked with a confession and expression of faith, "there is no church."[95] Where is the mention of the Word of God, obedience to Christ's commandments, and biblical organization? It is not difficult to see that Smyth could not have consented to such a radical reworking of his proposal.

An astounding move by Volf relates to his consideration of the relation of a church with all others. He states in unequivocal ecumenical language that a "discriminatory church is not merely a bad church, but no church at all . . . and that even if such a church were to assemble in the name of Christ, it could only expect rejection from its alleged Lord: 'I never knew you' (Matt. 7:21–3)."[96] This castigation of discriminatory attitudes leads him to an ecclesial minimum so that a local church must be open to all other churches and to all human beings who profess faith in Jesus Christ as universal Savior and Lord.[97]

94. Volf, *AOL*, 134.
95. Volf, *AOL*, 152–53.
96. Ibid., 158.
97. Ibid., 157–58.

The unstated conclusion of this development is the indirect rejection by Volf of the ecclesiology of Smyth and all the Separatist theologians who sought to identify the constitution of a true, visible church. According to Volf then, Smyth and his congregation in Amsterdam should be hearing from the lips of Christ, who is only "their alleged Lord," "I never knew you." It remains unclear as to whether Volf is consciously aware that his radical reworking of the doctrine of the church leads him to three points of departure from the *Works of John Smyth*, and his conclusion is in reality a discriminatory attitude toward many of the leaders of the English Separatist movement.

The Trinity and the Church

The theology of Smyth yields little regarding his doctrine of God, and there are no demonstrable links between his doctrine of the Trinity and the church.[98] There are similarly few discernible links on this theme by the other English Separatists or contemporary Puritans, and it is probably not until the later Congregationalist John Owen that we can see a greater correlation between the church and the Trinity.[99]

In handling this subject, Volf is only able to make two references to Smyth regarding his contribution to this discussion, which further illustrates the point already made. Volf establishes that Smyth "apparently advocated modalism," and he connects this statement about Smyth with his democratic principles for a nonhierarchical view of the church, and with that he explains that he "cannot be accused of clericalism."[100] This assertion by Volf appears tenuous, because Smyth's supposed tendency to modalism took place towards the end of his ministry in Amsterdam, several years after he had written his main works on ecclesiology. This raises the question: can it always be assumed that ecclesiology is a consequence and manifestation of the Trinitarian doctrine held by a theologian?

98. White, *Doctrine of the Church*. Even a basic study of this unpublished PhD thesis will demonstrate that the all-consuming passion of John Smyth was an ecclesiology for a true and pure visible church. The Trinity or the doctrine of God appears only faintly upon his theological radar.

99. Owen, *Works of John Owen*, and *Communion with God*.

100. Volf, *AOL*, 194; Smyth, *Works*, 733. The work cited by Volf is "Propositions and Conclusions," and this is chronologically placed by Whitely, probably post-1610(?), which was two or three years after "Principles and Inferences" (1607) and "The Differences of the Churches" (1608).

A further assertion is made by Volf that clarifies the issue at hand even more. He states that "for Smyth, the theological grounding of the church is not Trinitarian, but rather Christological" and that "his understanding of the church was that of the 'kingdom of Christ.'"[101] Doney observes a similar thought among the Elizabethan Separatists in what he calls their pursuit for the "Lordship of Christ" in the church.[102] Doney believes that there was a double emphasis at work at that time among its leaders, who "sought to restore the church [as the kingdom of Christ] to its original condition or integrity according to Scripture" and "Christ's immediate present rule over the Christian community."[103]

This christological grounding of the church was most probably a dominant motif for Smyth's ecclesiology also. Therefore a nonhierarchical doctrine of the church does not always correspond to a nonhierarchical doctrine of the Trinity. In Smyth's case, he arrives at his conclusions for the church by a different route other than by Trinitarian reflection. This provides some much-needed caution concerning the theological attempt to infer that one's doctrine of the Trinity is always superimposed onto one's doctrine of the church or that a Trinitarian theology is always the primary principle undergirding ecclesiology.

Volf concludes that the "correspondence between the church and the Trinity has remained largely alien to the Free Church tradition."[104] He claims that this is to be expected "if one understands the church as a covenant arising insofar as human beings make themselves into a church, as John Smyth suggests."[105] He raises a fair point because if the basis of a church's formation involves joining together with a covenant, then this could lean towards an emphasis on human responsibility at the expense of divine sovereignty. However it is probably unfair to place this weakness of the Free Church tradition mainly on the shoulders of Smyth. There were many other leaders who contributed to the richness of this tradition, and also a number of wider factors need to be considered.

Some of these wider factors include an overall weakness in the whole of Western Christianity towards its doctrine of God and the Trinity. Western Trinitarianism is by no means uniform, and the school

---

101. Volf, *AOL*, 196; Smyth, *Works*, 274, 740.
102. Doney, *Lordship of Christ*, 368.
103. Ibid., 1–2.
104. Volf, *AOL*, 196.
105. Ibid.

of thought that has dominated the theological landscape in the West, for centuries before Smyth's time, begins with the proposition that God is one and then proceeds to deal with this separately from the doctrine of the Trinity, often relegating the latter to a position of secondary significance. This mainstream tradition, stemming from Augustine, is further developed under the influence of the medieval works of Thomas Aquinas. Aquinas pursued this pattern in his *Summa contra Gentiles* and *Summa Theologiae* and separated the treatment of the one God (*de Deo uno*) and his attributes from the Triune God (*de Deo trino*).[106] Letham expresses an observation frequently made concerning this approach when he comments that "with the strong priority of the essence—the essence is before the Persons—a fundamentally impersonal doctrine of God results."[107]

Much evangelical Trinitarianism follows this format. A. A. Hodge completes eight chapters of his systematic theology, including a proof of God's existence and a description of his attributes, before dealing with the Holy Trinity;[108] Wayne Grudem similarly devotes five chapters to the doctrine of God before the Trinity is introduced;[109] and Bruce Milne, despite claiming that "just about everything that matters in Christianity hangs on the truth of God's three-in-oneness," consigns his doctrine of the Trinity to a rather isolated single chapter among thirty others.[110]

As we have demonstrated, the neglect of the Trinity within Western evangelical theology has commonly been a widespread phenomenon. A concluding thought is that much can be drawn from Smyth concerning ecclesiology but very little can be gleaned with respect to links between the Trinity and the church from his theological writings, and to do so is only speculative.

---

106. Torrance, *Christian Doctrine of God*, 10. He similarly laments the influence of Thomas Aquinas in this area of the doctrine of God where "the One God is divided from the doctrine of the Triune God, as though the doctrine of the One God could be set out rationally by itself, while the doctrine of the Triune God could only be accepted on the ground of divine revelation." He agrees with Karl Barth who argues that this led to splitting the fundamental concept of God.

107. Letham, "John Owen's Doctrine," 7–22.

108. Hodge, *Outlines of Theology*.

109. Grudem, *Systematic Theology*.

110. Milne, *Know the Truth*, 78.

The Structures of the Church

In this aspect concerning church structures Volf follows Smyth quite closely without engaging in the process of deconstruction and reconstruction to formulate his unique conclusions. He echoes Smyth's acknowledgment of the needed place for church officers and quotes him where he says that "members . . . received into communion are of two sorts 1. prophets 2. private persons."[111] Smyth appears to favor a democratic relationship between the officeholder and the congregation, in what Brachlow calls the opposite model of an "aristocratic" relationship.[112] Volf endorses Smyth's notion that "offices" are *charismata*, given by God, and they jointly believe that "the power of using those gifts they have is from the head, Christ, by the means of the body."[113] In following this line, ordination into office is seen as a vital link in the chain and an outward expression of a congregational model. Volf proposes that the process of ordination is "essentially a divine–human act" and that it is an "act of the entire local church led by the Spirit of God."[114] Smyth could wholeheartedly consent to this approach but offer disagreement with Volf's threefold pattern for church offices, comprising of bishops, presbyters, and deacons.[115]

With respect to the participation of the congregation in the decision making and election for ordination, Volf walks hand in hand with Smyth. This Separatist leader's premise was that pastors are "sent by God to preach whom the church sends," "election is by the most voices of the members of the church in full communion," and that "election, approbation and ordination must be performed with fasting and prayer."[116] Volf's participative model for the church, regarding office and ordination probably follows Smyth the closest at this point, with the exception of his threefold office pattern and more markedly, with his unhesitant support for a feminist ecclesiology and the ordination of women.[117] These latter matters would have been very strange to Smyth's ear, and

---

111. Volf, *AOL*, 245; Smyth, *Works*, 255.
112. Brachlow, *Communion of Saints*, 157–202.
113. Volf, *AOL*, 247–48; Smyth, *Works*, 424.
114. Volf, *AOL*, 249.
115. Ibid., 247–48.
116. Ibid., 249, 253, 256–57; Smyth, *Works*, 256.
117. Volf, *AOL*, 2.

the question remains, who is the most influenced by the culture of the day, Smyth or Volf?

Principles for Catholicity

A concept that promotes every local church with primacy over the universal church, with a status as being equally part of the whole church, and enjoying participation with the whole Christ is something expressed by Volf as a Free Church principle for catholicity. He backs Smyth's understanding of the local church in that "every true visible church has title to the whole Christ and all the holy things of God" and that the authority of the local congregation is derived from Christ: "the brethren jointly have all power both of the kingdom and priesthood immediately from Christ."[118]

Overall, however, the appeals to the theology of Smyth on matters of ecumenical development are sparse because Smyth's *Works* are a denial of catholicity to Episcopal churches. The very thought of an ecumenical movement would have been completely alien to his thinking, and if anything his ecclesiology is a wholesale rejection of any such move.

Does Volf Represent Smyth Accurately and Follow His Theology?

Our observations have found that there is no treatment by Volf concerning the historical or theological context of the times in which Smyth ministered. Volf simply assumes that his readers have a good working knowledge of Smyth, and more attention could have been given by him to explain who Smyth was and what were the theological issues he faced that led him to his Free Church ecclesiology.

For many, Smyth's writings will not be familiar because they were last reprinted in 1915, and almost a century has passed since his theology was in circulation. In studying Smyth's works, one cannot fail to be impressed by the voluminous Scripture references that literally saturate his handling of ecclesiology. His approach is systematic with abundant proof-texting; however he does not exhibit thoroughgoing and careful exegesis, as his handling of Matt 18:15–20 demonstrates. These aspects have been completely overlooked or downplayed by Volf in a way that is detrimental to our appreciation of his "chosen theologian," and this may cause people to misunderstand the "life-blood" of Smyth's lucid style.

118. Volf, *AOL*, 271–73; Smyth, *Works*, 267, 315.

Perhaps the Achilles' heel of Volf's usage of Smyth is that no reference is made to the evolutionary changes that occurred in most aspects of Smyth's theology, including his ecclesiology. In 1984, four respected historians attempted to identify the central theme in Smyth's theology, and they published their findings in the *Baptist Quarterly*, but they failed to reach a consensus.[119] In 2003, Lee, in writing *The Theology of John Smyth*, carefully explained the progressive changes in Smyth's theology from a Puritan, to a Separatist, and then Baptist before finally becoming a Mennonite.[120] These revisions in his thinking represent a moving theological feast, and therefore to quote one aspect of Smyth's thought simply fails to do justice to his final "Mennonite" position. Volf makes no reference to these changes in Smyth's theology, and this is a major omission both historically and theologically. Neither does he attempt to give his readers any insight into the corresponding difficulty in using his chosen representative in any dogmatic way. Despite this background, Volf uses Smyth as a launchpad on many fronts; either Volf has not sufficiently researched his "chosen theologian" or he has overlooked this aspect of progressive change in his ecclesiology, in a way that undermines the foundation of his thesis.

Following on from these general remarks, a glaring difference between Smyth and Volf relates to their differing theological goals, and this explains their differing conclusions on a number of points. For Smyth and his fellow Separatist leaders the need of the hour demanded a detailed explanation of the being, attributes, structure, and framework of a true visible church. He was certainly of plain speech in unhesitatingly declaring what he believed to be the difference between a true and false church. The context and theological aims for Volf are, however, markedly dissimilar. His background involves ecumenical engagement and much of the content of his thesis is, by his own admission, the fruit of ecumenical dialogue. He freely declares "the goal of my efforts is an ecumenical ecclesiology" and "all the great themes of this unmistakably Protestant ecclesiological melody are enriched by Catholic and Orthodox voices."[121]

---

119. Shantz, "Place of the Resurrected Christ"; Coggins, "Theological Positions"; Brachlow, "John Smyth"; White, "English Separatists."

120. Lee, *Theology of John Smyth*, xi–xiv. This section gives a summary of the changes outlined in each chapter in the book.

121. Volf, *AOL*, x–xi.

Their divergent purposes probably explain why they end up at very different places concerning their definition of the church and the identification as to where the church is. Despite this background their thoughts run parallel for the proposal for the ordination and election of church officers (*AOL*, chapter 6, "Structures of the Church") and the primacy and authority of a local church over against the universal church (chapter 7, "The Catholicity of the Church"). As has been previously outlined, Volf's proposal suggests rather tenuously that the heartbeat of Smyth's gathered church is the role of the "human will and activity" (chapter 4, "Faith, Person and the Church"). This raises some doubt as to whether Volf is interpreting Smyth accurately in this instance.

Is Smyth Representative of the Free Church Tradition?

This heading represents three questions rolled into one that now need to be addressed. They are: Is Smyth representative of any tradition? What is the Free Church tradition? Is Smyth representative of the Free Church tradition? It probably makes sense to deal with these questions in the order they are given, and concerning the issue as to whether Smyth is a representative of any given tradition, let us hear the voice of his contemporary leaders and secondly that of church historians or theologians.

In his day Smyth was a controversial figure, and his theological developments in the church at Amsterdam led to much heated controversy, not least his own self-baptism. On this matter Francis Johnson believed that "his view on baptism was heretical" and his former friend, Robinson, sadly but honestly wrote that "for Mr Smyth, his instability and wantonness of wit is his sin and our cross."[122] Governor Bradford similarly lamented that "his inconstancy and unstable judgment, and being so suddenly carried away with things, did soon overthrow him."[123] Additionally his associate pastor Helwys became so disillusioned with his ecclesiological practices that he and a number of the church seceded and the whole congregation imploded in 1610. The historical credibility and weight of these opinions cannot be easily dismissed, and it seems that his legacy in their eyes was more one of confusion—in no way did they consider him as representative of their movement.

---

122. White, *English Separatist Tradition*, 146; Dexter, *Congregationalism*, 3.
123. Dexter, *Congregationalism*, 3.

With the passing of time, church historians are sometimes able to reflect more accurately, but here also there is no widespread consensus as to Smyth's universal acceptance as a representative voice. The view of White cannot be quickly dismissed. He holds Smyth in high esteem as one in whom the Separatist tradition was remodeled and yet also climaxed, so much so, that the English (Arminian) Baptists owe their first beginnings to the exiled congregation in Amsterdam led by Smyth and Helwys.[124] Whitely, who was the last person to republish Smyth's complete works, is no less complimentary, and to support his own view he quotes Mandell Creighton saying: "none of the English Separatists had a finer mind or a more beautiful soul than John Smyth."[125]

The content of Smyth's ecclesiology is our main concern, and Burrage summarizes that his "work is crammed with still more astonishing views such as modern Separatists would find it difficult to comprehend, and much more difficult to put into practice."[126] Whitely is more affirming, as expected, and he understood that "the cause of separatism, as it was then termed, or of the Free Churches, as we speak today, gained from him impulse sufficient to carry it on for a generation till it stood firm."[127] In the light of this evidence it would be appropriate to only consider Smyth as a representative in a general sense, one among many leaders of the Free Churches and the Separatists, and specifically as one of the representatives of the early English General (Arminian) Baptists.

This conclusion partially answers the question as to the definition of this amorphous term, the Free Church tradition. This idiom is simply an umbrella term today that houses a somewhat fluid and loosely defined worldwide movement that encompasses a host of non-Episcopal church streams. Its diverse theologies and ecclesiologies means that it lacks homogeneity, thereby making it impossible for one theologian to be its primary or sole representative. Therefore Volf's assumption that Smyth is "the voice of the Free Church tradition" becomes impossible to defend, and the assertion that Smyth began that tradition is untenable. Brachlow brings to our attention the "dynamic and often fluid movement of the left-wing Puritan and Separatist convictions" in Jacobean England and arguably the same culture persists in so-called Free Churches in our

---

124. White, *English Separatist Tradition*, 116–41; White, *English Baptists*, 9–10.
125. Whitely, *Works*, cxviii.
126. Burrage, *Early English Dissenters*, 235.
127. Whitely, *Works*, cxviii.

day. Could any single leader, past or present, be realistically identified as the sole representative of the Free Church tradition?

Theologians reveal their presuppositions in many ways, and their choice of representative theologians is one of those ways that they are revealed. Franklin Littell offers a valuable insight to a perennial problem for historical studies in that "the ocean of facts is infinite" and that every historian reveals their presuppositions "by selecting certain persons to feature, certain reports to highlight, and certain events to emphasise in telling the story."[128] Quentin Skinner offers further blunt warnings for students of history and states:

> Besides the crude possibility of crediting a writer with a meaning they could not have intended to convey, there is the more insidious danger of too readily finding expected doctrines in classic texts. . . . The paradigm determines the direction of the entire historical investigation. . . . History then indeed becomes a pack of tricks we play on the dead. . . . It is also dangerous for historians of ideas to approach their materials with preconceived paradigms.[129]

Smyth is selectively applied by Volf in a way that reveals his own premises for a nonhierarchical government in his reconstructed Free Church model. Questions need to be faced as to whether Skinner's warnings also apply to Volf's treatment of Smyth. If Volf had a broader base of representation it would give more credibility to his case. Brachlow openly endorses the use of Jacob and Robinson to embody the ecclesiology of the radical Puritans and Separatists.[130] A threefold appeal to Smyth, Robinson, and Jacob would more likely cover the varied understandings of a Separatist church in their day and ours, to buttress the argument in *AOL* substantially. The use of a single theologian, like Smyth, paves the way for the accusation of discriminatory and weakened representation; as a prototypical theologian, Smyth will always lack credibility in some people's minds. This detracts from the noble aim of upholding the Free Church position that Volf hopes to reflect ecumenically.

---

128. Littell, "Periodisation of History," 18, quoted in Brachlow, *Communion of Saints*, 1.

129. Skinner, *Visions of Politics*, 61, 64–65, 77.

130. Brachlow, *Communion of Saints*. Each chapter concludes with a reflection on the ecclesiology of Henry Jacob and John Robinson as his chosen representatives.

Summary

"Is not the visible church of the New Testament with all the ordinances thereof, the chief and principal part of the gospel?"[131] Smyth underscores his concern for the vitality of local churches with this searching question, and Volf similarly expresses related sentiments in his proposal for Free Churches. The uncovering of the historical context of the Elizabethan-Jacobean period is essential in order to identify, broadly speaking, four ecclesial strands of church reformation. The Separatist movement, from which Smyth emerged, was very much associated with the crucial question as to the seat of church authority.

The democratic congregational model of church government adopted by Smyth leads Volf to name him as "the voice of the Free Church tradition," and we have critiqued and denied this declaration's legitimacy. We observe clear continuity but also marked discontinuity between Smyth and the accompanying Separatist leaders of his day. We expound where and how Volf uses Smyth to support his own case in *AOL*, but we also point out that Volf displays a number of significant points of departure from the ecclesial thinking of his chosen representative. Our analysis has required rigorous and extensive investigation, in order to ensure that we are hearing both Smyth and Volf accurately.

CONCLUSION

The previous chapters have sought to map out the theological paradigm of Volf in relation to *AOL*. The method that we have deliberately chosen is one that examines the theological influences upon Volf, so that we can then piece together a good understanding of his presuppositions before investigating the author's own writings. Eight assumptions that constitute the foundation of Volf's theological paradigm are gleaned from *AOL*.

The first is a nonhierarchical doctrine of the Trinity; secondly a communal and egalitarian ecclesiology; thirdly the existence of a direct relationship between the Trinity and the church, as the image of the Trinity; the fourth is a rejection of ecclesial individualism and hierarchical holism in favor of ecclesial sociality; the fifth is the endorsement of feminist ecclesiologies and women's ordination; sixthly an ecumenical approach; the seventh is the missiological value of his study; and the

---

131. Smyth, *Works*, 426.

eighth is a perceived need for a model that engages with the catholicity of the church.

The foundation of this theological construct rests on an egalitarian view of the Trinity, but it simultaneously dismisses monotheism and magnifies perichoresis to a center stage position. This social vision for the being of God looks forward to the reformation of Free Churches, into the image of a nonhierarchical of God, whose primary attribute is self-giving. The term "Trinitarian self-donation" is an expression seemingly coined by Volf to make vivid this attribute.

Volf draws upon a wide-ranging and eclectic mix of sources to formulate his proposal in *AOL*, but his doctrine of the Trinity is most influenced by the writings of, and in direct contact with, Moltmann. The starting point and foundation for Volf's model is an anthropological concern for identity. This pursuit for human identity becomes an all-controlling interpretive window through which all of his theology is projected. This Trinitarian paradigm informs his conception of the church, and he anticipates an ecclesial reconstruction that is moving towards the eschatological goal of an egalitarian new creation. A contextual theology is another key driving force behind much of Volf's work, and he openly places his conclusions within the framework of the Free Churches.

The theology and work of Smyth is Volf's chosen ecclesial representative, and "Smyth's voice" is a thread that runs through *AOL*. Our investigation of Smyth evaluates the accuracy with which Volf uses him, and we conclude that one chosen theologian cannot single-handedly represent a diverse global movement. One of the challenging statements in Volf's hypothesis is that Smyth is "the voice of the Free Church tradition."[132] Volf's declaration that Smyth is "the voice" of that tradition, a sole representative for such a fluid contemporary movement, remains as something of an unsolved mystery or perhaps too bold an assertion.

It has been advanced that the Achilles' heel of Volf's use of Smyth is that he makes no reference to the evolutionary changes that occurred in most aspects of his theology and ecclesiology. Smyth becomes a launching pad to support Volf's own proposals, but the theological snapshots that he presents of his chosen ecclesial representative fail to capture the whole panorama of Smyth's ever-changing theology. According to Lee, perhaps the most significant legacy of Smyth is that to his dying day he

---

132. Volf, *AOL*, 23.

remained faithful to his covenant to relentlessly pursue truth and to be willing to change his opinions where needed. Smyth saw this as fundamental in obeying God, and this explains the many changes in his doctrine and practice.[133] He was a pilgrim in his theology and ecclesiology, and if Volf had picked up on this legacy it could have been used to his advantage to greatly strengthen the eschatological goals in *AOL*. Had he done this, he would then have represented Smyth more accurately and also linked his own eschatological pursuit of egalitarianism to Smyth's goals more firmly.

---

133. Lee, *Theology of John Smyth*, 291; Smyth, *Works*, 1:271.

6

Volf's Dialogue with Joseph Ratzinger

INTRODUCTION

VOLF DELIBERATELY AND CAREFULLY chooses two theologians with whom he engages in critical dialogue. His choice is extremely significant because it reveals his aim to tackle two of the main bastions of hierarchical ministry, namely the Roman Catholic Church and the Orthodox Church (hereafter called OC). This opening move in *AOL* probably reflects a jointly held theological goal with Volf's supervisor, because Moltmann expresses in forceful terms his vision for liberation from the hierarchical structures in the RCC and the OC, and he states:

> Feminist theology . . . on the one hand motivates Christian women to participate in the general feminist movement, and on the other prepares the ground for those questions in the churches, which are even more patriarchally dominated than society—not to mention the rejection of women's ordination in the Roman Catholic and the Orthodox churches. Here, it seems to me, comes the hardest but most important challenge to the theology of liberation: the liberation of the church from "holy rule" so that it may become the community of the people.[1]

Volf grasps this liberation challenge with both hands, and part 1 of *AOL* is committed to counteracting the voices of these two theological opponents before he lays down a revisionist blueprint for theology and Free Church ecclesiology.

1. Moltmann, *Secular Society*, 56–57, 65–66.

Volf's first dialogue partner, Joseph Cardinal Ratzinger (1927–), now Pope Benedict XVI, was appointed prefect of the Congregation for the Doctrine of Faith by Pope John Paul II, a position he held for over twenty years. He is a prolific theologian, and while engaging with his writings we must recognize that we are handling one of the foremost theologians for the RCC in our day. J. K. S. Reid writes critically of Ratzinger in the light of the somewhat controversial *Ratzinger Report*,[2] and yet he concludes that: "Without doubt this figure is representative of the Church of which he is so distinguished a servant. But it is not totally representative."[3] This comment indicates that there is room for some diversity within the RCC, but overall we can securely say that Ratzinger's theology is a very safe guide to understanding contemporary Catholic thinking.

The second dialogue partner, John D. Zizioulas (1931–) is metropolitan of Pergamon in the Ecumenical Patriarchate of Constantinople and was previously professor of systematic theology at the University of Glasgow and visiting professor at King's College, London. He is recognized as an outstanding theologian: John Meyendorff believed him to be "one of the most influential Orthodox theologians of the younger generation";[4] and the Archbishop of Canterbury Rowan Williams says, that *Being as Communion* (hereafter called *BAC*) "has a fair claim to be one of the most influential theological books of the later twentieth century."[5]

These dialogue partners represent formidable opposition to the egalitarian understanding for theology and ecclesiology that is espoused by Volf. However intimidating this task may appear, Volf refuses to side step the challenge to be both enriched by the traditions of the Western and Eastern theologies, while sustaining critical evaluation of these theological paradigms, in order to put forward an ecclesial model for Free Churches worldwide. This sustained critical dialogue is the focal point of our study in chapters 6 through 9, and we begin firstly with an assessment of "Ratzinger: Communion and the Whole" (chapter 1 of *AOL*) in chapters 6 and 7 of this monograph. Next, we will assess "Zizioulas: Communion, One, and Many" (chapter 2 of *AOL*) in chapters 8 and 9.

2. Ratzinger and Messori, *Ratzinger Report*.
3. Reid, "Ratzinger Report," 132.
4. Meyendorff, foreword for *Being as Communion*, 11–12.
5. Williams, foreword for *Communion and Otherness*, xi.

AN INTRODUCTION TO RATZINGER'S THEOLOGY: *INTRODUCTION TO CHRISTIANITY*

One of the best places to commence an assessment of the theology of Ratzinger is his book *Introduction to Christianity* (1968, hereafter called *ITC*).[6] (It is this work by Ratzinger that Volf targets for critical evaluation in *EE*, and this indicates the measure of influence that Volf perceives this book has upon the Christian world.[7]) *ITC* is an exposition of the Apostles' Creed, which Ratzinger originally gave as a series of lectures at the University of Tübingen, and the content of this work forms something of a spinal column to his theological thought. Two themes that are particularly elucidated are his understanding of the Triune God and the church; this writing is perhaps the clearest expression of his doctrine of the Trinity, and we will examine that first.

The Doctrine of the Trinity

Ratzinger devotes the whole of chapter 5 to "Belief in the Triune God," but chapter 2 handles "The Ecclesiastical Form of Faith," which outlines his intention to develop a Trinitarian form of faith along the lines of the threefold structure of this creed. He explains that this creed "expresses the common ground of belief in the Triune God," one that is "within the framework of baptism (Matt. 28:19) as the triple answer to the triple question, 'Do you believe in God—in Christ—in the Holy Spirit?'"[8] Ratzinger explains that this creed (known as the *symbolum*, symbol) became the "unified symbol" of the Western "Latin-speaking area" and that "this unified text was adopted in the city of Rome in the ninth century."[9] His exposition answers his own rhetorical question: "What is really meant by the profession of faith in the Triune God?"[10] For Ratzinger the doctrine of God is the Trinity and vice versa; he asserts that the Christian's relation with God rests upon and is grounded in the doctrine of the Trinity.[11] In all of his writing, though, an element of theological mystery and wonder is upheld concerning the truth about God, in a way

---

6. Ratzinger, *Introduction to Christianity*.
7. Volf, *EE*, 128, 177–80, 321.
8. Ratzinger, *ITC*, 85–87.
9. Ibid., 84.
10. Ibid., 162.
11. Ibid., 162, 165.

that points to worship that is bathed in adoration. He guards against simple formulations that try to solve all of our theological conundrums for the Trinity, and he cautions:

> The doctrine of the Triune God, means at the bottom renouncing any solution and remaining content with a mystery that cannot be plumbed by man . . . the insolubility of the mystery of God. Every one of the main basic concepts in the doctrine of the Trinity . . . are accepted only inasmuch as they are at the same time branded as unusable and admitted simply as poor stammering utterances—and no more.[12]

His Trinitarian dogma starts by his own admission with "belief in Christ."[13] This reveals that the two guiding lights to his understanding of the Trinity are Christology and the Apostles' Creed.

Ratzinger fences off what we should not believe by exposing a number of heresies that have arisen in the historical development of this doctrine. He observes that:

> When one looks at the history of the dogma of the Trinity as it is reflected in a present-day manual of theology, it looks like a graveyard of heresies, whose emblems theology still carries around with it like trophies from battles fought and won.[14]

Nonetheless he proceeds to reject the Monarchians, Modalists, and Subordinationists; he also distances himself from those who attempt to use the Trinity as a political theology for a Marxist program of action.[15] He does move beyond the limitations of negative theology, though, and he proposes three paradoxical theses.

1. The paradox *una essentia tres persona* (one being in three persons) is associated with the question of the original meaning of unity and plurality.

    This first thesis maintains that unity is divine but that plurality is as well, not in the sense of dualism but as Ratzinger explains: "God stands above singular and plural. He bursts both categories," and for the one "who believes in God as tri-une, the highest unity is not the unity of inflexible

---

12. Ibid., 168, 171–72.
13. Ibid., 168.
14. Ibid., 172.
15. Ibid., 166–71; Ratzinger, *Church, Ecumenism and Politics*, 148–59.

monotony."[16] This model of unity is something that he envisages that Christians should strive for, a corporate oneness that is greater than its individual parts.

2. The paradox *una essentia tres persona* is a function of the concept of person and is understood as an intrinsic implication of the concept of person.

In this concept of personhood he clearly lays down that "there is no such thing as person in the categorical singular" because the Greek word *prosopon* from which this thought first developed literally means "look toward," which implies relatedness.[17] Ratzinger emphatically asserts, though, that the concept of person is "itself an inadequate metaphor" if it is regarded in an anthropomorphic way.[18]

3. The paradox *una essentia tres persona* is connected with the problem of absolute and relative and emphasizes the absoluteness of the relative, of that which is in relation.

This third thesis pulls together the twin concepts of substance and person. Ratzinger remarks that the biblical documents evidence a dialogue in God (Gen 1:26; Ps 110:1) who is therefore "not only *logos* but also *dia-logos*," thus meaning that "*relatio* stands beside the substance as an equally primordial form of being."[19] "Person," he declares, is the "pure relation of being related, nothing else," and Augustine is quoted to buttress this view because he wrote concerning the Trinity that "in God there are no accidents, only substance and relation."[20]

Where the First Person of the Trinity begets the Son, Ratzinger describes: "It is the act of begetting, of giving oneself, of streaming forth. It is identical with the act of self-giving."[21]

16. Ratzinger, *ITC*, 179.
17. Ibid., 179–80.
18. Ibid., 180.
19. Ibid., 182–83.
20. Ibid., 183–84, 184n11; Augustine, "On The Holy Trinity: Doctrinal Treatises, Moral Treatises," *NPNF*, vol. 3, 5.5, 6, 88–89.
21. Ratzinger, *ITC*, 184; Balthasar, "Self-giving," in *Epilogue*; Balthasar, *Credo*, 31. Here the Swiss-German theologian and writer Balthasar expounds "I believe in God the

This introduces the notion of divine attributes grounded in the mystery of begetting rather than in the economy of salvation. In christological terms, where Paul describes Christ (Phil 2:6), Ratzinger interprets this as the "openness of the one who willed to hold on to nothing of his own individuality," and this means that "clinging to individuality . . . hinders the coalescence into unity."[22]

Personhood and oneness are united together with statements from the Johannine Jesus who said: "The Son can do nothing of his own accord"; "I and the Father are one"; "for apart from me you can do nothing"; "that they may be one, even as we are one" (John 5:19, 10:30, 15:5, 17:11, 17:22); he deduces that "relation is at the same time pure unity," and he assumes that this "becomes transparently clear to us."[23] The notion for Trinitarian personhood that is expounded in thesis number 2 is applied as the pattern for Christian personhood that is based on "pure relations," where Christians are envisaged as "living completely open in the 'from' and 'toward.'"[24] The doctrine of the Trinity and anthropology are clearly connected in his mind with practical consequences, and he assumes that the doctrine of the Trinity helps us to "open up a new understanding of reality, of what man is and of what God is."[25]

He correctly makes the link between theology and mission, and he believes that this understanding of the Trinity should impact the church's pursuit for relatedness and hence unity. Ratzinger clearly expounds: "The doctrine of the Trinity, when properly understood, can become the reference point of theology that anchors all other lines of Christian thought."[26] Here he inserts an important guardrail against hasty moves that automatically link the Trinity to Christian thought with the clause "when properly understood." He does not assume that all Trinitarian constructions are suitable for application. Overall there is

---

Father" from the Apostles' Creed in similar words to Ratzinger. "[The generation of the Son is an act of] the unimaginable power of the Father in the force of his self-surrender, that is, of his love. What could surpass the power of bringing forth a God 'equal in nature,' that is equally loving and equally powerful, not another God but an other in God (In the beginning was the Word, and the Word was with God and the Word was God, Jn 1.1)?"

22. Ratzinger, *ITC*, 187.
23. Ibid., 185–87.
24. Ibid., 187.
25. Ibid., 190.
26. Ibid., 188.

a distinctly Western feel to his approach as we note that he only quotes one patristic source, that being Augustine, and his choice of the Western Apostles' Creed to explain the Christian faith. He also fails to warn against Tritheism, which is generally a danger that lurks behind many Eastern theologies.

In summary, the essence of Ratzinger's Trinitarian theology is something of an interconnected chain that embraces oneness–relatedness of persons–personhood as pure relations, nothing else. The threads of these three theses are intertwined, and none of the concepts can conceivably stand alone for a doctrine of God or for a doctrine of the church. Augustine is the only church father who seemingly informs this proposal, and he is directly referenced. This would suggest therefore that Augustine exerts the primary influence upon Ratzinger's understanding of the Triune God.[27]

The Doctrine of the Church

This leads us appropriately to Ratzinger's doctrine of the church, which comes to the fore when he unpacks the last statement in the creed, "I believe in . . . the holy, catholic church, the communion of saints." He reaffirms his belief that the content of the creed's faith "grew up out of the triple baptism question about faith" where its "tripartite arrangement is indeed one of the main roots of the Trinitarian image of God."[28] It is impossible to compress his RCC ecclesiology into convenient "bite-size" sentences, but he gives us some signposts by writing:

> Teaching about the church . . . which by no means exclude[s] the institutional form . . . the communion of saints refers, first of all, to the eucharistic community, which through the Body of the Lord binds the Churches scattered all over the earth into one church. Thus the church is not defined as a matter of offices and organisation but on the basis of her worship of God: as a community at one table around the risen Christ, who gathers and unites them everywhere.[29]

---

27. Ibid., 183, 184, 190. Note that Ratzinger quotes Augustine in Latin in *ITC*, which highlights his approval of Latin-based theological material (our quotations are in English for ease of reference).

28. Ratzinger, *ITC*, 331.

29. Ibid., 333–34.

For him the Trinity is no mere peripheral appendage to ecclesiological practice, it is to be at the very heart of the church's sacraments of baptism and the Eucharist, and the content of its faith to be confessed. It is for these reasons that Ratzinger can say that this "sacramental approach produces a completely theocentric understanding of the church" that manifests itself in "this theocentric image of the church."[30]

"Church and sacrament stand or fall together"[31] declares Ratzinger. For him the two are indivisible and indissoluble for the nature of the church. He spells out that his interpretation of "catholic" as referring first to "local unity—only the community united with the bishop is the 'Catholic Church,' not the sectional groups that have broken away from her, for whatever reasons."[32]

Secondly, the "many local Churches can only remain the church by being open to one another" thus the "forming of one church in their common testimony to the Word and in the communion of the eucharistic table which is open to everyone everywhere."[33]

Thirdly, it is clear that "episcopal organisation appears in the background as a means to unity" in the RCC.[34] This does not require much additional explanation because Ratzinger plainly sets forth that he singly refers to the RCC as the one true church, thereby excluding all other groups claiming the name church. The RCC Eucharist is set forth by Ratzinger as the single most important mark that identifies a true church in his eyes.

ITC introduces us to Ratzinger's doctrine of the Trinity and the church, alongside the connections that he makes between the two. Irrefutably he holds a robust Trinitarian theology for the church, and he proposes a "theocentric image of the church" that is "seen from the two angles of baptism (penance) and the eucharist."[35] Therefore, it is the Catholic administration of these two sacraments that gives the fullest expression to Trinitarian communion and a Trinitarian image in the church.[36] The notion of one substance in the Godhead is carried over

---

30. Ibid., 335–36.
31. Ibid., 338.
32. Ibid., 345.
33. Ibid., 346.
34. Ibid., 345–46.
35. Ibid., 336.
36. Ratzinger, *Spirit of the Liturgy*, 220–24. Ratzinger states that it is the "Catholic

into his theology for the church, which emphasizes our communion with the Lord as: "we all eat one and the same bread, to become in it 'one body' (1 Cor. 10:17) and, indeed, 'one single new man' (Eph. 2:15)."[37] We can deduce quite simply from his writings that he understands that it is the RCC that solely holds the keys to expressing a church in the image of the Trinity.

VOLF'S DIALOGUE WITH RATZINGER IN PART 1 OF *AFTER OUR LIKENESS*

An Overview

Volf asserts that for Ratzinger, the doctrine of the church is of significant importance. Volf states:

> The Church occupies the centre of the theology of Joseph (Cardinal) Ratzinger. What the young Ratzinger maintained about Cyprian[38] applies with virtually no restrictions to Ratzinger himself: "Regardless of where one begins, one always gets back to the church." From his dissertation on Augustine's ecclesiology to his most recent theological publications as Prefect of the Congregation for the Doctrine of the Faith, he has always tried to uncover and elucidate the inner logic of the Catholic form of ecclesiality, albeit from the perspective of this ecclesiality itself rather than from any neutral perspective.[39]

Certainly Aidan Nichols echoes Volf's thoughts, as he also writes concerning Ratzinger's persistent pursuit of doctrine focused on the church.[40] Nichols perceives that Romano Guardini's (1885–1968) discovery that "re-emphasised the central importance of the church" was something that gave impetus to Ratzinger's own theology.[41]

---

liturgy" that "is the liturgy of the Word made flesh (220)." C. J. McNaspy emphasizes the importance of the liturgy in the RCC, and he quotes Pope John Paul II who said: "The Liturgy was the first subject to be examined and the first too, in a sense of intrinsic worth and in importance for the life of the Church." McNaspy, "Introduction to the Liturgy," 133.

37. Ratzinger, *ITC*, 336.
38. Cyprian, *Ante-Nicene Fathers*, vol. 5, 261–596.
39. Volf, *AOL*, 29.
40. Nichols, *Thought of Pope Benedict XVI*.
41. Ibid., 29; Guardini, *Church and the Catholic*, 19.

"Ratzinger has not published a comprehensive ecclesiology" according to Volf, who discerns that his "ecclesiological thinking has remained remarkably consistent."[42] Perhaps a major reason that explains why Volf desires to critically engage with Ratzinger is their clash of views regarding the Free Church. While a key motivation behind *AOL* is to reformulate Free Church ecclesiology, Volf writes that "Ratzinger either explicitly or implicitly polemicizes against Free Church ecclesiology."[43] The central thread of Ratzinger's theology is what Volf calls the "*communio*-concept," and he asserts that "*communio* is the central concept" of his ecclesiology.[44]

The following sections will mirror the headings and outline used by Volf in chapter 1 of *AOL*, which culminates in an assessment of Ratzinger's relationship between the Trinitarian and ecclesial community.

Faith, Sacrament, and Communion

Here we consider Ratzinger's theology as one that envisages the church to be the mediator of faith and therefore of Christian existence. Volf explains that Ratzinger believes that the "church is a single subject with Christ" and "one subject with Christ" so that the "faith coming from Christ must simultaneously be the gift of the church acting with Christ."[45] Volf clarifies that this stems from Ratzinger's Trinitarian notion and writes:

> The God in whom one believes is the Triune God and thus is not a self-enclosed unity, but rather a community of the three divine persons.... Trinitarian faith accordingly means becoming community. One enters into the Trinitarian community through communion with Jesus Christ in faith. One can construct a private relationship with Christ as little as one can create a private relationship with the Triune God. Ratzinger interprets Gal. 2:20 from the perspective of his favourite ecclesiological passages, namely Gal. 3:16 and 3:28, which speak of "the seed" and "the one," and from which he alleges that the "one" is a new, single subject with Christ. Ratzinger believes that the deepest essence

---

42. Volf, *AOL*, 31.
43. Ibid., 30–31.
44. Ibid., 32.
45. Ibid., 36–37.

of the church consists in being together with Christ the *Christus totus, caput et membra* [the whole Christ, head and members].[46]

The consequence of this Catholic theology is that ecclesiology and soteriology are inseparable, and faith is essentially a gift of the church, and as such leads to communion with the RCC. The church is a collective subject, and Volf summarizes that for Ratzinger the "individual is integrated into the comprehensive ecclesial communion" and that "communal Christian existence must be conceived in correspondence to Trinitarian communion."[47]

The fundamental significance of this communal nature of faith is probably best illustrated in the administration of the sacraments[48] because Ratzinger states that faith that is not sacramentally mediated is "self-invented faith."[49] He further propounds that "church and sacrament stand or fall together . . . baptism, penance and eucharist are declared to be the framework of the church, her real content and her true mode of existence."[50] The mediation of faith is sacramental, and the sacraments are ecclesial in conjunction with the bishop of Rome and the priests. From beginning to end, wherever you dissect his theology, Ratzinger exudes the principle of *Mater Ecclesiae*.

Eucharist and Communion

There is no secret to the fact that Ratzinger holds a eucharistic ecclesiology, and Nichols records that this is a term that he has adopted for the church from Henri de Lubac.[51] Ratzinger explains that many refer to eucharistic ecclesiology as *communio*-ecclesiology and that "this be-

---

46. Ibid., 33.

47. Volf, *AOL*, 38–39; Ratzinger, *Theologische Prinzipienlehre*, 23.

48. The RCC has seven sacraments: Baptism, Confirmation, Holy Communion, Confession, Marriage, Holy Orders, and the Anointing of the Sick—these are the life of the Catholic Church. A sacrament is "an outward sign of an inward grace," and in their view they are only to be administered through the RCC: "The Seven Sacraments of the Church," in *Catechism of the Catholic Church*, 277–371.

49. Ratzinger, *Theologische Prinzipienlehre*, 41n69; Ratzinger, "Warum ich noch," 70.

50. Ratzinger, *ITC*, 338–39.

51. Nichols, *Thought of Pope Benedict XVI*, 31, 97–98, 103, 174; de Lubac, *Corpus Mysticum*; McPartlan, *Eucharist Makes the Church*.

came the centerpiece of Vatican II teaching on the church."[52] This leads us to the explicit assertion that the single most important mark of a true church is the administration of the Eucharist, in a Catholic sense, and this requires the connection with the collegiality of bishops. Ratzinger states that where a local church administers the Eucharist it is an "an immediate and actual realisation of the church itself" and it has the Lord totally.[53]

Volf disagrees with him but clarifies that Ratzinger means that "wherever the eucharist is celebrated, there too, is a church in the full sense of the word."[54] Volf interprets that this means that the communion at the Eucharist table locally is something that is derived from its received authority from the church's bishops; therefore this implies a "priority to the larger church."[55] Ratzinger takes for granted a unity between the bishopric in Rome and the Eucharist, and he assumes that "the word 'catholic' expresses the episcopal structure of the church."[56] Nichols makes plain that this "eucharistic ecclesiology naturally gives much attention to the church's ministerial pattern."[57]

Underlying the discussion of this *communio*-ecclesiology is the constitution of a true church, and on this matter Ratzinger and Volf are diametrically opposed to each other. Let us summarize their two positions before offering comment. In the documents of Vatican II, in the context of statements on the hierarchical structure of the church with special reference to the episcopate, *The Dogmatic Constitution of the Church* (Lumen Gentium) articulates: "The Church of Christ is truly present in all legitimate local congregations of the faithful which, united with their pastors, are themselves called churches in the New Testament."[58] Ratzinger expounds this assertion with particular reference to the phrases "all legitimate local congregations" and "united to their pastors." He writes:

> What does it mean? It means, first, that no one can make himself Church. A group cannot simply come together, read the New Testament, and say: Now we are the Church; after all, the Lord

---

52. Ratzinger, *Church, Ecumenism and Politics*, 17.
53. Ibid.; Ratzinger, *Theologische Prinzipienlehre*, 308, 315.
54. Volf, *AOL*, 43.
55. Ibid., 46.
56. Ratzinger, *ITC*, 345.
57. Nichols, *Thought of Pope Benedict XVI*, 139.
58. Abbott, *Documents of Vatican II*, 50.

is present wherever two or three are gathered in his name. One essential element of Church is receiving, just as faith comes from hearing and is not the product of one's own decisions or reflections. For faith is an encounter with something I cannot devise or bring about by my own efforts; instead, it is something that has to come to meet me. We call this structure of receiving, of encountering, "sacrament." And this is precisely why it is also part of the basic structure of the sacrament that it is *received* and that no one administers it to himself. No one can baptise himself; no one can confer priestly ordination on himself; no one can absolve himself of his sins.[59]

It is not hard to see why this causes Volf to respond accordingly, to defend his congregational church polity, and he answers:

> Ratzinger sets this *communio*-ecclesiology up against Congregationalist ecclesiology, whose basic idea is allegedly that "assembling in the name of Jesus itself produces the church."[60] From the Free Church perspective, of course, this is certainly a caricature that ignores the work of the Holy Spirit to which Free Church ecclesiology refers in this context. . . . According to his own principle, the church can be constituted only by "receiving itself from the whole and giving itself back to the whole."[61] Because Christ is himself is only with the whole, so also must the local church derive from the whole and be for the whole.[62]

There is a huge chasm between these two theologians concerning their respective views on the internal constitution of the church. Volf recognizes that Ratzinger's ecclesiology sidelines the place of the individual with respect to the whole, and he summarizes:

> Ratzinger's communal view of what is Christian is a view conceived from the perspective of the whole. This accommodates ecclesiologically the fact that biblical thinking, so Ratzinger, "seeks first the whole, and then the individual within the whole."[63]

---

59. Ratzinger, *Church, Ecumenism and Politics*, 19.
60. Ratzinger, *Zur Gemeinschaft gerufen*, 76.
61. Ratzinger, *Feast of Faith*, 59, 128; Ratzinger, *Theologische Prinzipienlehre*, 309.
62. Volf, *AOL*, 44.
63. Ibid., 47. The reference in quotation marks is from Ratzinger, *Das neue Volk Gottes*, 95.

The Word of God and Communion

Volf analyzes Ratzinger's ideas for the mediation of faith and states that if "faith is essentially a gift of the church" then the "content of faith must also be a gift of the church."[64] (This definition of the church refers to the RCC, as distinct from Orthodox and Protestant understandings of ecclesiology.[65]) When considering the whole concept of the Word of God, we do well to keep in mind that this subject is bound up with the complex themes of revelation, interpretation, hermeneutics, and tradition.

In commenting on *Dei Verbum*,[66] Ratzinger makes clear his position, and he claims that the "Holy Scriptures stand at our disposal as a standard."[67] At a conference on the Bible and the church, he claims, in plain contradiction to the Protestant principle of *sola scriptura*, "the Church must give the last word to the Bible."[68] He takes this a step further when he declares that without obedience to the "Christonomy of the *totus Christus*, there will be great abuses, and offices within the churches might become organs of the Antichrist."[69] Ratzinger believes that the RCC is God's sole steward of the interpretation of divine revelation, on behalf of Christ, in this world. This is something to be challenged, and Volf refutes Ratzinger on this point by quoting Reid, who asks: "Do the 20th century Roman bishops really have a 'deeper' and 'better' understanding than St. Paul, than the Apostles? Or is the difference not better described as 'other'?"[70]

Office and Communion

The interrelatedness of the church and its offices is critical to Ratzinger's understanding of communion. Volf adequately describes this theological position and writes:

> Ratzinger is a Catholic theologian, and accordingly he defines the concept of church not only through the sacraments and the word,

---

64. Volf, *AOL*, 48.

65. Ratzinger, *Church, Ecumenism and Politics*, 18–19.

66. Abbot, "Dogmatic Constitution on Divine Revelation (*Dei Verbum*)," in *Documents of Vatican II*, 137–78.

67. Ratzinger, *Offenbarung und Überlieferung*, 519.

68. Ratzinger, *Die Geschichtstheologie*, 69, 83.

69. Stallsworth, "Story of an Encounter," 167.

70. Reid, "Ratzinger Report," 125–33; Volf, *AOL*, 52–53.

but essentially also through the concept of office.⁷¹ Through the sacraments and the word, there occurs that unique interweaving of human "I" and divine "Thou" in the ecclesial "We" that actually constitutes the essence of the church . . . and considers the concept of office to be an inner requirement of the communality of Christian existence.⁷²

Ratzinger unreservedly asserts that "the Church, in fact is our Church," "we alone are the Church," and that her structures are "willed by Christ" and "willed by God."⁷³ Similarly he states that "her deep and permanent structure is not democratic but sacramental, consequently hierarchical. For the hierarchy based on the apostolic succession is the indispensable condition to arrive at the strength, the reality of the sacrament."⁷⁴

This brings the authority and necessity of the Petrine office and apostolic succession into clear view, for without this central "spoke to the wheel," metaphorically speaking, Ratzinger's ecclesiology cannot be sustained. Holy Orders are another hinge on which all else turns because a priest can only receive consecration from a bishop in communion with the bishop of Rome and the collegiality of bishops. Ratzinger's essay on "The Primacy of the Pope and the Unity of the People of God" illustrates the thrust of this ecclesiology. In short: No pope, no church. This particular piece of writing reveals the heart of the Roman-Petrine tradition, which is the essence of that ecclesiology. Despite the exclusive claims made by Ratzinger, he does signal a note of realism as he concludes:

> It would be foolish to expect that in the foreseeable future a general unification of Christendom will occur around the papacy, understood as an acknowledgment of the Successor of Peter in Rome.⁷⁵

Volf rightly concludes that much of Ratzinger's ecclesiology is cast in stone, and he explains that "spirituality is Ratzinger's answer to the desire for reform in the church."⁷⁶ Furthermore Volf critically states that

---

71. Volf, *AOL*, 53n137; the references Volf quotes are Rahner and Ratzinger, "Ein Versuch zur Frage des Traditionsbegriff," in Ratzinger, *Offenbarung und Überlieferung*, 27; Ratzinger, *Das neue Volk Gottes*, 119.

72. Volf, *AOL*, 53–54.

73. Ratzinger and Messori, *Ratzinger Report*, 49.

74. Ibid.

75. Ratzinger, "Primacy of the Pope," in *Church, Ecumenism and Politics*, 49.

76. Volf, *AOL*, 61.

the notion of *Christus totus*[77] means that "all of Christ's activity must proceed through the narrow portals of the office of Peter."[78] This drives Volf to challenge the ecumenical implications of Ratzinger's theology, and he asserts:

> If the relation to all other churches is essential for the ecclesiality of the local church, and if the bishop of Rome is essential for the unity of the church, then the bishop of Rome is essential for the unity of the church, then the bishop of Rome is also essential for the ecclesiality of individual local churches. Loss of this element of unity with the successors of Peter wounds the church "in the essence of its being as church."[79] That this ecumenically so offensive thesis could come from Ratzinger's pen can surprise only those unfamiliar with his theology.[80]

Ratzinger's conception of the relationship between the one and the whole leaves no room for a Free Church ecclesiology; he is not naive, and he readily acknowledges that once *sola scriptura* becomes reduced to an individual's perception then an alternative ecclesiology to that of the RCC will of necessity be sought.[81]

What is refreshing concerning Ratzinger's writings is that he is easy to understand, straightforward, and honest in expressing his theological position. In discussing the challenge of ecumenism from a Catholic perspective he repeatedly returns to the question of ecclesiology and raises three matters that make the barrier with Protestantism impassable. Firstly he identifies the initial cleavage with Luther as decisive, and he explains that this means that the "authority of the exegete is put over the authority of the Church and her tradition."[82] This is utterly contrary, he states, to the "Catholic conviction that the Church is the authentic interpreter of Revelation's real meaning."[83]

---

77. Benedict XVI, "Eucharistic Celebration." This article explains that the RCC takes Augustine's teaching for the eucharistic mystery and believes that the church/Christians become one with Christ through the Eucharist (see Augustine, "Homilies on the Gospel of John," *NPNF*, vol. 7, 21.8).

78. Volf, *AOL*, 60.

79. Ratzinger, *Zur Gemeinschaft gerufen*, 88.

80. Volf, *AOL*, 59.

81. Ratzinger and Messori, *Ratzinger Report*, 156–57.

82. Ibid., 158.

83. Ibid. Note that Ratzinger capitalizes *church* to indicate equivalence between church and the RCC. For him the two terms are synonymous.

A second "insuperable barrier" concerns how the church is understood, and Ratzinger insists that: "It will be hard, if not impossible for a reformed Christian to accept the priesthood as a sacrament and an indispensable precondition for the eucharist."[84] He reminds his hearers that the dividing line is the Eucharist and that Rome refuses to tolerate intercommunion and participation in the Eucharist of a Reformed Church.[85] Standing behind this ecumenical intolerance is a third roadblock, and he declares: "The Catholic confession is that without the apostolic succession there is no genuine priesthood, and hence there can be no sacramental eucharist in the proper sense. We believe the Founder of Christianity himself wanted it this way."[86]

Sometimes Volf seems to pin all of the ecclesial ills of Ratzinger upon the single issue of hierarchy.[87] However, Catholic ecclesiology cannot be condensed into one concept because the theology of the RCC is holistic with an interconnected doctrine of the church. The three insuperable barriers with Protestants, as Ratzinger highlights, are the Catholic claims that the RCC is the sole interpreter of revelation, that their priesthood should solely administer the Eucharist, and thirdly, standing behind everything, that it upholds apostolic succession. Many other matters could be raised, such as the position of the bishop of Rome as the perceived center of unity, but we have established so far some of the main ecumenical issues with Protestantism in general, from which Volf's Free Church ecclesiology has emerged.

Communio Fidelium

In this section of the chapter, Volf attempts to pinpoint Ratzinger's understanding of the place of the laity in the liturgical events of the church, the community of the faithful (*communio fidelium*). He quotes from one of Ratzinger's articles that states that the laity are not passive because the liturgical subject is the "assembled congregation as a whole; the priest is the subject only in so far as he co-embodies this subject and is its interpreter."[88] Therefore the priest is understood to be the person who

---

84. Ibid., 160.

85. Ibid., 161. Ratzinger does concede that the OC has a "genuine episcopate and Eucharist" (162).

86. Ibid.

87. Volf, *AOL*, 72, 214, 217–18, 253–54.

88. Ratzinger, "Demokratisierrung der Kirche?" 39.

represents the authority of the entire church and the *Christus totus*. Volf claims that "like Augustine, however, Ratzinger understands the salvific acts of the church acting with Christ as proceeding 'through the visible instrumental acts of the official church hierarchy.'"[89]

Accordingly for Ratzinger, laypersons cannot lead the congregation because they do not possess the authority from the whole church, and therefore he believes that the "concept of charisma should disappear from the debate concerning democratisation."[90] Similarly the liturgical acts of individual congregations are not self-enclosed units, but their participation in the Eucharist connects and unites them with the whole church. Volf rightly points out that this means that "Ratzinger's basic conviction that the salvific encounter between a person and the Triune God is always realised by way of universal communion."[91] In other words the local church can never be discussed in isolation from the universal church.

Unsurprisingly, this leads Volf to clash again with the ecclesial worldview of Ratzinger with respect to the communion of an individual and a local church with the Triune God. Volf's Free Church ecclesiology is simply not tolerated by Ratzinger. With anti-Free Church polemic Ratzinger asserts that "a faith, a church, the word of God, a liturgy not received from the larger church is 'self-invented faith,' a 'self-constructed congregation.'"[92] Ratzinger places an unyielding emphasis on the church as he writes that one cannot "start a conversation with Christ alone, cutting out the church,"[93] and he gives expression to Guardini's vision for the "awakening of the church in people's souls."[94]

Trinitarian and Ecclesial Communion

The foregoing discussion paves the way for a summary of some of Ratzinger's potential connections between the church and the Trinity. Volf asserts that despite the fact that Ratzinger has "written little about the Trinity" he believes that he gives a priority to the one substance of

89. Volf, *AOL*, 62; Ratzinger, *Volk und Haus Gottes*, 149.
90. Ratzinger, "Demokratisierrung der Kirche?" 26.
91. Volf, *AOL*, 64.
92. Ratzinger, "Warum ich noch," 70; Volf, *AOL*, 64.
93. Ratzinger, *Feast of Faith*, 30.
94. Guardini, *Church and the Catholic*, 19; Ratzinger, *Church, Ecumenism and Politics*, 13.

God that leads him to a Catholic ecclesiology—an ecclesiology that gives priority to the whole at the expense of individuals.[95] Volf suggests that Ratzinger's basic principle is *Christus totus*, which implies that the "church, constituting one subject with Christ, is integrated into the Trinitarian life of God."[96]

Volf understands that for Ratzinger there is a clear link between his model of Trinitarian personhood and the relationship between an individual and the collective subject of the church. Volf explains that this model of relations between the divine persons has to be drawn almost completely from *ITC*, which teaches that "person is the pure relation of being related, nothing else"[97] and that the Father is the begetter and the Son, in his own self-emptying (Phil 2:6), "willed to hold on to nothing of his own individuality."[98] Ratzinger concludes that in the relations between the Father and the Son that there is "no kind of fenced-off private ground," and this means that the Son "coincides with the Father, is 'one' with him."[99]

It is this construction of personhood by Ratzinger that collapses the relations into pure unity along with the notion that divine communion exists simply as "being from and being toward"[100] each other, that is for Volf totally untenable. Criticism is leveled by Volf at Ratzinger's theology of the Trinity and his anthropology of self-divestment, which he claims moves human personhood in the wrong direction; Volf endorses Robert A. Krieg's evaluation of Ratzinger's relational view of personhood, where Krieg denounces this notion of person as relation because it evades clear understanding.[101] Volf discerns that Ratzinger's repeated emphasis upon the "pure unity" between the Father, Son, and Holy Spirit means that "the one substance gains the upper hand over the three relations."[102] This ecclesiology effectually aims to "take human beings up into the Trinitarian life of God" according to Volf, who comments that Ratzinger

---

95. Volf, *AOL*, 67–70.
96. Ibid.
97. Ratzinger, *ITC*, 183.
98. Ibid., 187.
99. Ibid., 186.
100. Ibid., 187; Volf, *AOL*, 57.
101. Volf, *AOL*, 67–70, 68n210; Krieg, "Kardinal Ratzinger, Max Scheler," 121.
102. Volf, *AOL*, 70; Ratzinger, *ITC*, 135.

is aware of Erik Peterson's *Monotheism as a Political Problem* but that he still fails to take divine perichoresis seriously.[103]

Regarding the conception of ecclesial structures Volf asserts that Ratzinger thinks "by way of the one substance of God" and a "monistic structure for the church emerges from this."[104] Volf interprets that Ratzinger "understands the church from the perspective of the whole" where the one substance of God the Father is over Christ; therefore a hierarchical structure with pope and bishops over the church emerges.[105]

Summary

The church is clearly of significant importance to Ratzinger, and we cannot fully comprehend his theology without understanding his ecclesiology. At most points of the discussion in *AOL*, Volf's Free Church model is diametrically opposed to Ratzinger's conception of the church. The latter considers soteriology, the interpretation of revelation, and unity as being impossible without the existence of the RCC in Petrine succession, under the direct authority of Christ, the head of the one Church.

At the heart of Ratzinger's *communio*-ecclesiology are the sacraments and most especially the Eucharist. The Protestant view of the Eucharist is rejected outright, which includes Volf's Free Church view, and Volf protests against Catholic hierarchy, the lack of democratic principles in local churches, and the seeming priority given to the universal church over the local church and the individual.

HOW DOES VOLF INTERACT WITH RATZINGER IN PART 2 OF *AFTER OUR LIKENESS*?

In part 2 of *AOL*, Volf proposes a fivefold thesis for "the church as the image of the Trinity." In each of these five chapters he introduces and engages with the relevant aspects of Ratzinger's ecclesiology while he simultaneously puts forward his own proposals. The first theme he takes up is "The Ecclesiality of the Church," and to this we now turn.

---

103. Volf, *AOL*, 71; Ratzinger, *ITC*, 52, 168, 171; Peterson, "Der Monotheismus," 45–147.

104. Volf, *AOL*, 71.

105. Ibid., 72.

The Ecclesiality of the Church (Chapter 3)

This chapter explores what it is that makes a church the church. Volf explains that Ratzinger understands the "church as constituted in the Spirit through the sacraments, above all through baptism and the eucharist"; "the *office of bishop* represents the indispensable condition of the sacraments . . . standing in apostolic succession and in communion with all the other bishops."[106] It is therefore the local believers who are united to their Catholic pastors who represent churches, and even though Ratzinger accepts that the OC "seems to be an anomaly" it is only the churches of the RCC that "qualify as churches."[107]

The phrase "united to their pastors" (a term borrowed from Vatican II), with all that stands behind that expression, is identified by Volf to be the first condition of a church in the Catholic tradition. The second condition is the people, who supposedly participate in the whole liturgical event. Volf rationalizes that the individual priest represents the larger church, so that the congregation receives the liturgy from the universal church.[108] Volf reminds his readers that Ratzinger emphasizes "the priority of the universal church"[109] in a way that interprets that the local church as the realization of the universal church. Volf proposes that Ratzinger appropriates the "Augustinian notion that Christ and the church constitute a single person, the whole Christ," alongside the idea that the church is a "single subject with Christ."[110]

The Free Church and the Catholic position (including the OC) are "mutually exclusive" according to Volf, who explains that there are three points of impassable difference. The first point is the supposed episcopal idea that the presence of Christ is mediated through a bishop standing in apostolic succession,[111] secondly the notion that "Christ's presence is mediated sacramentally," and thirdly the idea that the presence of Christ is constituted through liturgical activities.[112] Volf rejects all three of these

106. Volf, *AOL*, 130.
107. Ibid., 130–31.
108. Ibid., 131.
109. Ibid., 140.
110. Ibid., 141. Ratzinger, "Kirche II, III," 519.
111. Ratzinger, *Principles of Catholic Theology*, 288–90; Ratzinger does not tolerate any supposed church community or local church Eucharist that exists outside of the communion of the universal church and its apostolic succession.
112. Volf, *AOL*, 133–34.

points; instead he supports a Free Church model that believes that the presence of Christ is not dependent on a bishop. This is because he believes that Christ's direct presence is "unmediated to the whole church" in some measure subjectively (as opposed to objective elements of bishop, Eucharist, and ministry) through "genuine faith and obedience to God's commandments."[113]

Faith, Person, and Church (Chapter 4)

Volf explains that in the Catholic tradition "salvation is communion with God and human beings" where soteriology and ecclesiology are fundamentally intertwined.[114] Volf insists that this "understanding of the church as communion is unpersuasive," but he affirms Ratzinger's opinion that the character of faith is something that should be affirmed.[115] He rejects the notion that salvation is mediated through the sole agency of the church, and he prefers to think of the church as an "external aid for a fuller experience of salvation."[116] Volf endorses the value of church membership as a "consequence of communion with God."[117] We must not forget that Volf's thinking is constrained by a Free Church pattern, which is an altogether different view on the mediation of salvation to the RCC.

In consideration of human identity in relation to the church, Volf is again highly critical of Ratzinger because of the "tendency to lose 'person' within the 'whole Christ,' a tendency evident in . . . [his] soteriology and ecclesiology."[118] Human identity is a passionate concern regularly expressed by Volf, and he proposes that Ratzinger's notion of person confined to relations actually corresponds to the influence of Augustine's concept of the Trinitarian persons, where "the person consists completely and totally of its relations and possesses nothing of its own."[119] Volf believes that Ratzinger fails to distinguish sufficiently

---

113. Ibid., 133–35.

114. Ibid., 172; Ratzinger, "On the Relationship of Structure and Content in Christian Faith," in *Principles of Catholic Theology*, 15–84.

115. Volf, AOL, 172.

116. Ibid.

117. Ibid., 173.

118. Ibid., 181.

119. Ibid., 186. In this reference, Volf asserts that Ratzinger's theology is Augustinian, but he does not provide any supporting reference for his proposition from Augustine's writings.

between anthropology and soteriology in his view of the church as a collective subject because he collapses personhood into pure relations. A phrase that Volf repeats to summarize Ratzinger's notion of personhood is that of "pure relationality."[120]

Trinity and Church (Chapter 5)

Volf draws explicit conclusions between Ratzinger's doctrine of the Trinity and his doctrine of the church, and he asserts that Ratzinger's emphasis on the one substance of God with the dominance of unity then controls how he constructs his theme of the divine persons to be understood as relations. Volf evaluates that for Ratzinger the "relationship between the universal and local church is then determined in analogy to the relationship between substance and Person in God" where the "one universal church takes precedence over the many local churches."[121] Volf also rejects the opinion of Ratzinger that the universal and local church simultaneously are the image of the Trinity, and he dissents from Ratzinger's doctrine of the Trinity that dissolves the divine persons into relations.[122] Volf summarizes:

> Ratzinger conceives relations within the church in a Trinitarian fashion; he conceives the structure of the church monistically. The paradox is only apparent. Hence for both the Trinity and for the church, the "one" is structurally decisive: the one divine nature, the one Christ, the one pope, and the one bishop. The strictly hierarchical structure of the church derives from the systemic dominance of the one and from the precedence of the whole. Because only the one can ensure the unity of the totality, the pope must rank above the bishop, just as the bishop must rank above the congregation.[123]

The hypothesis proposed by Volf is that Augustine's doctrine of the Trinity places priority on the oneness of God, and this becomes the predominant influence upon Ratzinger's doctrine of the Trinity; the priority

---

120. Ibid., 187.

121. Ibid., 201.

122. Ibid., 204–5.

123. Ibid., 214, 214n100. At this footnote Volf writes that he believes that this doctrine of the church is derived from Augustine's doctrine of the Trinity, and he references Hill, *Three-Personed God*, 61; Studer, "Der Person-Begriff," 174.

on the one substance of God then in turn becomes the primary influence upon Ratzinger's doctrine of the church.[124] This bold assertion requires careful critical evaluation, but we will hold back on critical assessment of this proposition until we have described Volf's dialogue with Ratzinger from the remaining two chapters of *AOL*.

Structures of the Church (Chapter 6)

The title of this chapter is self-explanatory, and Volf describes Catholic ecclesiology as episcopocentric and Ratzinger as one who emphasizes that the "church is one subject with Christ"; Volf complains that the liturgical activity of the Catholic priest "ascribes too much soteriological significance to the church."[125] Ratzinger writes that the church participates in Christ's own mediatorship in the liturgical activity of the priest at a local level; the priest receives his authority from the whole church.[126] Volf describes the structure of the RCC as a "monocentric-bipolar community," but he prefers to think of the church as a "polycentric community structure."[127]

Again Volf accuses Ratzinger of holding to a hierarchical doctrine of the Trinity, one that is monocentric (Volf infers that Ratzinger's monocentricity connects to the one substance of God to the center of the Trinity), constituted of asymmetrical relations (the act of begetting, being begotten, and procession) and that this is manifested in his doctrine of the church.[128] It is proposed that Ratzinger's doctrine of the Trinity shapes his Catholic doctrine of the church.

Regarding the structures of the church it is inconceivable for Ratzinger to think of the totality of the congregation without the unity of office, and Volf repeats that he understands that this stems from Ratzinger's supposed hierarchical doctrine of the Trinity where the one is dominant. Volf puts forward that such a doctrine that places priority on the one substance and hierarchical relations leads to a stress on the whole, universal church at the expense of the local church and individual;

---

124. Volf, *AOL*, 71.
125. Ibid., 223.
126. Ratzinger, *Theologische Prinzipienlehre*, 287.
127. Volf, *AOL*, 224.
128. Ibid., 236.

therefore the election of the officeholders and ordination stands as part of a united hierarchical act of the whole church.[129]

The Catholicity of the Church (Chapter 7)

The Catholic tradition contrasts with Free Churches according to Volf, in that the latter believes that "the local church has all the ministries necessary for life" whereas the former perceives that ministry is only valid when it "stands in synchronic and diachronic communion with other bishops."[130] It is not necessary to repeat what Volf has stated elsewhere in *AOL* that Ratzinger's position on the catholicity of the church is objectionable on the grounds that the RCC is a self-enclosed and unyielding system. Again Volf remarks that for Ratzinger the catholicity of an individual person is only recognized when they stand in union with the universal church because the church and Christ constitute "a single mystical person, the whole Christ."[131]

These chapters in *AOL* summarize Volf's interpretation of the theology of Ratzinger and a number of significant hypotheses are suggested by him. These propositions now require examination as to their validity, and this forms the material for our next discussion (in the next chapter of this monograph), where the overarching pursuit for the ecclesial image of "the church as the image of the Trinity" is kept in mind as our intended goal.

---

129. Ibid., 247, 252, 254.
130. Ibid., 273; Ratzinger, *Das neue Volk Gottes*, 116.
131. Volf, *AOL*, 279, 281.

7

A Critical Evaluation of Volf's Dialogue with Ratzinger

VOLF'S PROPOSITIONS CONCERNING RATZINGER

SO FAR, IT HAS become clear that on most points regarding the doctrine of the Trinity and the doctrine of the church, Volf and Ratzinger are in serious disagreement. It is worthwhile highlighting at this juncture that any Protestant theologian who studies Ratzinger, or indeed any Roman Catholic theologian, must exercise great caution. This is because a Catholic teacher may use the same words or terminology as a Protestant but fill them with a very different meaning. For example when Rome prays for, or speaks of unity, they envisage that all churches will come under the headship of the RCC's Petrine authority. This is very far from the typical Protestant notion of unity that commonly desires better dialogue, a common understanding between two groups, or simply good and friendly relations. Another example could be given concerning the NT concept of "the body of Christ" (1 Cor 12:27; Eph 1:22, 4:12), which in Protestant circles commonly indicates a metaphor for the church,[1] but which Ratzinger describes as a twofold mystery of the church and a sacramental gift.[2]

As we look carefully at Volf's thesis in *AOL* we are able to discern four clear propositions that he makes concerning Ratzinger's doctrine of

---

1. Cole, *Body of Christ*; Minear, *Images of the Church*; Newbigin, *Household of God*; Dulles, *Models of the Church*.
2. Ratzinger, *Church, Ecumenism and Politics*, 137.

A Critical Evaluation of Volf's Dialogue with Ratzinger 115

the Trinity, the church, and the connections that he supposedly makes between the two. Each proposition is explicitly stated in *AOL*, but they are not always substantiated with clear-cut evidence or footnote references to back up each claim. Time and space do not permit an exhaustive survey of each of these hypotheses suggested by Volf; however each of them requires critical evaluation and comment because they undergird Ratzinger's attempt to formulate a vision of the church in the image of the Trinity. This vision is something that is shared by this researcher (and Volf) and hopefully due consideration to each of these four propositions will yield valuable material for our study.

Proposition 1: The Primary Influence upon Ratzinger's Doctrine of the Trinity Is Augustine's Conception of the Trinity, Which Places Priority on the Oneness of God

The clearest expression of Ratzinger's conception of the Triune God appears in *ITC*, and the patristic source that is used to buttress his doctrine of the Trinity is Augustine. There are three specific quotations from the writings of Augustine that are selectively woven into this presentation of the Trinity, and we will outline them to confirm that Volf's assertion that Augustine's influence is primary upon Ratzinger's thought on the Trinity is indeed accurate.

The first two Augustinian quotations apply to the concept of person in relation to the Triune God, where Ratzinger attempts to demonstrate that substance and relations are coequal partners for the inner-Trinitarian relations. The first reference is from part of Augustine's exposition of a messianic psalm (Ps 69) where he teaches: "He is not called Father with reference to himself but only in relation to the Son; seen by himself he is simply God."[3] This comment forms an excursus by Augustine in his exposition of Ps 69:2, where he takes the time to expound the doctrine of the one substance of God. Augustine writes:

> God is a sort of substance: for that which is no substance, is nothing at all. To be a substance then is to be something. Whence also in the Catholic Faith against the poisons of certain heretics thus we are builded up, so that we say Father, Son and Holy Spirit are of one substance.[4]

---
3. Augustine, "Expositions on the Book of Psalms," *NPNF*, vol. 8, Psalm 69, 301; Ratzinger, *ITC*, 183.

4. Augustine, "Expositions on the Book of Psalms," *NPNF*, vol. 8, 301.

Ratzinger explains that Augustine balances his emphasis on the priority of the one substance in God with the concept of relations among the persons.

The second quotation comes from Augustine's majestic work *On the Holy Trinity* where he unfolds that "nothing is spoken of God according to accident, but according to substance or according to relation."[5] Again Augustine places the two concepts of "substance" and "relation" side by side in his attempt to explain the doctrine of the Trinity. Ratzinger echoes this conception of the Trinity and affirms that "the sole dominion of thinking in terms of substance is ended; relation is discovered as an equally valid primordial mode of reality."[6]

The third reference arises from Augustine's exposition of John's Gospel and the sentence spoken by Jesus, "My teaching is not mine, but his who sent me" (John 7:16). Augustine asks: "What is so much yours as yourself, and what is so little yours as yourself?"[7] Ratzinger quotes this phrase and underlines that "the concept of mere substance (= what stands in itself!) is shattered, and it is made apparent how being that truly understands itself . . . only comes to itself by moving away from itself and finding its way back as relatedness."[8] This last reference, Ratzinger uses to ascertain "of what man is and of what God is,"[9] and he concludes that the twin notions of substance and relation must be simultaneously and inseparably held side by side for a doctrine of the Triune God that is then to be applied to the church or human relations.

Volf proposes that Augustine's doctrine of the Trinity exerts a primary influence upon Ratzinger's theology for the Trinity. This is seen to be accurate, and furthermore Ratzinger demonstrates that Augustine is the sole influence upon his understanding of the Trinity. Volf also assumes that Augustine's priority on the one substance of God is mirrored by Ratzinger's pursuit for his own model for the Trinity, which is then applied to the church.[10] Ratzinger unequivocally deduces from Augustine's writings a coequal priority for the one substance and relatedness for a

---

5. Augustine, "On The Holy Trinity: Doctrinal Treatises, Moral Treatises," *NPNF*, vol. 3, 89.

6. Ratzinger, *ITC*, 184.

7. Augustine, "Homilies on the Gospel of John," *NPNF*, vol. 7, 184.

8. Ratzinger, *ITC*, 190.

9. Ibid.

10. Volf, *AOL*, 71, 236.

doctrine of God. Volf overstretches his assertion concerning Ratzinger's application of the priority of one substance of God, and he fails to do justice to the coequal weight that Ratzinger gives to relations. In all three of the references by Augustine that Ratzinger quotes, all of them are used to reinforce a belief in the Triune God where the one substance in God and the relatedness of the persons stand side by side.

Proposition 2: Ratzinger's Concept of Personhood Corresponds to Augustine's Trinitarian Concept of Person

The discussion for the previous proposition paves the way for our consideration of this second proposal. In writing on the subject of "Faith, Person and Church" in *AOL*, Volf asserts:

> Ratzinger offers the understanding of person as "total relationality" in correspondence to the Augustinian Trinitarian concept of person. The person consists completely and totally of its relations, and possesses nothing of its own.[11]

As is often the case, Volf does not substantiate his claims, and there are no footnotes or references given to explain how or why he has come to this conclusion. Our investigation of Ratzinger's doctrine of the Trinity does show that it corresponds to Augustine's writings on the Trinity and that Ratzinger especially applies Augustine's thought for the concept for Trinitarian personhood. Therefore Volf's proposition is verified even though he does not qualify it himself.

The concept of personhood is developed by Ratzinger in respect to the persons of the Trinity, and while the parallel ideas of unity and relations are held together by him, an emphasis on unity appears to gain the upper hand. In contemplating Christ's earthly ministry Ratzinger apparently stresses unity with the Father at the expense of the distinction of the Son. He quotes a string of verses that magnify the Son's oneness with the Father (John 5:19, 15:5, 17:11, and 17:22),[12] and he develops a model of personhood that collapses into unity. Ratzinger writes:

> [Christ] willed to hold on to nothing of his own individuality (Phil. 2:6), follows the complete "at-one-ness"—"that they may be one, even as we are one" (Jn. 17:11). All not-at-one-ness, all division, rests, on a concealed lack of real Christliness, on a cling-

11. Ibid., 186.
12. Ratzinger, *ITC*, 184–87.

ing to individuality that hinders coalescence into unity. It is the nature of the Trinitarian personality to be pure relation and so the most absolute unity.[13]

This conception for Trinitarian relations is then applied by Ratzinger to his theology for missions, the church, and anthropology.[14] It is this stress on the unity of relations that is rejected by Volf, who rightly understands that Ratzinger's vision of persons leads to a somewhat depersonalized ideal where the concept of person is stripped of distinction.[15] This ideal flows from the influence of Augustine upon Ratzinger's concept of person in the doctrine of the Trinity.

Proposition 3: Ratzinger's Doctrine of the Trinity Is a Monocentric Model That Constitutes Hierarchical Relations of the Persons

It needs to be stated at the outset that Volf paints Ratzinger's doctrine of the Trinity and the church in a consistently negative light. Volf's crusade against all forms of hierarchy seems to blind him to some of the many valuable lessons that can be drawn from Ratzinger's theology. He repeatedly asserts throughout *AOL* that Ratzinger believes in a Trinity that is monocentric, something that means having a single center, and this is in reference to the supposed priority given to the simplicity of God. At the same time Volf emphatically accuses Ratzinger of holding to a notion of hierarchy among the persons of the Trinity, which he believes are used to justify the hierarchical structures in the RCC. As we scrutinize these two postulates we will see that in reality they are mutually exclusive.

Volf asserts that "for Ratzinger, relations in the Trinity and in the church are monocentric; since the persons are 'pure relations,' the Trinity can have but one centre."[16] Again he states that "although Ratzinger considers the one substance of God and the three divine Persons equiprimal, he takes the dominance of unity as his point of departure."[17] "Pure unity" is a term that Volf employs to capture the heartbeat of Ratzinger's doctrine of the Trinity, and Volf again writes that though the "one substance gains the upper hand over the three relations," he does "maintain

---

13. Ibid., 187.
14. Ibid., 187–90, 221, 345–46.
15. Volf, *AOL*, 168n53, 185–86, 189, 204–6, 214.
16. Ibid., *AOL*, 236.
17. Ibid., 201.

A Critical Evaluation of Volf's Dialogue with Ratzinger 119

that the relations represent a form of being equiprimal with that of substance."[18] These assertions are in harmony with the discussion on the first proposition that the Trinity has one center and that all three persons are united in the one substance.

Running alongside this description, Volf puts forward another angle to his perception of Ratzinger's theological construction of the Trinity. Volf advances that Ratzinger understands "the Trinity hierarchically" and that he grounds "the hierarchical relations within the church in part on that basis."[19] There is no evidence given by Volf in *AOL* to support this assertion that Ratzinger upholds a hierarchy within the Trinity, and Ratzinger's own teaching in *ITC* on the Triune God offers no evidence along this line.[20] This represents a contradiction because the persons of the Trinity cannot be equiprimal with a priority given to a monocentric substance and hierarchical at the same time, as Volf claims.

Proposition 4: Ratzinger's Doctrine of the Trinity Shapes His Doctrine of the Church

It is correctly put forward by Volf that Ratzinger connects the Trinity to the church, and he expounds:

> All the crucial elements in his [Ratzinger's] ecclesiology and entire theology are rooted in the doctrine of the Trinity. The entire life of the church, including its spirituality and structures is shaped in correspondence to a certain understanding of the Trinity.[21]

Nichols confirms this idea that Ratzinger believes that "the doctrine of the Trinity should become the 'nodal point' of all Christian thinking" and that "unity is the foundation of reality."[22] While Volf maintains that both unity and hierarchy are guiding lights that direct Ratzinger's doctrine of the Trinity, which in turn shapes his view of the church, we reject the inclusion of hierarchy but agree with the inclusion of the con-

---

18. Ibid., 70; Ratzinger, *ITC*, 229, 131, 135.

19. Volf, *AOL*, 236; Here also (72) Volf asserts that Ratzinger holds to a hierarchy in the Trinity.

20. Ratzinger, "Belief in the Triune God," *ITC*, 162–90. There is no description by Ratzinger to relate his doctrine of the Trinity hierarchically.

21. Volf, *AOL*, 67.

22. Aidan Nichols, *Thought of Pope Benedict XVI*, 84.

cept of unity. The doctrine for church hierarchy in Ratzinger's theology is founded on Christology (Christ's teaching to Peter, Matt 16:18), not the Trinity.[23] Perhaps it is better to think of "unity and relations" as the two aspects of his doctrine of God that then radiate through all aspects of his theology.

Nichols perceives that the theme of unity runs through the works of Ratzinger, and he remarks:

> Cardinal Joseph Ratzinger, writing in the preface to a work by a Dominican author, remarks: *c'est le tout qui est la verité*. "Truth is *the whole*." And referring back to Irenaeus of Lyons—the first great theologian in the church's history—he reminds his readers that theology needs to express unity: the unity of the covenants, the unity of the Creator with the Redeemer, the unity of philosophy and faith.[24]

The significance of unity is observed by Volf as he comments that Ratzinger appropriates the "Augustinian notion that Christ and the church constitute a single person, the Whole Christ."[25] The works of Augustine and especially *The City of God* have undoubtedly enriched Ratzinger's ecclesiology;[26] however Volf gives insufficient attention to the contemporary influences of de Lubac, Guardini, and Balthasar.[27] It is probably from de Lubac that Ratzinger receives impulse to develop what is, according to Nichols, the central motif of his ecclesiology—eucharistic ecclesiology.[28]

The metaphor "the church as the image of the Trinity" is not directly employed by the contemporary Catholic theologians such as Ratzinger or Avery Dulles.[29] However, it would be wrong to assume that

---

23. Joseph Ratzinger, "The Primacy of Peter and the Unity of the Church," in *Called to Communion*.

24. Nichols, *Thought of Pope Benedict XVI*, xiii; Ratzinger, preface to *Synthèse dogmatique*, 5; Irenaeus, "Irenaeus Against Heresies," *ANF*, vol. 1, 33.8, 508.

25. Volf, *AOL*, 36–39, 141.

26. Augustine, "City of God," *NPNF*, vol. 2; Nichols, "Augustine and the Church," in *Thought of Pope Benedict XVI*, 17–33.

27. Guardini, *Church and the Catholic*; Ratzinger, *Church, Ecumenism and Politics*, 13; Ratzinger, *Spirit of the Liturgy*, 7; Balthasar, *Mysterium Pascale*.

28. Nichols, *Thought of Pope Benedict XVI*, 31, 96–99; de Lubac, *Christian Faith*; Ratzinger, *Church, Ecumenism and Politics*, 38n6.

29. Dulles, *Models of the Church*.

the doctrine of the Trinity does not inform and enrich the ecclesiology of the RCC.

WHAT CAN WE LEARN FROM RATZINGER'S VISION FOR "THE CHURCH AS THE IMAGE OF THE TRINITY"?

There are three general principles that we can learn from Ratzinger's approach to theology that are helpful for us to consider. Firstly he maintains in his exposition of the Apostles' Creed that "belief in Christ [is] the starting point of the doctrine of the Trinity."[30] Christology and church tradition form two anchors to his whole theology, and while he maintains a priority to the one substance in God, this does not hinder him from developing a rich understanding of Christ, as his book, *Jesus of Nazareth*, demonstrates.

A second learning point from Ratzinger's theology is the unity that exists across his whole system of thought. His theology is consistent and harmonious to form a united whole. This emphasis on unity clearly connects with his understanding of the Trinity but also for the church, as Volf observes that, for Ratzinger, "the church is a single subject with Christ."[31] This is just one example of how this theme of unity plays out in Ratzinger's thought to produce a total unity between Christ and the church, and we could say it forms one undivided theological substance.

The third precept we can glean from Ratzinger's example is what Nichols calls the "ecclesial or churchly character" of his theology.[32] Volf reminds us that "regardless of where one begins" with Ratzinger, "one always gets back to the church."[33] This is a timely admonition for a fresh reflection of the subject of ecclesiology, especially in the light of contemporary challenges. Ratzinger reports of the need to recover the art of catechizing that is "organised around four fundamental elements: the *Credo*, the *Our Father*, the *Decalogue*, [and] the *Sacraments*."[34] It is these four elements in the current RCC catechism that offer practical insight as to how Ratzinger envisages the church in the light of the Trinity.

---

30. Ratzinger, *ITC*, 168.
31. Volf, *AOL*, 36.
32. Nichols, *Thought of Pope Benedict XVI*, xiii.
33. Volf, *AOL*, 29.
34. Ratzinger and Messori, *Ratzinger Report*, 72–73.

SUMMARY

Volf aptly describes the ecclesiology of Ratzinger in chapter 2 of *AOL* as "Communion and the Whole." Ratzinger's book *ITC* is a primary source material for any researcher who attempts to gain an appreciation of Ratzinger's doctrine of the Trinity and the church. Volf explores this book along with many other writings by Ratzinger in order to critically evaluate this outstanding theologian, and at most points they firmly disagree. The Trinity for Ratzinger is summarized as embracing three concepts simultaneously: oneness–relatedness of persons–personhood is pure relations, nothing else. This understanding of the church is a eucharistic ecclesiology, and it is the sacrament of the Eucharist that Ratzinger believes is the apex of revelation for a "theocentric image of the church."

Our analysis of Volf's evaluation of Ratzinger's theology is labeled under the headings of four propositions. We sustain Volf's assertion that Augustine is the primary influence upon Ratzinger's doctrine of the Trinity and ecclesiology. Similarly we uphold Volf's opinion that Ratzinger's doctrine of the Trinity shapes his doctrine of the church but not with respect to the RCC's hierarchical structures. There appears to be no evidence that Ratzinger's doctrine of the Trinity holds the explanatory key to the church's structures, as Volf insists. On the contrary the RCC structure is understood christologically from the Petrine commission, and this highlights that Volf has pushed this ecclesial metaphor for "the church as the image of the Trinity," in this instance, beyond reasonable bounds.

Ratzinger appears to offer alternative lines of development to understand "the church as the image of the Trinity." In the RCC catechism, the Trinity is connected to the church in relation to the profession of faith, the liturgy, the Ten Commandments, and prayer. These four aspects of ecclesiology offer rich potential for their further development for any section of the church that attempts to develop a correspondence between the Trinity and the church.

8

Volf's Dialogue with John Zizioluas

AN INTRODUCTION TO THE THEOLOGY OF ZIZIOULAS

Being As Communion: Studies in Personhood and the Church

Being As Communion (1985) is the primary source for Volf's examination of Zizioulas's theology in *AOL*, especially with respect of the connections that are suggested between the church and the Trinity.[1] The key thread to Zizioulas's proposal is communion, as the title of his book suggests, and he states: "The church is not simply an institution. She is a 'mode of existence,' a way of being."[2]

Zizioulas puts forward a neopatristic synthesis of the concept of communion, one that contemplates the Holy Trinity as a relational being in dialectical relationship to ontology, ecclesiology, and anthropology.[3] He expresses:

a. There is no true being without communion. Nothing exists as an "individual," conceivable in itself. Communion is an ontological category.

b. Communion which does not come from a "hypostasis," that is, a concrete and free person, and which does not lead to "hypostases," that is concrete and free persons, is not an "image" of the

---

1. Volf, *AOL*, 74n9.
2. Zizioulas, *BAC*, 15.
3. Ibid., 15–19.

being of God. The person cannot exist without communion; but every form of communion which denies or suppresses the person is inadmissible.

These statements lay the foundation for his thesis and the assumption he makes, that the two decisive events and actions for the church are baptism and the Eucharist. It is through baptism that a person experiences the "new birth from on high" according to Zizioulas, and this "hypostasises the person according to God's way of being," which is "what makes the church the image of the Triune God."[4] Zizioulas suggests that the notion of the church as "the image of God" is not "founded simply on triadology" but rather "man in the church is the 'image of God' due to the economy of the Holy Trinity."[5]

"It is in the eucharist that the church would contemplate her eschatological nature" asserts Zizioulas (because Sunday is the "day of the *eschata*") and "taste the very life of the Holy Trinity; in other words she would realise man's true being as the image of God's own being."[6] This eucharistic ecclesiology held by Zizioulas insists that "wherever the eucharist is, there is the church,"[7] but he differs from that of the modern Orthodox theologian Nicholas Afanasiev at two critical junctures.[8] Zizioulas puts forward that Afanasiev proposes two errors: the first of these errors is that a local eucharistic parish is a complete catholic church and the second is that the local church can be the holy catholic and apostolic church independently of other local churches.[9] Zizioulas explains that Afanasiev confuses the necessity for a robust understanding between the universal and the local church because it is the Eucharist that expresses the mystery between the local and universal church.[10]

---

4. Ibid., 19.

5. Ibid.

6. Ibid., 21; 61n62, Maximus the Confessor, "Mystagogy." Zizioulas explains that "Maximus understood the holy eucharist as movement, as progress towards the goal (τὸ πέρας)."

7. Zizioulas, BAC, 24, 60n59. Here Zizioulas explains: "The term ἐκκλησία is not unrelated in its original usage to the fact of the Eucharistic community" (Zizioulas references his own work written in Greek: *Eucharist, Bishop, Church*, 29–59).

8. Afanasiev (also Afanassieff), "Church Which Presides," 57–110; Afanassieff, "Statio Orbis," 65–75; Afanasiev, "L'Eglise de Dieu," 19.

9. Zizioulas, BAC, 23–25.

10. Ibid. Ratzinger agrees with Zizioulas that Afanasiev is confused at this point. Ratzinger, *Principles of Catholic Theology*, 292.

Zizioulas rejects "purely humanistic" understandings of a concept for person, and he claims that this subject is "indissolubly bound up with theology."[11] The thesis in *BAC* attempts to distance itself from the ontological monism of Platonic thought, and instead it explores the possibility that the notion lying behind hypostasis is a platform for understanding personhood and being.[12]

In *BAC*, Zizioulas explores the interrelation between truth and communion, and he provides a synopsis of the range of historical approaches to truth that existed in the patristic era. He outlines that these are: the Logos approach, the eucharistic approach, the Trinitarian approach, the apophatic approach, the christological approach, and the approach through *Eikon*.[13] In the approach through *Eikon*, Zizioulas describes that truth has christologically unfolded in history, and he writes:

> How can this be expressed in theological terms? It will suffice to quote here a passage of Maximus [the Confessor].[14] "The things of the Old Testament are shadow (σκιά); those of the New Testament are image (εἰκών); and those of the future state are truth (ἀλήθεια).[15]

Zizioulas develops this iconological language further and uses Athanasius to support his suggestion that "the Son is the εἰκών of the Father" and that *Eikon* is communicated to the church liturgically through the Eucharist.[16] He firmly asserts that the "mystery of the church is essentially . . . 'One' and 'many' at the same time,"[17] and it is this phrase that is picked up by Volf for the title of chapter 2 in *AOL* ("Zizioulas: Communion, One, and Many").

The Eucharist is both the locus of truth and communion for the OC in Zizioulas's opinion, and he does not fail to highlight the ecclesial significance of apostolic succession and the role that the linear

---

11. Zizioulas, *BAC*, 27.

12. Ibid., 27–65.

13. Ibid., 67–101.

14. Scholion, "Ecclesiastical Hierarchy," 3, 3.2; Zizioulas, *BAC*, 62n63, 99n91.

15. Zizioulas, *BAC*, 99.

16. Ibid., 101; Athanasius, "Against the Arians," *NPNF*, vol. 4, 1.20–21. It is interesting to note that quite often Athanasius uses the word "Triad" in his writings instead of Trinity.

17. Zizioulas, *BAC*, 112.

development of ministry plays: "Christ–the apostles–bishops."[18] The role of the bishop in the OC's Eucharist is indispensable, and it is at the Eucharist that the bishop is ordained. Zizioulas summarizes that "the bishop in his function is the apostles' successor inasmuch as he is the image of Christ within the community."[19] To conclude the thought of Zizioulas, it is evident that the Eucharist is the locus of communion (*koinōnia*) and the locus of truth (*alētheia*), and it is this liturgical event where the eucharistic community experiences the freedom of truth.[20]

In reflecting on the place of pneumatology in ecclesiology, Zizioulas prefers the emphasis of Boris Bobrinskoy and Nikos Nissiotis; they stress that the "work of the Holy Spirit and that of Christ belong together and should never be seen in separation."[21] This communion ecclesiology is associated with the significance that Zizioulas places upon the Corinthian benediction, and he states:

> Another important contribution of the Holy Spirit to the Christ event is that, because of the involvement of the Holy Spirit in the economy, Christ is not just an individual, not "one" but "many." This "corporate personality" of Christ is impossible to conceive without pneumatology. It is not insignificant that the Spirit has always, since the time of Paul, been associated [2 Cor 13:14] with the notion of *communion* (κοινωνία).

This statement helpfully summarizes this synthesis in *BAC* of the "one" and "many" for the Trinity and the connection that Zizioulas makes from this for the church, through the communion of the Holy Spirit (2 Cor 13:14).

Communion for the church centers on the Eucharist, in the theology of Zizioulas. He believes that this liturgical event points to the simultaneous "priority of the local and universal church"; he rebuffs any proposal that would lead to an ecclesiology that magnifies the local church at the expense of the universal church.[22] At the same time he explains that the difference between the ecclesiology of the RCC in the West and that of the OC in the East is due to the differing lines of theological

---

18. Ibid., 112.
19. Ibid.
20. Ibid., 114–22.
21. Nissiotis, "Doctrine of the Trinity," 62; Bobrinskoy, "Le Saint-Esprit," 47–60.
22. Zizioulas, *BAC*, 133.

development of their respective understandings of the Trinity.²³ He asserts that there appears to be an "exact correspondence between the Trinitarian theology as it was developed particularly by the Cappadocian Fathers—especially St Basil—and Orthodox ecclesiology."²⁴

He puts forward that Basil replaced the notion of substance as an ontological category with that of *koinōnia* so that Basil preferred to speak of the communion of persons rather than the unity of God.²⁵ Zizioulas writes that "communion is for Basil an ontological category" where the "nature of God is communion."²⁶ He brings out that for Orthodox ecclesiology the bishop represents the "one" (Christ) and the congregation the "many" (Church), and that baptism and ordination require both parties. He states that this contrasts to the Roman Catholic ecclesiology because for the OC the "one" cannot exist without the "many" and vice versa.²⁷ He concludes that it is pneumatology that constitutes the being of the church in Orthodox theology, hence "all pyramidal notions disappear in ecclesiology: the 'one' and the 'many' co-exist as two aspects of the same being."²⁸ However in consideration of ministry and communion he leans in favor of hierarchy, and he elucidates that the "church becomes hierarchical in the sense in which the Holy Trinity itself is hierarchical."²⁹

This whole ecclesiology with its emphasis upon the apostolic succession of the bishops as the essential component for the Eucharist has obvious ecumenical implications. Zizioulas understands apostolic succession as "historical and eschatological" (here, now, and in the future fulfillment of Christ's mandate to the "ends of the earth"), and he states that the bishops"primary function is always to make the catholicity of the church reveal itself in a certain place," so that there can be "no

---

23. Ibid., 132–42.

24. Ibid., 134.

25. Ibid.

26. Ibid., 134n23; on this footnote Zizioulas supports his view with a number of references. These are: Basil of Caesarea, "On The Spirit" and "Letters," *NPNF*, vol. 8, 18.45, 28 and 38.4, 139 respectively.

27. Zizioulas, *BAC*, 134–42. This theme of the "one" and "many" is recurring in *BAC*, for example 145–54. The corresponding relationship between Christ–church is supposedly seen in the relationship between bishop–church, because the bishop in apostolic succession represents Christ to the congregation.

28. Ibid., 139.

29. Ibid., 223.

ministry in the catholic church that can exist *in absoluto*."[30] Similarly, there are missiological implications because, in short: no bishop in apostolic succession and communion with the congregation, no church.

Furthermore Zizioulas expounds that this relational view of ministry means that the "only acceptable method of mission for the church is the incarnational one."[31] He clarifies that the "nature of mission" is not the church "addressing the world" but the church "being fully in *compassion* with it"; and he does not permit preaching to be understood as a ministry itself.[32] He prefers to think that the "Word of God permeates the entire ministry" and that "Paul (1 Cor. 11:26) understood the eucharist as 'proclamation.'"[33] It is significant that in the context of an ecclesiology that magnifies the *koinōnia* of the Spirit (2 Cor 13:14) so much that Zizioulas should identify a divine attribute (compassion, cf. 2 Cor 1:3–4) as the church's primary means of addressing the world in its mission.

Communion and Otherness: Further Studies in Personhood and the Church

Communion and Otherness (2006, hereafter called *CAO*)[34] was published eight years after *AOL* (1996); therefore it does not form part of the reference material that informed Volf's thesis. However it is beneficial to summarize some of the key elements from this book because it provides valuable clues to understanding the theology of Zizioulas and, indeed, Eastern Orthodox theology. This book also offers valuable gleanings for any potential future model that attempts to understand "the church as an image of the Trinity."

As in *BAC*, Zizioulas takes it a priori that there are connections between the Trinitarian and ecclesial communities. He asserts:

> There is no model for proper relation between communion and otherness either for the church or for the human being other than the Trinitarian God. If the church wants to be faithful to her true self, she must try to mirror the communion and otherness

---

30. Ibid., 165–66, 172–75.
31. Ibid., 224.
32. Ibid.
33. Ibid., 224n42; Ignatius, "Ephesians," *ANF*, vol. 1, 19.1, 57.
34. Zizioulas, *Communion and Otherness*.

that exists in the Triune God. The same is true of the human being as the "image of God."³⁵

This statement sets the stage and outlines that the thesis in *CAO* is concerned with the implications that the doctrine of the Trinity has for ecclesiology and anthropology. Zizioulas plainly and concisely sets out his theological framework for the Trinity with three propositions. Firstly he establishes the *monarchia* of the Father, secondly he writes that this monarchy is "expressed through unbreakable *koinōnia* that exists among the three Persons," and thirdly he maintains that the "Father, the Son and the Spirit are absolutely different (*diaphora*)."³⁶ It is not without significance that the two patristic theologians who are most frequently quoted by him are Basil of Caesarea (330–379) and Maximus the Confessor (580–662).³⁷ Indeed the source materials utilized by any theologian invariably reveals how and why they reach specific conclusions.

Zizioulas explains that the two concrete forms of ecclesial communion that reflect faith in the Trinity, Christ, and the Spirit are baptism and the Eucharist. But he spells out that it is the Eucharist that is the "heart of the church, where communion and otherness are realised *par excellence*" and that if it is not "celebrated properly, the church ceases to be the church."³⁸ Furthermore in stating that "there can be no church without a bishop" he expounds that true communion with the Triune God is only found in and through the communion of the OC.

In this book, Zizioulas specifically critiques the theology of Volf's presentation in *AOL*, and it is worthwhile outlining the theological junctures at which they disagree. Firstly, Zizioulas declares that Volf's ecclesiology is congregational, one that gives "priority to the local community," where Volf does not even bother about the "one church, at least in its visible form."³⁹ Secondly, he believes that Volf demonstrates a kind of ecclesiology that proposes that "all hierarchical notions are suspected as threatening communion as well as otherness."⁴⁰ Zizioulas expounds

---

35. Ibid., 4–5.

36. Ibid., 5. *Diaphora* indicates that which is significant whereas *adiaphora* implies secondary issues that are nonessentials.

37. Zizioulas, *CAO*. Basil of Caesarea, "On The Spirit" and "Letters," *NPNF*, vol. 8, 18.45, 28 and 38.4, 139 respectively. Maximus the Confessor, *Selected Writings*.

38. Zizioulas, *CAO*, 7.

39. Ibid., 38, 38n73.

40. Ibid., 145; 145n91, here Zizioulas specifically criticizes and names both Volf,

that congregational models tend to the extreme end of antihierarchical Protestantism. He disfavors the Protestant view that ministry should be seen in terms of function, "centred mainly on the ministries of the Word and Sacrament," at the expense of the "establishment and experience."[41] It is for these reasons that he explains that it is natural that Volf (and Moltmann) so strongly react against the "Cappadocian teaching of the Father as 'cause.'"[42]

The Trinitarian doctrine of the Father as cause (*monarchia*) is central to Zizioulas's doctrine of God, and he carefully explicates the consequences that this presents for anthropology, ecclesiology, and monotheism.[43] For anthropology, he explores what the idea of the Father as the cause of the Son and Spirit "tells us about our way of being 'in the image and likeness of God.'"[44] His theology does not accept that theologians should transpose their ideas of personhood onto God but rather that a true doctrine of God should inform our doctrine of man in relation to each other.[45] He concludes that the Father as cause means firstly that persons are not self-existent because they have a cause ("causality in Trinitarian existence reveals to us a personhood which is constituted by love"), secondly "our personal existence is caused by a person and not nature (whether human or divine)," and thirdly that "personal otherness is not symmetrical but a-symmetrical."[46]

It is this last point of "a-symmetrical" relations that leads Zizioulas to openly rebut the Moltmann theological school of thought (of which Volf belongs), which rejects any notion of hierarchy in God, the church, humanity, or society. Zizioulas accepts that for the modern mind, hierarchy can often equate to the oppression or suppression of freedom, and he recognizes that commonly it acquires a pejorative sense.[47] However he explains that to apply the doctrine of God to humanity as the "im-

---

AOL, 215–17, and Moltmann, *Trinity and the Kingdom*, 200.

41. Zizioulas, CAO, 145.

42. Ibid.

43. Zizioulas, "Father as Cause" (chapter 3), CAO, 113–54.

44. Ibid., 140.

45. Ibid., 140–41. Others have expressed the concern regarding Trinitarian projection onto society: Peterson, "Der Monotheismus"; Schwöbel, "Radical Monotheism," in *Neue Zeitschrift*, 54–74; and Kilby, "Perichoresis and Projection," 432–45.

46. Zizioulas, CAO, 140–43.

47. Ibid., 143.

age of God" does not mean that the "a-symmetry of hierarchical *taxis* (order) is *per se* problematic."⁴⁸ He insists that "hierarchical ordering is inherent in all personhood" and that asymmetry is not "incompatible with equality."⁴⁹ Zizioulas rejects the egalitarianism of Moltmann-Volf outright, and he accuses them of constructing an otherness that is "finally reduced to functionalism" and a "personal identity to personality based utilitarianism."⁵⁰

It is assumed that the theology of the Father as cause is a Cappadocian concept, but Zizioulas acknowledges that his own theology refers more to Basil of Caesarea as opposed to Gregory of Nazianzus; the latter by Zizioulas's own admission held that the whole Trinity has divine rule—*monarchia*.⁵¹ In discussing the consequences of Trinitarian theology for ecclesiology, Zizioulas dismisses the egalitarian church models of Moltmann-Volf and also Ratzinger's ecclesiology.⁵² He accuses Ratzinger of transferring his "substantialist Trinitarian theology" into his ecclesiology to produce a "priority of the 'one' over the 'many,' or of substance over personhood," to enforce unity.⁵³ (Volf would wholeheartedly consent to Zizioulas's critique of Ratzinger's doctrine of the Trinity and its consequence for the church.)

Taxis is a key theological term for Zizioulas's doctrine of the Trinity and the church. He maintains that it is possible to construct a doctrine of the Trinity that "points to a notion of hierarchy that is free from monistic

---

48. Ibid., 143–44.

49. Ibid., 144.

50. Ibid., 145; 144n88; 145n91. Utilitarianism is the system of thought which believes that the best action or thought is the one that benefits the most people.

51. Ibid., 144. Here Zizioulas equates the idea of the "Father as cause" as a Cappadocian doctrine, but earlier in the chapter he acknowledges that Gregory of Nazianzus held that the divine monarchy belongs to the whole Trinity (126–34). There was some diversity among the three Cappadocian theologians, therefore caution should be exercised in the use of blanket term "the Cappadocians" that could mislead readers to think that their doctrine of the being of God was homogeneous—this was not the case. Gregory of Nazianzus, "Orations," *NPNF*, vol. 7, 2.28.1, 288; Gregory of Nazianzus, "Orations," *NPNF*, vol. 7, 29.2; 31.13–16; 39.12 also 31.14 and especially 322.

52. Zizioulas, *CAO*, 145.

53. Ibid., 145–46; 145n91–92. Zizioulas specifically rejects Volf's *AOL*, 215–17, Moltmann's *Trinity and the Kingdom*, 200, and Ratzinger's *Church, Ecumenism and Politics*. Zizioulas accepts Volf's critique of Ratzinger where Volf states that, for Ratzinger, "Persons are 'pure relations' and ecclesial structures are conceived by way of the one substance of God (Volf, *AOL*, 67)."

and legalistic or pyramidal church structures, and it is such a kind of hierarchy that systematic theology should consider and discuss."[54] By this he implies that the "*taxis* of the immanent Trinity" becomes the ordering and work of the economic Trinity applied to us in the church where everything proceeds from the Father to the Son and to the Spirit, which is "returned finally to the person of the Father."[55]

Any Trinitarian understanding that supports the idea of the Father as a cause, as in Eastern Orthodoxy, inevitably has consequences for monotheism. Zizioulas explains that Christianity arose out of the milieu of a Hebraic concept of monotheism and that this doctrine of God came under pressure with the NT revelation concerning the deity of Jesus.[56] The three solutions to the problem between monotheism and the Trinity, according to Zizioulas, are the "modalist, Cappadocian and the Augustinian solution."[57] Zizioulas dismisses the Augustine–Aquinas formulation that he believes focuses on the one substance of God, and he counts this solution as "responsible for the eclipse of Trinitarian theology in the West for such a long time."[58]

Furthermore Zizioulas blames the Augustinian model for the Trinity for the rise of existential approaches to the doctrine of the Trinity that reject the "substantialist approach to God and thus God as such."[59] He names the proponents of this modern solution to be Moltmann, Barth, and Rahner, and Zizioulas suggests that these theologians embrace a "Hegelian idea of God as the absolute subject (one subject, three modes of being) that relates to itself by an eternal process of self-differentiation and self-identification."[60]

Moltmann represents a departure from historic Christianity and Orthodox understandings of the Trinity in Zizioulas's opinion, who prefers to hold fast to the Cappadocian solution that brings "Christian monotheism into harmony with the biblical equation of God with

---

54. Zizioulas, *CAO*, 147.

55. Ibid., 148–49.

56. Ibid., 149–51.

57. Ibid.

58. Ibid., 151. Zizioulas even blames this solution for the "emergence of modern atheism" (151).

59. Ibid.

60. Ibid., 151n105. Moltmann, *Trinity and the Kingdom*, 17, 139.

Father."⁶¹ Zizioulas seems to take it for granted that the Cappadocian teaching on the Trinity is homogeneous regarding the Father's primacy, and this proposition requires critical scrutiny. There are nuances in the way the Cappadocian theologians balance the different dynamics that constitute the inner-relations of the Triune God, and this leads to differences in their doctrines of the Trinity.⁶²

A SUMMARY OF CHAPTER 2 (*AOL*): "ZIZIOULAS: COMMUNION, ONE, AND MANY"

The analysis of Zizioulas's ecclesiology in *AOL* is based on the "essays as they appear in *BAC*," and Volf discerns that the "inner logic of Zizioulas's thinking" is to "begin with the Trinity itself, and then to make the transition to the eucharistic community."⁶³ According to Volf, *BAC* maps out the "clear contours of an intended 'neopatristic synthesis'" with a presupposed vision of the "church as *imago trinitatis*."⁶⁴ The method chosen by Volf in his examination of this particular theologian is to begin with a study of the "ontology of person at the Trinitarian and anthropological levels" and then to conclude by assessing the impact upon the "essence and structure of the ecclesial communion."⁶⁵

Trinitarian Personhood

The background to Zizioulas's doctrine of the Trinity in *BAC* is encapsulated by Volf, who describes:

> According to Zizioulas, it was the Greek Fathers, especially the Cappadocians, whose efforts to formulate Trinitarian theology laid the groundwork for an ontology of person. They effected what amounts to a "revolution" within monistic Greek philosophical thinking by identifying "hypostasis" (ὑπόστασις, substantia) with "person" (πρόσωπον, persona), that is, with a concept to which no

---

61. Zizioulas, *CAO*, 150. Kelly, *Early Christian Doctrines*, 267; Kelly comments that a stress on the ontological integrity of the Persons of the Trinity "risks the possibility of Tritheism." Zizioulas believes that the "Cappadocians avoided this risk by introducing the principle of ontological origination and making the Father the 'cause' of Trinitarian existence" (150).

62. Hanson, *Christian Doctrine of God*, 787; Letham, *Holy Trinity*, 146–66.

63. Volf, *AOL*, 73–75, 74n9, 75n15; Zizioulas, *BAC*, 27–65.

64. Volf, *AOL*, 74–75.

65. Ibid., 75.

ontological content could be attributed within the framework of this particular thinking.⁶⁶

According to Volf this move by the Greek fathers shattered the traditionally held monistic ontology for the doctrine of God, and this enabled a fresh conception of the being of God with respect to God's personhood and "the communion that God is."⁶⁷ In other words, this leads us to the conclusion that "Personhood is God's essence," as Volf states, and that "the statement 'God is person' acquires its full significance only if it is also reversible: 'person is God.' "⁶⁸

Volf correctly asserts that "Zizioulas insists on the monarchy of the Father," but this conception of God is troublesome to Volf, because he believes that this leads to a "kind of subordination" of the Son and the Holy Spirit to the Father and that the "concept of hierarchy . . . inheres in the idea of person."⁶⁹ This leads to an inner-communion of the persons of the Trinity, which Volf describes as an "asymmetrical-reciprocal relationship between the one and many."⁷⁰ Volf foresees how Zizioulas's model of the Trinity will play out as a paradigm for human communion and ecclesiology, and he expresses his concern about this model and writes:

> This arouses the suspicion that he [Zizioulas] is not actually grounding the necessity of the one for the unity of the church by way of the Trinity, but rather quite the reverse is [his] projecting the hierarchical grounding of unity into the doctrine of the Trinity from the perspective of a particular ecclesiology.⁷¹

This raises a significant question for any theologian, including Volf, when attempts are made to link their doctrine of the Trinity with their own particular understanding for the doctrine of the church: Which

---

66. Ibid., 76; Zizioulas, *BAC*, 36. These following articles are given by Volf to support this comment in *AOL*, 76n18: Zizioulas, "Christologie et existence," 155–61; Zizioulas, "La Relation," 60–72; Zizioulas, "Contribution of Cappadocia," 23–37.

67. Volf, *AOL*, 77.

68. Ibid., 78. Volf also footnotes two other reference in *AOL*, 78n29 and 78n31: Zizioulas, "Second Ecumenical Council," 29–54; Zizioulas, "Human Capacity and Incapacity," 401–447.

69. Volf, *AOL*, 78; Zizioulas, *BAC*, 89; Zizioulas, "Die pneumatologische Dimension," 141.

70. Volf, *AOL*, 78.

71. Ibid., 79.

informs which? Does our ecclesiology inform our doctrine of God, or vice versa?

Ecclesial Personhood

For Zizioulas the incarnation has great significance, and he postulates that the doctrine of the "two natures of Christ" teaches us that "in Christ human personhood became historical reality."[72] Volf surmises that "Christ is the person *par excellence*" and that in Zizioulas's mind the divine nature of Christ refers to the eternal begetting of the Son by the Father and that the virgin birth teaches us that "personhood cannot be derived from biological procreation."[73] Volf concludes that the theological implication for Zizioulas is that "only the uncreated God is a person in a full sense of the word, and only in communion with the Triune God can human beings become free 'catholic' persons living in communion."[74] Furthermore Volf suggests that Zizioulas develops a "deindividualisation of Christ" because "one can speak of Christ meaningfully only in relation to the church."[75]

Baptism is pivotal to the understanding of personhood for Zizioulas, because he believes that it is at baptism that regeneration takes place (1 Pet 1:3, 1:23) and that then the individual enters the ecclesial communion and becomes a new "hypostasis."[76] Zizioulas asserts that baptism is simultaneously a "baptism in the Spirit" while giving "human beings the possibility of being hypostasised in Christ" into the "one body (1 Cor. 12:13)."[77] Baptism is understood to be the initiation into Trinitarian communion, but Zizioulas defines the communal event of the Eucharist as where our communion with the life and communion of the Trinity itself is actualized.[78]

Volf critically evaluates this ecclesiology, and he concludes that "strikingly, faith plays no role in Zizioulas's soteriology and ecclesiology" and that *sola gratia* is conceived in such a way that "not only human

72. Zizioulas, *BAC*, 54.
73. Ibid., 55; Zizioulas, "Human Capacity and Incapacity," 436; Volf, *AOL*, 84.
74. Volf, *AOL*, 84.
75. Ibid., 85.
76. Zizioulas, *BAC*, 53.
77. Ibid., 56, 113; Zizioulas, "Human Capacity and Incapacity," 441; Zizioulas, "Some Reflections," 645.
78. Zizioulas, *BAC*, 94.

origination of faith is excluded (as with the Reformers), but also human experience of faith."[79] The exclusion by Zizioulas of all human choice from his model for ecclesial personhood and salvific grace leads Volf to conclude that this framework for anthropological communion is implausible.[80]

Ecclesial Communion

The heartbeat and locus of Orthodox ecclesiology is the eucharistic celebration. The theology of Zizioulas mirrors this view as he writes that "the church is in the eucharist and through the eucharist."[81] It is at this celebration that the eucharistic community receives, in this means of grace, "the person of Christ in its totality."[82] Zizioulas teaches that "to eat the body of Christ and to drink his blood means to participate in him who took upon himself the 'multitude' . . . in order to make of them a single body, his body."[83] Volf sheds further light on this eucharistic ecclesiology as he explains:

> In the eucharistic celebration, the many become one body of Christ, and do so in such a way that Christ takes them up "into himself." This is why in the eucharist, the body of the one (Christ) and the body of the many (the church) are identical.[84]

This theological intertwining between the church and Christ, soteriology and ecclesiology, in and through the Eucharist is the reason why, according to Volf, that Zizioulas ignores all the NT metaphors that indicate a difference between Christ and the church (for example the church as a bride or as a flock).[85]

Zizioulas expounds that a local church is the celebration of the Eucharist at a specific place (1 Cor 11:20), and he writes:

---

79. Volf, *AOL*, 96; 96n128; Volf appeals for support to his argument in this footnote to Joest, *Ontologie der Person*, 234.

80. Volf, *AOL*, 97.

81. Ibid.; Zizioulas, "Die Welt," 342.

82. Zizioulas, "L'Eucharistie," 55.

83. Ibid., 69.

84. Volf, *AOL*, 98; Zizioulas, "Ecclesiological Presuppositions," 342; Zizioulas, "La Mystére de l'Église," 147.

85. Volf, *AOL*, 100.

> A metropolis, an archdiocese or a patriarchate cannot be called a church in itself, but only by extension, i.e., by virtue of the fact that it is based on one or more episcopal dioceses—local churches which are the only ones on account of the Episcopal eucharist properly called churches.[86]

The difference between Ratzinger's understanding of ecclesiology and that of Zizioulas is highlighted by Volf, who explains that for the latter "the local church is the whole church" and that relationships between local Orthodox churches are "fundamentally symmetrical, with no superiority or subordination."[87]

The Structure of the Communion

The one indispensable element for Zizioulas is the bishop who acts as the head of the eucharistic congregation, and this office is essential to the Eucharist, which is central to Orthodox ecclesiology.[88] Volf observes that "since the eucharistic gathering is the εἰχών ('image') of Christ, so also is the bishop, as its head, the εἰχών of Christ"; this inevitably leads to the bishop having priority over the congregation.[89] This means that "the church is episcopocentric" according to Volf, because the "presence of Christ in the church and the catholicity of the church are mediated through the bishop."[90]

This does not mean that the laity are simply passive or that they have no meaningful place in the church but that a hierarchical structure is imposed on the congregation in the ecclesiology of Zizioulas, and Volf calls this liturgy a "bipolar event."[91] Volf observes that for Zizioulas this "bipolarity allegedly corresponds to the Pauline church order, according to which the people are to speak the 'amen' in the charismatic worship services (1 Cor. 14:16)."[92] Volf proposes that another decisive element in Zizioulas's understanding of the church is

86. Zizioulas, *BAC*, 247, 252.
87. Volf, *AOL*, 107; Volf, "Trinity, Unity, Primacy."
88. Zizioulas, *BAC*, 138, 205–7, 256.
89. Volf, *AOL*, 110–12; Zizioulas, "La Mystére de l'Église," 329; here he states that "in the eyes of his people, the bishop is Christ."
90. Volf, *AOL*, 113; Zizioulas, "Bishop in the Theological Doctrine," 23.
91. Volf, *AOL*, 116.
92. Ibid.; Zizioulas, "L'Eucharistie," 43; Zizioulas, "Early Christian Community," 140.

the "eschatological continuity of the church with Christ" where the bishop acts as *alter Christus* and *alter apostolus* to uphold eschatological and historical continuity. Zizioulas writes:

> [The bishop] is the instrument of the catholicity of the church not only in terms of eschatology (*alter Christus*) and of history (*alter apostolus*), but also in terms of catholicity in space; for each local church in order to be catholic must be in communion with all the other local churches in the world.[93]

The comment that bishops enjoy "equality and sovereignty" among each other is correctly inserted into *AOL* by Volf, who then asserts that in this model, the "one constitutes the many and the many are conditioned by the one; at the level of the relations between the churches and the bishops."[94]

In conclusion, Volf sets down that in the theology of Zizioulas the "local church stands at the centre of his ecclesiology,"[95] and he summarizes:

> Just as in the Trinity the one (the Father) constitutes the many (the Son and the Spirit) and at the same time is conditioned by them, so also does the one (Christ and bishop as *alter Christus*) constitute the many (the church) and at the same time is conditioned by them.[96]

This structure is a reflection of a Trinity that envisages a monarchy of the Father according to Volf, and this is mirrored in the OC by asymmetrical relations between the one (the bishop) and the many (the congregation).[97] This hypothesis deserves attention because if it is correct, it provides important clues for our pursuit of "the church in the image of the Trinity."

---

93. Zizioulas, "Bishop in the Theological Doctrine," 31–33.
94. Volf, *AOL*, 118, 120; Zizioulas, *BAC*, 134.
95. Volf, *AOL*, 123.
96. Ibid.
97. Ibid.

HOW DOES VOLF INTERACT WITH ZIZIOULAS IN PART 2 OF *AFTER OUR LIKENESS*?

The Ecclesiality of the Church

Volf attempts to summarize Orthodox ecclesiology from the writings of Zizioulas, and he concludes that it is a wholly eucharistic and episcopocentric church; the bishop mediates the presence of Christ, secures the catholicity of the church, and connects all the local churches in time (apostolicity) and space (concilarity).[98] Volf recognizes that in the Orthodox tradition that the people are also an indispensable condition for the church, as they say the liturgical "amen." He explains that in this tradition that the "relation "bishop–laity" at the level of the local church corresponds to the "relation 'Christ–church' at the level of the universal church."[99]

Regarding the interpretation of the church as the "body of Christ" (1 Cor 12:12), Volf claims that Zizioulas is similar to Ratzinger in appropriating the "Augustinian notion that Christ and the church constitute a single person—the whole Christ."[100] However he distinguishes Zizioulas's view of "total identification of Christ with the church" from Ratzinger's idea that the "church is a single subject with Christ."[101] Regarding the relationships between local churches, Volf correctly points out that Zizioulas differs from Ratzinger in this matter also. He explains that Zizioulas "rejects any hierarchical subordination between local churches" and that a local church is "capable of passing final judgment on everything."[102] Volf comments that there is a surprising similarity between Orthodox ecclesiology at this point and his own notion of congregational independency.[103] Ultimately the constitutive presence of Christ in the OC depends on the bishop standing in communion with the other Orthodox bishops, in time and space; this is unlike Volf's congregational believers' church model where the presence of Christ is mediated independently of office.

---

98. Ibid., 131; Zizioulas, "Die pneumatologische," 140.
99. Volf, *AOL*, 131.
100. Ibid., 141.
101. Ibid.; Zizioulas, "La Mystére de l'Église," 328.
102. Volf, *AOL*, 155; Zizioulas, "Episkope and Episkopos," 33.
103. Volf, *AOL*, 155.

Faith, Person, and Church

The only comment that Volf makes concerning Zizioulas's view of the transmission of faith is that he understands him to insist on the "essential sociality of salvation" where "salvation is communion with God and human beings."[104] This communal perspective of ecclesiology leads Zizioulas to a corporate doctrine for the mediation of salvation to the individual, and this framework is persuasive for Volf. The majority of Volf's dialogue with Zizioulas in this chapter considers, unsurprisingly, personhood and the church because this theme is a major emphasis in Zizioulas's theology. Volf rebuts a supposed tendency in Zizioulas where in relation to ecclesiology and soteriology the person is lost within the concept of the church as the "whole Christ."[105]

Volf asserts that Zizioulas understands that it is "through baptism" that personhood is initiated (with a christological grounding), which means that "human beings are simply isolated individuals before they experience salvation."[106] Volf identifies two mistakes in this theology on personhood, and he writes:

> Zizioulas accordingly has committed two mutually determinative anthropological mistakes in his understanding of Christian initiation. By understanding human beings who live without Christ as isolated individuals, and by negating the cognitive and volitional mediation of salvation, he negates both the essential sociality and the subjecthood of human beings. The way one becomes a person (anthropology) and the way one becomes a Christian (soteriology) both differ and correspond to one another.[107]

Volf is particularly careful to maintain a person's independence while affirming that people are socially conditioned entities, and he senses that

---

104. Ibid., 172. Zizioulas, *BAC*, 53n47. Zizioulas states: "Soteriologies which are not inspired by genuine patristic theology have created the following dilemma: either hypostasis without ecstasy (a kind of individualist pietism), or ecstasy without hypostasis (a form of mystical escape from the body, an ecstasy of the type of Hellenistic mysteries). The key to the soteriological problem lies in the safeguarding of both the ecstatic and the hypostatic dimensions of the person equally, without the 'passions' of ontological necessity, individualism and death." Clearly Zizioulas holds a very different view of soteriology to Volf's individualistic approach to salvation.

105. Volf, *AOL*, 181.

106. Ibid., 185; Zizioulas, "Human Capacity and Incapacity," 438.

107. Volf, *AOL*, 185.

Zizioulas is in danger of violating these two principles by his construal of personhood as "undifferentiated multiplicity."[108]

Trinity and Church

Volf agrees with Dorothea Wendelbourg, who states that "in so far as for the West, the unity of the divine essence is primary, whereas in the East it is the triplicity of the divine persons."[109] The remark by Volf that the "unity of God is grounded not in the divine substance of God" for Zizioulas, but "in the person of the Father"[110] is accurate. This means that the correlation between the church and the Trinity is understood on the basis of the primacy of the person of the Father whereby the "monarchy of the Father" is reflected by the "hierarchical relations within the church."[111] There is a correspondence of asymmetrical relations between the one and the many where the bishop constitutes the church according to Volf and similarly the Father constitutes the Trinity.[112]

Structures of the Church

The OC is "episcopocentric" according to Volf because he states that the "bishop acts *in persona Christi* and simultaneously *in persona ecclesiae.*"[113] This means that the bishop represents Christ to the congregation, and Volf understands that this structure is asymmetrical and bipolar, something he profoundly disagrees with.[114] Volf reasons that this bipolar OC structure is, as Zizioulas describes, grounded in the "Trinity hierarchically" and that therefore he apparently grounds the "hierarchical relations within the church, in part on this basis."[115] The single connection that Volf insists is relevant for "the church as the image of the Trinity" in the theology of Zizioulas is singularly the reflection of hierarchical relations in the Trinity and in the church. It appears quite clearly that Volf

---

108. Ibid., 185, 189.
109. Wendelbourg, "Person und Hypostase," 503; Volf, *AOL*, 200.
110. Volf, *AOL*, 201.
111. Ibid., 215.
112. Ibid.
113. Ibid., 223.
114. Ibid., 224.
115. Ibid., 236, 247, 252–54. Volf's polemic against hierarchical relations is well illustrated when he critiques Ratzinger and Zizioulas because he utilizes the word "hierarchy" four times (236).

attempts to repeatedly and persistently polemicize against any notion of hierarchy in any aspect of theology, in favor of total egalitarianism.

The Catholicity of the Church

There is no extensive reference to Zizioulas in chapter 7, but Volf points out that he "has contested the priority of the universal church over the local church"[116] and that this clashes with his own Free Church model for catholicity. For Zizioulas the indispensable requirement of episcopal ordination is the presence of the bishop for the eucharistic gatherings to function, and this pattern of ministry excludes all congregations outside of their Orthodox affiliation.[117]

CONCLUSION

In these five theses in *AOL*, Volf persistently critiques the writings of Zizioulas but not with the same intensity as he does with Ratzinger. This is probably because Volf rejects Ratzinger's doctrine of the Trinity and ecclesiology almost in its entirety, but by contrast, Zizioulas's construction of the Trinity and the church is much closer to his own paradigm. However a theological gulf remains between Zizioulas and Volf, and this forms part of the discussion in the next chapter of this book.

---

116. Ibid., 271–73.
117. Ibid., 273.

9

A Critical Evaluation of Volf's Dialogue with Zizioulas

THE THEOLOGICAL PARADIGM OF THE ZIZIOULAS SCHOOL

THE ZIZIOULAS SCHOOL,[1] as we shall refer to it, exhibits a clear theological outline with seven main distinctive assumptions. The first of these is a doctrine of God that is wholly Trinitarian with a single focus on the being of God that is underpinned by four theological concepts. These are *monarchia* (the monarchy and rule belongs exclusively to the Father), *taxis* (a clear order in God, where the Father is the fountainhead of everything), *koinōnia* (this is what exists among the three persons), and *diaphora* (the three persons are distinct).[2]

The second assumption is that there is a clear paradigmatic difference between the Eastern (as represented by Zizioulas) and Western (as represented by Ratzinger, Moltmann, and Volf) conceptions of the Trinity and therefore ecclesiology. In our own examination in this chapter it is self-evident that Zizioulas and Ratzinger present two Trinitarian (and ecclesiological) constructions with marked differences between them. Zizioulas explains that this is due to the differing lines of theological development: the West follows an Augustinian lineage and the

---

1. The term the "Zizioulas school" is employed to demonstrate a certain theological paradigm. Zizioulas is representative of Eastern Orthodoxy and the most influential "Zizioulas school" advocate in the West is probably Colin Gunton, but the school also includes Robert W. Jenson, Christoph Schwöbel, and Wolfhart Pannenberg.

2. Wilks, "Trinitarian Ontology."

East a Cappadocian model, with Basil of Caesarea seemingly exerting the strongest influence upon their doctrine of the Trinity.

A third conjecture is the presupposition that the church is the image of the Trinity and that the Eastern doctrine of the Trinity is the interpretative key for an understanding of the OC. The being of God is connected to the being of the church almost without qualification. The four concepts of monarchy, order, communion, and the distinction of the three persons are transposed upon the doctrine of the church, and this reveals that the doctrine of the Trinity is the starting point for ecclesiology.

A fourth tenet is a concept for the "one" and the "many" that is reflected by the OC structures, as a result of their understanding of the existence of the "one" and the "many" in the communion of the Triune God. This ideal apparently manifests itself around the office of the bishop who represents the "one (Christ)" to the "many (the congregation)." Zizioulas concedes that there is a hierarchy in God and therefore in the church also, but he rebuts the Moltmann school proposition that upholds the notion that hierarchy should be seen negatively. He rejects Catholic and congregational ecclesiologies simultaneously, and he especially renounces the egalitarian models for the Trinity, the church, and theology that are put forward by Moltmann and Volf.

A fifth assumption of this paradigm is the significance that Zizioulas places upon the office of bishop, without which there can be no apostolic succession, no connection with the universal church, and therefore no communion with God or each other. Without a legitimate bishop there can be no Eucharist, and without the Eucharist there can be no church. However the Eastern Church differs in its conception of apostolic continuity and succession to that of RCC. The OC understands the twelve apostles as forming "a college," and apostolicity is determined from the whole body of the twelve apostles and not singularly Peter, as understood by the RCC.[3]

Sixthly, communion is the central thread of ontology, the Trinity, ecclesiology, and anthropology. The concept of communion, also referred to as *koinōnia*, has its locus in the church's liturgical participation by the community in the Eucharist.

---

3. Zizioulas, *BAC*, 174–75, 176–208. This approach in the Eastern Church is close to the idea of "a college of presbyters," (177) which has some parallels with a Presbyterian form of church government.

A seventh assumption is the equal ultimacy of the local and universal church whereby each is mutually interdependent; no priority is given of either over the other. The Zizioulas school differs greatly from Ratzinger, who magnifies the universal church at the expense of the local church, and also from Volf, who conversely focuses his whole theology on the local church.

It is interesting to point out that some of the other advocates of the Zizioulas school include Gunton, Jenson, Christoph Schwöbel, and Pannenberg. The inclusion of Pannenberg in this list is quite remarkable because Volf simultaneously critiques Zizioulas, and yet he claims that Pannenberg's doctrine of the Trinity has informed his own construction for the Trinity. Pannenberg himself holds to the monarchy of the Father and a hierarchical (in Volf's eyes) model for the church.

WHAT ARE THE POINTS OF AGREEMENT AND DISAGREEMENT BETWEEN ZIZIOULAS AND VOLF?

While Volf almost entirely dismisses the doctrine of the church and that of the Trinity that is espoused by Ratzinger, the same cannot be said of Volf's treatment of Zizioulas. In chapter 4 of this monograph a summary is given of Volf's Trinitarian and ecclesial paradigm that includes a description of eight assumptions that are visible in *AOL*.[4] Volf and Zizioulas occupy common ground in three areas of their respective theologies, and these are: the recognition that there exists clear paradigmatic differences between the Eastern and Western Trinities and ecclesiologies, the explanatory significance of the Trinity for the church alongside the unquestioned use of the metaphor of "the church as the image of the Trinity," and the importance of the concept of communion for a theology of the Trinity and the church.

In the next subsection of this monograph we will examine the debate as to whether there is a difference between Eastern and Western Trinities and ecclesiologies, and in chapter 10 of this monograph we

---

4. In chapter 4 of this monograph, these eight assumptions are: (1) an egalitarian Trinity; (2) a communal and egalitarian ecclesiology; (3) an unquestioned employment of the ecclesial metaphor of the church as the image of the Trinity; (4) the rejection of ecclesial individualism and old style hierarchical holism; (5) the endorsement of feminist theologies and women's ordination; (6) an ecumenical ecclesiology; (7) the recognition that the transmission of faith is crucial to the doctrine of the church; (8) a recurring eschatological theme.

will explore the question: is the metaphor of "the church as the image of the Trinity" valid? It must be pointed out that while Volf agrees with the principle that Zizioulas maintains for the centrality of communion for the Trinity and the church, in practice Volf takes perichoresis as the spinal column for his Trinitarian, ecclesial, and anthropological conclusions.

Timothy Ware outlines that it is common for the OC to contemplate the church as the image of the Trinity, and he writes:

> Just as each man is made according to the image of the Trinitarian God, so the church as a whole is an icon of God the Trinity, reproducing on earth the mystery of unity in diversity. In the Trinity the three are one God, yet each is fully personal; in the church a multitude of human persons are united in one, yet each preserves his personal diversity unimpaired.[5]

However, Volf and Zizioulas, who simultaneously adopt a stance that the Trinity explains ecclesiology, both fall into the trap of projecting this assumption on to Catholic theology. They both view the RCC through this hermeneutical lens that "the church is the image of the Trinity," and they take this as their interpretative key; they equally, but in different ways, overstep the mark in asserting that Ratzinger's (and the Catholic) emphasis upon the Augustinian notion of the one substance in God accounts for the conclusions made for that church.[6] We have seen that the Trinity is part of the holistic doctrine of the RCC but that the doctrine of the Trinity does not explain everything in the Catholic Church.

Volf correctly labels the theme of Zizioulas's theology in chapter 2 of *AOL* as one that embraces "communion, one, and many" with regard to the Trinity and the church. However Volf fails to give a sustained critical analysis of the assumption made by Zizioulas for an equiprimal view of the local and universal church. While Volf consistently upholds the primacy of the local church, he fails to answer his critics who charge that he does not even bother to give a reasoned account of the connection between the "one" and the "many" (1 Cor 10:17) or between the "general" and the "particular."[7] Volf assumes that individualism is flawed, but

---

5. Ware, *Orthodox Church*, 244.

6. Zizioulas, *CAO*, 150–51; Volf, *AOL*, 70–72, 201. Zizioulas writes of his agreement with Volf that the RCC's "ecclesial structures are conceived by way of the one substance of God" (Zizioulas, *CAO*, 145n92; Volf, *AOL*, 67).

7. Zizioulas, *CAO*, 38, 38n73.

his omission to explicate an adequate defense of the connection between local churches opens the door to the accusation that his theology leads to corporate individualism.[8] In other words a local congregation is communal in Volf's ecclesiology, yet it is potentially isolated from the universal church.

The fundamental point of disagreement between Zizioulas and Volf is in their dramatically different constructions of the Trinity. Volf's insistence on egalitarian relations between the Trinitarian persons flattens out Zizioulas's concepts for the monarchy of the Father and an ordered constitution of a communion centered on the Father. This leads Zizioulas to lament that Volf's (and Moltmann's) nonhierarchical church structures represent an aberration from Protestant ecclesiology and a divergence from Western Trinitarian theology by their rejection of the "substantialist approach to God."[9]

IS THERE A DIFFERENCE BETWEEN THE EASTERN AND WESTERN CONCEPTIONS OF THE TRINITY AND HENCE ECCLESIOLOGY?

Until recently there has been universal academic and ecclesiological consensus that there are significant differences in the conceptions of the Trinity between the East and the West. While both wings of the church remain equally committed to the historic creeds and most especially the Niceno-Constantinopolitan Creed (381), the insertion of the *filioque* clause at the Council of Toledo, Spain, in 589 eventually led to the great schism and the papal bull of excommunication that was delivered to the church at Constantinople in 1054. Ware summarizes the reasons as to why the Eastern Church took exception to the addition of the *filioque* clause, something that claims a double procession of the Holy Spirit from the Father and the Son, and he writes:

> The Creed is the common possession of the whole Church, and part of the Church has no right to tamper with it. The West, in arbitrarily altering the Creed without consulting the East, is guilty (as Khomiakov put it) of moral fratricide, of a sin against

---

8. Volf, *AOL*, 25. Volf states that "the central focus of my constructive interest is the local church, and only on the periphery do I address the theme of the relationships obtaining between various local churches and between these and their surrounding social reality."

9. Zizioulas, *CAO*, 145, 150–51.

the unity of the Church. In the second place, Orthodox believe the *filioque* to be theologically untrue. They hold that the Spirit proceeds from the Father alone, and consider it a heresy to say that he proceeds from the Son as well.[10]

The healing of this breach that has spanned a millennia is no small challenge to any potential advance in ecumenical relations between the East and West. Given that there are significant differences also in almost all areas of theological, ecclesiastical, and missionary development of the two sections of the church, the doctrine of the Trinity is only one of a number of divergences.

The Protestant theologians Gerald Bray, Kärkkäinen, and G. C. Berkouwer, the Catholic writer Dulles and the Orthodox churchmen Vladimir Lossky and Ware, are all in agreement as to the existence of two fundamentally different doctrines of the Trinity and the church in the East, compared with the West. Letham summarizes the differences in the doctrine of the Trinity and writes:

> Beginning with a focus on the Three Persons, the East has sometimes tended to see the Father as the source not only of personal subsistence of the Son and the Spirit but also of their deity. In this way, it is easy to see how the Son could be viewed as a little less divine than the Father, possessing his deity by derivation rather than of himself. The best of Eastern theology has avoided these dangers.
>
> The West, for its part, has fallen more towards modalism. By this is meant the blurring or eclipsing of the eternal personal distinctions. Generally—Western Trinitarianism has been based on the priority of the one divine essence and has had some difficulty doing justice to the distinctions of the Three Persons.[11]

Letham summarizes the practical implications of the dominance of this Aquinas–Augustine Western model: "The West has divorced the Trinity from much of the life and worship of the church, unlike the East where the Trinity is more central."[12]

Despite these clear paradigmatic differences on the Trinity, there has been a lesser-known school of thought in the West that treats the

---

10. Ware, *Orthodox Church*, 59.

11. Letham, *Holy Trinity*, 3.

12. Ibid. The two chapters "East and West: The *Filioque* Controversy" and "East and West: The Paths Diverge" offer excellent summaries.

doctrine of God in wholly Trinitarian terms and sees the Triune God as the main thread running through all its theology. Notable representatives of this school include Peter Lombard, Bonaventure, Calvin, Owen, Barth, Torrance, and Gunton. Richard A. Muller's claims that the Reformers followed the Thomist doctrine of God must be treated with caution;[13] his refusal to except Calvin from this conclusion is not well founded,[14] and Owen's work on *Communion with God* clearly broke the traditional mold.[15]

Therefore a real opportunity exists to redress the balance in the West by making the Trinity the theological starting point and ontological foundation that informs not only the doctrine of God but all that the church says and does. This renewed focus on the Triune God is intended to encourage us to think of God and God's attributes in personal terms, and not as an abstract or impersonal subject.

For our own purposes in relation to *AOL*, it must be highlighted that Volf makes clear his position that in the East and West—and he takes Ratzinger and Zizioulas as representative theologians of these two traditions—there are distinctly different understandings of the Trinity and the church. Ratzinger echoes these differences in *ITC*[16] and states:

> The Roman creed (and with it the Western creed in general) is more concerned with the history of salvation and with Christology. The East, on the other hand, has always sought to see the Christian faith in a cosmic and metaphysical perspective.[17]

Zizioulas similarly underscores these differences in *BAC*.[18] Despite this historic consensus, a number of authors have emerged who have

---

13. Muller, "The Unity of Existence, Essence and Attributes in God" in *Post-Reformation Reformed Dogmatics*, vol. 3, 173, 153–226.

14. Butin, *Revelation, Redemption and Response*, 128–29. Butin concludes that for Calvin, the doctrine of the Trinity is the doctrine of God and that "this position has been seldom noticed by 'Calvinistic' interpreters" (129).

15. Muller, *Post-Reformation Reformed Dogmatics*, vol. 4. Here only a cursory reference is made to Owen's significant work on *Communion with God* (154, 156, and 375) and vol. 3 omits this work altogether.

16. Ratzinger, *ITC*, 84–85, 86–87, 89–90.

17. Ibid., 85. Balthasar, *Credo*, 77–78; and Kehl, "Introduction." Balthasar, *Credo*, 13–14; both of these authors accept without question that there are significant theological differences between East and West.

18. Zizioulas, *BAC*, 74–75, 88, 95, 100, 123, 234–35. Kelly, *Early Christian Creeds*, 181. Kelly makes the same argument as Ratzinger, Volf, Zizioulas et al.

begun to mount a serious challenge to what they believe is a stereotype of a supposed polarity in the approach to the Trinity between the East and the West.

According to Letham, M. R. Barnes[19] has spearheaded a challenge against the acceptance of a distinction between Eastern and Western Trinitarianism.[20] Sarah Coakley similarly blames Theodore de Régnon in part, for giving much momentum to what she believes is a misreading of the divergence between the Eastern and Western Trinities, and she questions:

> Could it be, as an important earlier article by Michael René Barnes[21] has documented fully (and André de Halleux had already earlier suggested[22]) that the lurking influence of de Régnon's classic work on the Trinity[23] has fixated both Easterners and Westerners, and for over a century now, on a reading of Gregory [of Nyssa] as "starting from the three and proceeding to the one"; and so—according to a further elaboration, most famously associated with John Zizioulas[24]—normatively instantiating the so-called "social Trinity of the East," a "communitarian" understanding in which "personhood" is somehow *prior* to "substance"?[25]

If Coakley is firm, then David Bentley Hart is furious in his castigation of this suggested cumulative misreading of the Eastern and Western traditions with respect to the Trinity, and he declares:

> The notion that, from the patristic period to the present, the Trinitarian theologies of the Eastern and Western catholic traditions have obeyed contrary logics and have in consequence arrived at conclusions inimical each to the other—a particularly tedious, persistent, and pernicious falsehood—will no doubt one day fade away from want of documentary evidence. At present, however, it serves too many interests for theological scholarship to dispense with it too casually: Eastern theologians find in it a weapon to wield against the West, which they believe has tradi-

---

19. Barnes, "Rereading Augustine," 145–53.
20. Letham, "Trinity," 42–56.
21. Barnes, "De Régnon Reconsidered," 51–79.
22. de Halleux, *Patrologie et Oeuménisme*, chapters 5, 6.
23. de Régnon, *Études de théologie*, vol. 1.
24. Zizioulas, *BAC*.
25. Coakley, "Introduction," 4.

tionally—so alleges for instance, John Zizioulas—forgotten the biblical truth that the unity of the Trinity flows from the paternal *arche*, which is entirely "personal," and come to believe instead "that that which constitutes the unity of God is the one divine substance, the one divinity."[26]

Other authors also join this chorus of support, such as Lewis Ayres,[27] to propose a revision of our understanding of the division between the East and the West on the Trinity, and this is something that they perceive to be an entrenched mainstream hypothesis. Among these is Lucian Turescu, who specifically targets Zizioulas and rebukes him for misrepresenting the Cappadocian theologies on the Trinity.[28] While it is true that Zizioulas rests most of his thought on Basil while claiming to hold to a Cappadocian theology (which he could better term Basil's doctrine of the Trinity), there are subtle Trinitarian nuances between the three Cappadocian fathers (Basil of Caesarea, Gregory of Nyssa, and Gregory of Nazianzus).[29] However, Turescu objects to the reality of these supposed differences between the East and West on the Trinity, and he asserts that these claims are tenuous. Karen Kilby follows a similar pattern to Turescu, but she focuses her attack on a seeming overemphasis of the social Trinitarians such as Moltmann and Gunton; she disagrees in that they "distinguish sharply between the way the doctrine of the Trinity was worked out in the East, and how it developed in the West."[30]

There is a legitimate place for challenging some of the overstatements of Gunton and Zizioulas regarding the influence of Augustine in the West. Gunton claims in "Eastern and Western Trinities" that "the real difference lies not in the starting point but in the way the oneness and threeness of God are weighted in relation to one another."[31] The validity of this opinion must be questioned because it is probably an oversimplification. According to Louis Berkhof, "the Western conception of the

---

26. Hart, "Mirror of the Infinite," 111, 111n1.

27. Ayres, *Nicaea and Its Legacy*. Ayres propounds a similar idea to Coakley et al., and Ayres claims that his own "paradigm attempts to move beyond simplistic East/West divisions and to respect the diversity of "pro-Nicene" theologies better than available accounts" (1).

28. Turescu, " 'Person' Versus 'Individual,'" 97.

29. Zizioulas, *CAO*, 118–34.

30. Kilby, "Perichoresis and Projection," 434, 434n4.

31. Gunton, "Eastern and Western Trinities," 43–44.

Trinity reached its final statement in the work of Augustine of Hippo";[32] however, the North African's enormous influence has left a questionable Trinitarian legacy. His emphasis on the oneness of God's *ousia* (being and substance) and the use of psychological analogies (memory/understanding/will), according to Gunton, express the relations of the three persons with modalist tendencies that have influenced Western theology through the centuries.[33]

Zizioulas likewise suggests that the psychological analogies employed by Augustine have contributed to the "emergence of modern atheism" in the West.[34] This kind of assertion opens the door for accusations that Zizioulas and Gunton engage in a Trinitarian misreading of this patristic theologian, and though they are well-meaning, their conclusions probably reflect a flawed hermeneutic—one that believes that a particular doctrine of the Trinity has explanatory significance for all ecclesiology.

In what way does this discussion concerning the potential differences of Eastern and Western Trinities have an impact on Volf's thesis in *AOL*? If Coakley et al. are correct then much of Volf's thesis in *AOL* collapses because his assertions rest on the assumption that Ratzinger and Zizioulas represent two radically different doctrines of the Trinity and therefore of the church. This thread forms a spinal column throughout *AOL*, alongside Volf's egalitarian social Trinity and his egalitarian, congregational church model. We need to distinguish between the general criticisms of social Trinitarian, with any theological suggestion, whatever their Trinitarian persuasion, that there is little difference between Eastern and Western Trinities.

Do the Eastern and the Western churches' conceptions of the Trinity differ? If there is one area of theology where Ratzinger, Zizioulas, and Volf concur, it is on this point. The most brilliant theologians from the East have argued consistently from Photius (the patriarch of Constantinople, 815–897) in the ninth century to Metropolitan Kallistos (Ware) of Diokeleia (1934–), Lossky and Meyendorff, that the East and

---

32. Berkhof, *History of Christian Doctrines*, 92.

33. Gunton, *Promise of Trinitarian Theology*, 31–57. Gunton asserts that "this is a pneumatological matter: the Achilles' heel of all Western theology is Augustine's failure to make the Spirit a person": *Becoming and Being*, 238. This is probably overstated but an understanding that the Spirit is a person is very important.

34. Zizioulas, *CAO*, 150–51.

West have diverged. The strength of theological weight and emotion that is evoked with regard to the *filioque* question cannot be hastily swept aside;[35] certainly not in the eyes of the East because they regard this departure by the West as heresy and tantamount to a declaration of theological departure.[36]

The historical developments of the Eastern Church, which has survived centuries of Islamic occupation in distinct contrast to Christendom in the West out of which the Western Church has emerged, cannot be overlooked. This proves the point that these two wings of the church have two very different histories and two very different contexts out of which their respective theologies have unfolded.[37] The radical difference between the liturgies of the Eastern and Western church visibly manifests a stark contrast between them both and especially considering that the liturgy is the very heart of the church in the East.[38]

Time and space do not permit an extensive commentary on the differing understandings of apostolic succession, including Rome's insistence on the primacy of Peter and the primacy of the Church of Rome over Christendom; this papal debate alone justifies the conclusion concerning ecclesial divergence. Augustine's use of psychological illustrations in *The Holy Trinity*[39] contrasts markedly with Gregory of Nazianzus's *Orations*,[40] and the latter plainly denies that anything in creation can be an adequate illustration of the Trinity.[41] The legacy of these two theological giants upon the differing lines of Trinitarian development is all too obvious, and Letham argues persuasively that de Régnon's thesis, which puts forward that the East exemplifies a different paradigm to the West, with significant divergence to each other, has validity.[42] Letham summarizes these differences and concludes:

35. Louth, *Greek East and Latin West*.

36. Ware, *Orthodox Church*, 218–23.

37. Roman Catholic Church, *Catechism of the Catholic Church*, 2.2.1.2.1, 291, hereafter called *CCC*; this catechism recognises that there are two traditions: East and West.

38. Antiochian Orthodox Christian Archdiocese of North America, *Service Book*; *Catholic Prayer Book*; Letham, *Through Western Eyes*, 162–71.

39. Augustine, "The Holy Trinity," *NPNF*, books 8–15.

40. Gregory of Nazianzus, "Orations," *NPNF*, Fifth Oration.

41. The difference in the understandings of the Trinity in the East and West is explained in more detail by Letham, *The Holy Trinity*, chapter 10, and *Through Western Eyes*, chapter 9.

42. Letham, "Trinity," 42–56. Hayes, "Introduction," 35. Hayes makes the same

> In the East the doctrine of the Trinity has remained a vital part of belief and worship, in contrast to the West, where for the vast majority it is little more than an arcane mathematical riddle, of no real consequence for daily living. Eastern liturgies are full of Trinitarian prayers, hymns and doxologies. Elsewhere I have referred to the sad lack of appreciation of the Trinity by Western Christians in general. This is all the more tragic in view of the fact that this is the God we worship and serve.[43]
>
> If a random selection of Western Christians were asked what the Trinity meant to them, the chances are overwhelming that the questioner would receive a blank response. What a contrast the Byzantine liturgy provides! The Trinity saturates the prayers and acclamations. Right at the heart of Eastern piety—and thus Eastern theology—is a clear and articulated realisation that the God we worship is Triune.[44]

The observations that are made by Letham point to a critical issue—namely the need for a fresh appreciation of the Trinity, irrespective of our tradition, to enrich our liturgy and therefore our worship.

In conclusion of this current debate, we can safely assume that there is indeed a vast gulf of difference historically, theologically, and liturgically with respect to the doctrine of the Trinity, something that remains to this present day between the church in the East and West. Therefore, Volf's assertions in *AOL* are sustainable in this matter, albeit there are many voices of dissent concerning his social model of the Trinity. This model now comes under the theological microscope in our next section.

IS VOLF'S "SOCIAL TRINITY" A DEPARTURE FROM BOTH THE EASTERN AND WESTERN CONCEPTIONS OF THE TRINITY?

We need to examine a single question: does Volf's (and Moltmann's) social doctrine of the Trinity depart fundamentally from the traditions of the East and West with respect to their Trinitarian formulations? In order to answer this question, we need to establish the criteria that are to be applied for critiquing Volf's doctrine of the Trinity, especially as it is presented in *AOL*. There are five criteria that are going to be applied, tests that hopefully represent a spectrum of theologies that attempt to be faithful to historical developments in theology and the doctrine of

---

argument as Letham to support de Régnon's thesis.

43. Letham, *Holy Trinity*, 407–24.
44. Letham, *Through Western Eyes*, 271–72.

the Trinity. These tests or hermeneutical lenses are the Apostles' Creed, the Niceno-Constantinopolitan Creed (381, hereafter called NCC), the Westminster Confession of Faith (hereafter called WCF), the use of patristic sources, and the biblical documents.

For Ratzinger the Apostles' Creed shapes his ecclesiastical form of faith, and this approach is consistent with the Catholic hermeneutic that takes the deposit of faith as resting on church tradition. Ware comments that the Apostles' Creed does not have the same weight of influence (further evidence of the divergence of East and West) for the OC, and he writes:

> In the eyes of the OC, the statements of faith put out by the Seven [Ecumenical] Councils[45] possess, along with the Bible, an abiding and irrevocable authority. The most important of all the Ecumenical statements of faith is the Niceno-Constantinopolitan Creed, which is read or sung at every celebration of the eucharist, and also daily at Compline. The other two creeds used by the West, the Apostles' Creed and the Athanasian Creed, do not possess the same authority as the Nicene, because they have not been proclaimed by an Ecumenical Council. Orthodox honour the Apostles' Creed as an ancient statement of faith and accept its teaching; but it is simply a local Western Baptismal Creed, never used in the services of the Eastern Patriarchates.[46]

The NCC (without the *filioque* clause) is a crucial declaration of faith for the East, and therefore any critical evaluation of any theologian must include a measurement against these two standards of the faith (Apostles' Creed and NCC) in order to meaningfully represent the Catholic and Orthodox Churches.

Our ultimate goal in this monograph is to develop an understanding of the church from a reformed perspective, and our chosen representative document for this tradition for the English speaking world is the WCF.[47] It is critical to point out that the reformed movement has never operated independently of tradition or without reference to patristic sources. A. N. S. Lane demonstrates that this was the case for

---

45. Percival, "Seven Ecumenical Councils." The seven ecumenical councils are: Nicea (325), Constantinople (381), Ephesus (431), Chalcedon (451), the Second Council of Constantinople (553), the Third Council of Constantinople (680–81), and the Second Council of Nicea (787).

46. Ware, *Orthodox Church*, 210.

47. Westminster Assembly, *Westminster Confession of Faith*.

Calvin,[48] and Letham contends that the members of the Westminster Assembly were constantly referring to the church fathers in their theological discussions.[49] The distinctive of Protestant reformed theology is that the Bible is the final source of authority but never the only source of theology.[50]

There are seven tenets of the doctrine of the Holy Trinity that are manifested in the creeds and patristic writings. These are: one being–three persons; one essence (*homoousios*); three distinct persons (*hypostases*); mutually indwelling persons (*perichōresis*); order among the persons (*monarchia, autotheos, taxis*); three-personal communion (*koinōnia*); knowable and yet unknowable persons. Arguably all these seven facets to the Trinity need to be held with equal ultimacy to avoid a slide into heresy or a departure from a historically agreed upon formulation for this precious doctrine. Augustine correctly warns us that "in no other subject is error more dangerous or inquiry more laborious, or the discovery of truth more profitable,"[51] but this does not exclude further doctrinal developments.

The WCF, for example, makes space for theological advances by the church, and it states:

---

48. Lane, *John Calvin*; Lane, "Scripture, Tradition and Church," 37–55.

49. Letham, *Westminster Assembly*; Letham, *Through Western Eyes*, 94–98.

50. Clark, *Recovering the Reformed Confession*, 8–11, 27. To be Reformed means holding to a Reformed confession as a basis for church membership, preaching, and interpreting Scripture. It is not uncommon to hear some Christians boldly assert that "all I need is the Bible." It sounds right, and yet it is profoundly mistaken because the real question centers on how we interpret the Bible. There are three options when it comes to church tradition. Tradition is something that is sometimes seen in a negative light by Evangelicals, as if all tradition is ugly and something to be rejected as utterly false. According to Heiko Oberman there are two ways to understand the relation between Scripture and tradition, called tradition 1 and tradition 2 (Oberman, "Quo vadis, Petre?" 269–96). Tradition 1 is the Reformed principle of *sola scriptura*, which accepts the Scripture as the single and unique authority in the church while maintaining a high regard for tradition to learn from the past, so that we can more accurately interpret Scripture. Tradition 2 would represent the Roman Catholic Church that places church tradition on an equal footing with the Bible. Alistair E. McGrath observes a third category called tradition 0, which is a "fundamentally individualistic approach to Scripture and tradition." McGrath explains that this places the "private judgement of the individual above the corporate judgment of the Christian church concerning the interpretation of Scripture," and furthermore he believes it is "a recipe for anarchy" (*Reformation Thought*, 144–45).

51. Augustine, "On the Trinity," *NPNF*, 1.3.5, 19.

> The whole counsel of God concerning all things necessary for his own glory, man's salvation, faith and life, is either expressly set down in Scripture, or by good and necessary consequence may be deduced from Scripture. (1.6)

However all theological developments need to remain within the ancient boundaries of Scripture, and the historic creeds and councils. The WCF again clarifies:

> The supreme judge by which all controversies of religion are to be determined, and all decrees of councils, opinions of ancient writers, doctrines of men, and private spirits, are to be examined, and in whose sentence we are to rest, can be no other but the Holy Spirit speaking in the Scriptures. (1.10)

> All Synods or councils, since the Apostles' times, whether general or particular, may err; and many have erred. Therefore they are not to be made the rule of faith, or practice; but to be used as a help in both. (31.4)

Therefore it is contended that any new developments of the doctrine of the Trinity must remain within the limits of the established tenets of this truth, and it is put forward that the aforementioned headings suitably summarize seven Trinitarian boundary markers. Our question remains: does Volf's doctrine of the Trinity remain within this established theological tradition?

Volf's social Trinity is explained in *AOL* and in the article "The Trinity Is Our Social Program."[52] There are three main postulates that underpin his understanding for the inner-relations of the Trinity, and these are: relational personhood, perichoretic personhood, and nonhierarchical Trinitarian relations.[53] This proposal for the Trinity by Volf rejects monotheism, the concept of *homoousios*, and any thinking in terms of the one substance in God, thereby squeezing its paradigm into a nonhierarchical communion of perichoretic relationships between the three persons. Volf's theology only engages with two out of the seven tenets that are required for any doctrine of the Trinity to remain within historical and theological boundaries.

This wholesale rejection of monotheism by Volf, and similarly by Moltmann (chapter 4 of this monograph observes that their theologies

---

52. Volf, *AOL*, 204–17; Volf, "Trinity Is Our Social Program," 407–12.
53. Volf, *AOL*, 204–17.

on the Trinity are almost identical), is a full-blown rejection of the first two ecumenical councils in 325 and 381. This means that they both render the NCC as virtually obsolete and the councils' settlement concerning the concept of *homoousios* as containing little relevance for contemporary theology. This marks a dramatic departure from the traditions of both East and West, and their (Volf and Moltmann) writings on the Trinity produce nonecumenical conclusions, ones that are deemed to be heretical in the eyes of the RCC and the OC. Within *AOL*, there is almost no engagement with any of the patristic essays on the Trinity, no mention of historic creedal settlements, and Volf's bibliography in *AOL* contains virtually no patristic Trinitarian references[54]—startling omissions.

The WCF upholds that "in the unity of the Godhead there be three Persons, of one substance" (2.3); again this confessional statement would be rejected by the adherents to the Moltmann school. We may ask, where does Volf's doctrine of the Trinity arise from? His starting point is resolutely an anthropological inquiry of human identity based on philosophical questions.[55] He argues that "in recent decades the issue of identity has risen to the forefront of discussion in social philosophy" and that one of the "major concerns of the nineties seem to be about identity."[56] The resulting Trinitarian synthesis that he outlines in *AOL* is somewhat mysterious because it does not follow Hegelian logic either; there is no thesis, but only a suggested antithesis.

Finally on the matter of hermeneutics and its relation to tradition, it is difficult to identify the guiding principles of Volf's system of interpretation. A. E. McGrath explains that in the sixteenth century there were three main understandings of the relation between Scripture and tradition. He summarizes them as follows:

> Tradition 0: The radical Reformation
>
> Tradition 1: The magisterial Reformation
>
> Tradition 2: The Council of Trent[57]

---

54. Ibid., 283–306.

55. Volf, "Trinity Is Our Social Program," 408.

56. Ibid., 408 and 408n22; here he appeals to Menand, *Culture Wars*, and Taylor, "Politics of Recognition," 25–73.

57. McGrath, *Reformation Thought*, 144.

According to this schema "Tradition 0" was pursued by Smyth and the Anabaptists who followed a strict "*scriptura sola* principle," which "allocate[d] no role whatsoever to tradition."[58] Luther, Calvin, and the Westminster divines adopted "Tradition 1": this meant that "Scripture could not be interpreted in a random way; it must be interpreted within the context of the historical continuity of the Christian church. The parameters of its interpretation were historically fixed and given."[59] "Tradition 2" by contrast favored a "dual-source theory of doctrine,"[60] that of Scripture and tradition, and this represents both Ratzinger and Zizioulas.

It is evident that Volf and Moltmann fit none of these three paradigmatic methods of interpretation. Volf departs from Smyth's principle of consistent adherence to the examination of the Scriptures, and even a brief analysis of Smyth's *Works* demonstrates that his writings are saturated with Bible references; this contrasts significantly with Volf's own style. Our conclusion is that Volf and Moltmann's social doctrine of the Trinity exhibits a departure from both Eastern and Western conceptions of the Trinity, the Reformers, historic creeds, and the church fathers. The consequent result is that Volf's newly conceived doctrine of the Trinity remains remarkably isolated from the majority of Christendom, and it is still far from being compatible with the broader scholarly consent.

SUMMARY

In our analysis of Volf's handling of Zizioulas's theology in *AOL*, we have seen that *BAC* is a primary source material for Volf, but we have also discovered that *CAO* yields valuable insight into the theological paradigm of Zizioulas (even though this book was written eight years after the publication of *AOL*). These two theologians agree on some points, notably their mutual appreciation for the ecclesial metaphor for "the church as the image of the Trinity," their consent that there exists clear paradigmatic differences between Eastern and Western constructions of the Trinity, and their anticipation that the doctrine of the Trinity always has explanatory significance for ecclesiology.

Our summary of the theological assumptions of Zizioulas is outlined under seven headings, and these clearly demonstrate significant

---

58. Ibid.
59. Ibid., 135–36.
60. Ibid., 136.

differences between Zizioulas and Volf. Zizioulas rejects Volf's egalitarian Trinity and his nonhierarchical congregational doctrine of the church. Reciprocally Volf polemicizes against Zizioulas's hierarchical Trinity for the church and the constitution of the church centered on the bishop. Free Church and Orthodox ecclesiologies are seen to be fundamentally different, and Volf does not appear to succeed in his attempt to produce an ecumenical thesis. Rather he magnifies the many areas of disagreement that exist between these two theologians.[61]

Our final discussions centered on the conclusion that there are indeed clear paradigmatic differences between Eastern and Western conceptions of the Trinity and that Volf represents a radical departure from both of these traditions regarding the Trinity.

CONCLUSION

This chapter and the previous three of this monograph, critically evaluate Volf's engagement with his two chosen representatives: Ratzinger and Zizioulas. Volf specifically dialogues with Ratzinger (chapter 1) and Zizioulas (chapter 2) in *AOL*, and he persistently rejects every vestige of hierarchy in their doctrines of the Trinity and their ecclesiologies. The second section of *AOL* consists of five further chapters, and each of these contains a specific aspect of Volf's own proposal to connect the Trinity to communion in the church. In each of these proposals Volf also engages with Ratzinger and Zizioulas, and this material also forms the content of this chapter and the three previous ones.

For ease of purpose we have chosen to analyze Volf's interaction with Ratzinger separately to his engagement with Zizioulas. In many ways Volf handles his assessment with Ratzinger more intensely than with Zizioulas, and it becomes evident that he disagrees with the former on almost every point. Our analysis of Volf's treatment of Ratzinger attempts to capture Volf's thought by summarizing his ideas under the headings of four propositions that he makes clear in *AOL*. While a number of the points that Volf raises in these assertions have validity, it appears that Volf has misread Ratzinger on a number of matters.

Volf misinterprets Ratzinger when he fails to recognize that Ratzinger gives equal priority to the one substance of God and the relatedness of persons; this leads to Volf overemphasizing the priority that

---

61. Volf, *AOL*, 19–25.

Ratzinger gives to the one substance in God. Similarly Volf does not seem to pick up that Ratzinger's ecclesiology and especially the RCC pattern for ministry is driven primarily by Christology. Volf repeatedly insists that the Trinity holds explanatory significance for Ratzinger's ecclesiology. While this is true for Zizioulas and Volf, the same cannot be said of Ratzinger; however Ratzinger's theology is a united and consistent whole and the doctrine of the Trinity forms part of this harmonious whole.

As for Zizioulas, his neopatristic synthesis makes much of supposed explicit connections between the church and the Trinity, and along the same vein as Volf, Zizioulas sees that the Trinity is the interpretative lens to understand the church. Zizioulas's Orthodox ecclesiology is eucharistic with an apostolic succession based on all the apostles, and not just Peter, as in the RCC. This doctrine of the Trinity is founded upon the concepts for monarchy, communion, and hierarchical order among the three persons. This leads him to openly rebut the Moltmann theological school of thought (of which Volf belongs) because they reject any notion for hierarchy in God, the church, or society.

Volf's own ecclesiology deals almost exclusively with the notion of the local church, and he fails to adequately respond to the clear framework offered by Zizioulas, where equal ultimacy is upheld for the universal and local church. We have observed that the Zizioulas school, one that asserts the importance of the monarchy of the Father, is also expounded by Gunton, Jenson, Schwöbel, and Pannenberg. Pannenberg is of particular interest because Volf claims to "adopt the general features of the social model of Trinitarian relations as proposed by Moltmann (though also by Pannenberg)."[62] On the one hand Volf endorses a supporter of Zizioulas's theology while on the other hand rejecting Zizioulas's work in *AOL*; he must have misread Pannenberg's systematic theology. Free Church and Orthodox ecclesiologies are two different constructions and ecumenically, *AOL* does not provide substantial conclusions to resolve these differences.

62. Volf, *AOL*, 198.

10

A Critical Evaluation of "The Ecclesiality of the Church"

INTRODUCTION

THE CONNECTION BETWEEN THE Trinity and the church offers many fruitful lines of enquiry, and Volf does not miss the opportunity to explore a whole range of theological avenues in part 2 of *AOL*. He puts forward five successive proposals that expound his understanding of links that can be made, but he does this from the vantage point of his own particular understanding of the social doctrine of the Trinity and his interpretation of how Free Churches should operate.

The first proposal for critical analysis is "The Ecclesiality of the Church" (chapter 3 of *AOL*); the second is "Faith, Person, and Church" (chapter 4 of *AOL*); thirdly, "Trinity and Church" (chapter 5 of *AOL*); the fourth thesis, "Structures of the Church" (chapter 6 of *AOL*); and lastly "The Catholicity of the Church" (chapter 7 of *AOL*).

Throughout Volf's theses he takes it for granted that the doctrine of the Trinity should inform our ecclesiology, and in many cases he anticipates that his revised appreciation of the Triune God should automatically lead to the remodeling of local churches. However, this stance also deserves critical assessment concerning the validity of the ecclesial symbol, "the church as the image of the Trinity." This is our starting point in this chapter in order to establish the appropriateness of this metaphor for ecclesiology prior to scrutinizing Volf's specific doctrine of the church. Hopefully valuable material will be gleaned from the overall thrust of Volf's aim in *AOL*, which can then be used by different branches of the church to enable them to freshly appreciate the Trinity in their worship and mission within their own multicultural context.[1]

IS THE METAPHOR OF "THE CHURCH AS THE IMAGE OF THE TRINITY" VALID?

At this point we need to investigate the ecclesial metaphors that are commonly used to describe the mystery of the church. It is important to examine afresh the theological validity of the "the church as the image of the Trinity" as an ecclesial symbol. It is an almost obvious expectation of Volf, in that he should handle this matter in *AOL*, but he does not do so, and he simply assumes unquestionably that the church is an image of the Trinity.[2]

However, there is a plausible explanation behind this. *AOL* originated as a postdoctoral dissertation, with the German title *Trinität und Gemeinschaft: Eine ökumenische Ekklesiologie* (Trinity and Communion: An Ecumenical Ecclesiology), and this title more accurately reflects Volf's intention in his thesis as compared with the publisher's title in English for *AOL*. This probably explains why he does not outline the connection between the communion in the Trinity and the anticipated communion in the church. It is therefore needful to explore the appropriateness of this metaphor because this may provide vital clues to our overall ecclesiological pursuit.

Paul S. Minear observes in *Images of the Church in the New Testament* that there are more than eighty of them, in one way or another.[3] In his survey of ecclesiological imagery he helpfully classifies these under five headings: minor images of the church, the people of God, the new creation, the fellowship of faith, and the body of Christ.[4] In spite of his excellent work he does not specifically identify that the church is to be a reflection of the Trinity.

Similarly, Dulles's study in *Models of the Church* does not expound on the relation between the Trinity and the church,[5] and Lesslie Newbigin

1. Kärkkäinen, *Trinity and Religious Pluralism*.
2. Volf, *AOL*.
3. Minear, *Images of the Church*, 28.
4. Ibid., 10, 268–69.
5. Dulles, *Models of the Church* emphasizes the church as the "people of God" and "eschatological nature of the pilgrim church," 24–37, 78–85; Abbott, *Documents of*

likewise overlooks this potentially rich metaphor.[6] However, in writing on the topic of mission Newbigin does focus on the importance of the doctrine of the Trinity, and he invites the "missionary movement to bind to itself afresh the strong name of the Trinity."[7] He relates this more to the content of the church's message than to the church modeling itself after the Triune God.

Reformed systematicians do not generally pick up on the potential use for this metaphor. G. C. Berkouwer focuses on the four creedal attributes of the church (unity, catholicity, apostolicity, and holiness).[8] Herman Bavinck follows the same line as Berkouwer, while also including the idea of the church as the "people of God" and the "communion of the saints,"[9] and Grudem omits ecclesial metaphors altogether.[10] Edmund P. Clowney constrains his ecclesiology to the same pattern as Berkouwer and Bavinck, but he perceptively states that "for a fresh look at the biblical doctrine of the church, a full Trinitarian approach serves best."[11] Unfortunately he does not expound further on this theme.

Schwöbel, a Lutheran scholar, is a good example of a theologian who firmly connects the ecclesial and Trinitarian communities, but he does so in way that moves the discussion along abstract, metaphysical, and academic lines, that demonstrates a lack of functional application for the church.[12] This pattern appears to be all too common in the West, so that even when a theologian grasps the significance of the Trinity for the church, the Trinity remains somewhat isolated from practical worship. This brief survey confronts us with a key question because Western ecclesiology seems to virtually overlook the need for the Trinity to

---

Vatican II.

6. Newbigin, *Household of God*.

7. Newbigin, *Trinitarian Doctrine*, 33.

8. Berkouwer, *Church*. James Bannerman also does not offer any detailed analysis of the metaphors and images of the church: Bannerman, *Church of Christ*.

9. Bavinck, *Reformed Dogmatics*, 273–325. Robert L. Reymond also only focuses on the four attributes of the church in line with Berkouwer: Reymond, *New Systematic Theology*, 837–60.

10. Grudem, *Systematic Theology*, 853–1088.

11. Clowney, *Church*, 29. John Stott and Donald Macleod similarly make little connection between the Trinity and the church: Stott, *Living Church*; Macleod, *Priorities for the Church*. It must be noted, however, that Macleod does place more attention on the Trinity in his small book, *Shared Life*.

12. Schwöbel, "Die Suche nach Gemeinschaft Gründe."

inform its understanding of the church. Either this pursuit is irrelevant or there is a fresh need for a Trinitarian approach to systematic theology and ecclesiology.

Perhaps Ware was right when he asserted in 1963 that "Western Christians, whether Free Churchmen, Anglicans, or Roman Catholics, have a common background in the past. All alike have been profoundly influenced by the same events."[13] Western theology displays an ecclesiological framework that does not generally place the Trinity at the heart of its discussion, worship, and practice. Newbigin admits that he himself makes "one very large omission" in his contemplation of the doctrine of the church, and he states that "I have said nothing about the Eastern Orthodox interpretation of the life in Christ."[14] It is not coincidental that when the Anglican Church issued a statement in 2006 to affirm that we must think of *The Church of the Triune God* that it did so in the context of Anglican–Orthodox theological dialogue.[15]

The Anglican Consultative Council pursues the use of this metaphor, but it carefully explains that "theology and worship alike control the way these words [when God is called Father, Son and Holy Spirit] are understood."[16] This document applies the doctrine of the Trinity to the sacraments of baptism and the Eucharist because it outlines that the church should "always be a visible sign of her inner reality as the mystery of communion with and in the Blessed Trinity."[17] With respect to the relationship between church structures and communion (*koinōnia*), a guarded phrase is used against ecclesial independency, and it states: "The doctrine of the Holy Trinity implies that to be 'in the image and likeness of God' is to be in communion, to be simultaneously 'one' and 'many.' "[18] This latter phrase explicitly distances itself from theologians that make

---

13. Ware, *Orthodox Church*, 9.

14. Newbigin, *Household of God*, ix–x.

15. Anglican Consultative Council, *Church of the Triune God*. The British Council of Churches similarly published a book in 1989 that seems to have been in response to the Russian Orthodox Church in the UK. British Council of Churches, *Forgotten Trinity*, 1, 27–34.

16. Anglican Consultative Council, *Church of the Triune God*, 22.

17. Ibid., 14–15.

18. Ibid., 13, 18. British Council of Churches, *Forgotten Trinity*, 27–34; this book similarly encourages the recovery of the Trinity as something to be realized as central in worship and in the understanding of the church as primarily communion, not as an institution.

little sense of the interrelation between the "one" and the "many," and this would include Volf's conception of the church in *AOL*.

John Behr's *The Trinitarian Being of the Church*, proposes that the "three primary scriptural images for the church—that is, the church as the people of God, the body of Christ and the temple of the Holy Spirit" thereby links the church "in a particular way to one member of the Trinity."[19] Christoph Gregor Müller and John Stott[20] have recognized that Paul employs three ecclesial metaphors (1 Cor 3:5–17) that are set within a Trinitarian framework; these pictures are God's field, God's building, and God's Temple. Müller explains that a Trinitarian ecclesiology can be deduced from this passage as well as from 1 Cor 12:4–6 and 2 Cor 13:14.[21] However Müller and Stott do not offer practical theological answers as to how these insights can be worked out in the church's worship, liturgy, faith, practice, and mission. This approach contrasts dramatically with Eastern theology. Zizioulas explains that "ecclesiology in the Orthodox tradition has always been determined by the liturgy [and] the eucharist,"[22] and the doctrine of the Trinity literally saturates Eastern liturgy.

One of the most significant portions of the Orthodox liturgy comprises what is known as the Trisagion prayers, which are used at the opening and near the end of every service, except the Divine Office. They are the ladder by which the priest's mind and heart ascend to God and then bring them down again to serve their brethren in the Divine Liturgy. They form a composite hymn of praise to God, the thrice holy God, and they commence with the prayer: "In the name of the Father, and of the Son, and of the Holy Spirit. Amen."[23] A Trinitarian form of the Christian faith is repeatedly affirmed as the NCC is confessed in each Divine Liturgy, both St. John's and St. Basil's.[24] God is addressed using many biblical titles, but also the names "All-holy Trinity" and "O Holy Trinity" are considered to be equally valid, and the prayer, "Glory to the Father, and to the Son, and to the Holy Spirit; now and ever and unto

---

19. Behr, "Trinitarian Being of the Church," 70.
20. Müller, *Gottes Pflanzung*; Stott, *Calling Christian Leaders*, 85–106.
21. Müller, *Gottes Pflanzung*, 119.
22. Zizioulas, *BAC*, 131.
23. Antiochian Orthodox Christian Archdiocese of North America, *Service Book*, 7–12.
24. Ibid., 9, 13, 110, 133.

ages of ages, Amen," is regularly repeated.²⁵ The Eastern liturgy is the Trinity in practice, par excellence, and it provides a living symbol for the validity of the metaphor of the church as the image of the Trinity.

The Eastern liturgy appears to provide a cogent defense for any attempt to connect the Trinity to the church for practical and pastoral theology. Before we conclude this investigation, it is prudent to comment on some of the Eastern patristic writings and some contemporary Eastern theologians. The church father Origen (185–?232), according to F. Ledegang, stresses that "once people have acquired an insight into the mystery of the Trinity, the church becomes a temple."²⁶ While Ledegang observes that Origen does not explicitly utilize a Trinitarian metaphor to describe the church, he explains that Origen places a "great importance" on the "belief of the Trinity: With it the church stands or falls."²⁷ Gregory of Nazianzus (329–374) places the Trinity at the heart of the Christian faith, and he famously writes: "When I say God, I mean Father, Son and Holy Spirit."²⁸ As bishop of Constantinople where he preached his *Orations* in the midst of the Arian controversy, Gregory's "constant theme was the worship of the Trinity," suggests Philip Schaff.²⁹

Maximus the Confessor (580–662) is in Andrew Louth's view "the greatest of Byzantine theologians."³⁰ According to Adam G. Cooper he was a "learned monk who is one of the profoundest of Byzantine saints and a faithful and fertile representative of the Greek patristic tradition."³¹ Jaroslav Pelikan writes that Maximus is the "leading theologian of his era in the Greek East, probably in the entire church,"³² and Lars Thunberg asserts that he is "one of the greatest thinkers of all time."³³ It is perhaps in the thought of Maximus the Confessor that the Orthodox understanding of the church as the image of God reached its theological climax.

---

25. Ibid., 7–8.
26. Ledegang, *Mysterium Ecclesiae*, 342.
27. Ibid.
28. Gregory of Nazianzus, "Select Orations of Gregory Nazianzen," *NPNF*, 38.8, p. 347.
29. Schaff, "Prolegomena," *NPNF*, vol. 3, 197.
30. Louth, *Maximus the Confessor*, 3.
31. Cooper, *Body in St. Maximus*, 1.
32. Pelikan, " 'Council or Father or Scripture,' " 277.
33. Thunberg, *Man and the Cosmos*, 7.

Louth explains that "Maximus wrote no work expressly on the church, the nearest being his work, the *Mystagogia*,[34] on the Divine Liturgy."[35] However it is Maximus's insights about the liturgical activity that brings a fresh appreciation of the church. Louth summarizes:

> The notion of the church presented in the *Mystagogia*, which focuses on the action of the *Divine Liturgy*, and the way in which what happens in the Church is reflected at every level of reality, from the transcendent reality of God, through the manifold unity of the cosmos, to the depths of the human soul. This vision of the church—at once cosmic, eschatological, eucharistic and ascetic—is then related to Maximos' views on the institutional church.[36]

Maximus held a Trinitarian framework for divine revelation, and Cooper expounds:

> It is therefore the implicitly Trinitarian structure of revelation, centred upon the revelation of the Word in the flesh, that shapes Maximus' understanding of the need to advance through the flesh of the incarnate Word to lay hold of the "naked" Word himself. For the whole Spirit and the whole Father are substantially united with the Word. . . . The vision of the glory of the Father—in the Son—through the Spirit.[37]

For Maximus, this encounter with the Triune God takes place in the liturgy, which "constitutes a progressive series of unfolding symbolic, theandric activities through which the hidden, eschatological union of the cosmos in and with God is manifested."[38] The church's architecture, furniture, layout, the nave (accessible to all the faithful), the sanctuary (accessible exclusively by the bishop, priests, and deacons), and the liturgy are a demonstrative parable of the holy church of God as an image of the cosmos.[39]

---

34. Maximus the Confessor, *La Mystagogie*. "Mystagogy" means the celebration of the Eucharist.

35. Louth, "Ecclesiology of Saint Maximos," 109. In this article Louth deliberately uses the Greek name Maximos in preference to the commonly used Anglophone name Maximus.

36. Ibid.

37. Cooper, *Body in St. Maximus*, 35.

38. Ibid., 198.

39. Ibid., 198–200.

Melchisedec Törönen similarly explains Maximus's understanding of the "church as an image reflecting God" where the "celebration of the eucharist [is] a movement [that] takes place, a movement from nave to the sanctuary."[40] Törönen further describes Maximus's interpretation of the Eucharist in connection to the ecclesial metaphor of temple (1 Cor 3:16–17), and he writes:

> Maximus views the liturgy thus: the first entrance of the bishop signifies the first coming of Christ and his saving passion; the bishop's entering the sanctuary and mounting the throne is nothing less than Christ's ascension into heaven and sitting on the heavenly throne, the reading of the Gospel signifies the end of this world, and the bishop's descent from the throne, his second and glorious coming: the dismissal of the catechumens is the final judgment; and all that follows belongs to the life of the future kingdom of heaven. It is the eschaton made present: union of all with God as He is.[41]

It was Balthasar who popularized the term "Theo-Drama"[42] to explain the redemptive activity of Christ, and we could describe the theology of Maximus as a weekly liturgical "Theo-Drama," a visual aid for the gospel, all centered on the Eucharist.

We may not all hold to an Orthodox pattern for worship, but there are many valuable lessons to be learned from the insights of Maximus. All that is done in public worship is an image of some underlying conviction, conscious or otherwise. Contemporary Christian worship requires careful reexamination to determine the theological roots of the traditions that are practiced, in order to ensure that they are biblical and God centered. Paul warned the Corinthian church regarding their public meetings, and he instructed them to do "all things . . . decently and in order" (1 Cor 14:40). Why? Because to permit disorder is to misrepresent God: Paul explains that "God is not a God of confusion but of peace" (1 Cor 14:33). The unstructured meetings at Corinth were in danger of promoting actions that did not reflect the right image of God, that being the peace of God; Paul's concern was that the congregation should strive to display this in the church's public worship.

---

40. Törönen, *Union and Distinction*, 143–45, 150.
41. Ibid., 151.
42. Balthasar, *Theo-Drama*.

It is through the church that we encounter Christ, and it is through Christ that we then encounter the Triune God. Therefore, Cooper asserts that the church is the "concrete locus whereby Christ is universally identifiable and tangibly accessible in all his salvific splendour."[43] Perhaps the most explicit teaching by Christ on the Trinity is found in John's account of the Last Supper (John 13:1—17:24), and it is through Christ that we have access to the Triune God. Bruce D. Marshall wrestles with these complex matters, and in contemplating the "epistemic primacy of belief in the Trinity" he then proposes that the NT characteristic is to portray "Jesus as the image of the unseen God" (Col 1:15).[44]

Vladimir Lossky (1903–1958) was a formidable representative of the OC in the twentieth century, and he states: "The Trinity is for the OC, the unshakeable foundation of all religious thought, of all piety, of all spiritual life, of all experience."[45] How many Protestant or Catholic congregations could make the same claim? Eastern Orthodoxy has much to teach the universal church concerning the integration of the knowledge of the Triune God into the fabric of daily worship and piety. Lossky ensures that a careful balance is upheld between a focus on the Trinity and simultaneously on the Son.[46] He expounds his "theology of the image" and "the Trinitarian theology of images" by reminding us that it is Christ who "is the image of the invisible God" (2 Cor 4:4; Col 1:15).[47] We could describe his theology as a Triune-christological balancing act, one that attempts to uphold a coequal emphasis on the Trinity and on the Son.

One of the dangers for any metaphor for the church is the tendency to develop an unbalanced theology. A vision for the church, however, must logically be expected to mirror the being and attributes of the Triune God, and this factor has been absent from many attempts to formulate a biblical ecclesiology. Calvin, in commenting on the Psalms, illustrates this concept by remarking that "the church is a distinguished

---

43. Cooper, *Body in St. Maximus*, 167.

44. Marshall, *Trinity and Truth*, 110.

45. Lossky, *Mystical Theology*, 65.

46. A similar balancing act appears to be demonstrated in the Russian Orthodox theology of A. S. Xomjakov; O'Leary, *Triune Church*, 58–82. O'Leary states that "Xomjakov's ecclesiology is dominated completely by the conviction that the Church is the creation of the Holy Trinity" (58).

47. Lossky, *Image and Likeness*, 133, 135–36.

theatre in which the divine glory is displayed" and that the "church . . . is a mirror of the grace and justice of God."[48] These statements raise the question: is our appreciation of the Trinity fully taken into account and reflected in our understanding of the church?

Much has been written to promote a Christ-centered conception of the church, but this often gives the impression that the Trinity is peripheral and nonessential. A new paradigm is needed, one that marries Christology with the Triune God to form a new interpretive lens; hence our proposed Christo-Trinitarian hermeneutic. This could also be called a Trinitarian–christological hermeneutic because its philosophic thrust is to develop a way of thinking about Christ that leads to the Trinity, and vice versa.

As in all theology we are on a cliff edge. A metaphor that fixes on "the church as an image of the Trinity" can itself be potentially problematic if it marginalizes God's ultimate self-revelation in Christ. Calvin's ecclesiastical wisdom has a valuable caution: "Whenever we think of God or want to speak of him, we ought to avoid dwelling on his infinite essence. This form of thinking is dangerous, since human understanding becomes confused by it. Rather, we should constantly return to Jesus Christ, in whom the Father has revealed himself to us."[49]

Our findings lead us to propose that we should adopt the pursuit of "the church as the image of Christ and of the Trinity," not simply "the church as the image of the Trinity" or "the church as the image of Christ." Christ and the Trinity should be consistently connected simultaneously and inseparably, in a way that should hopefully avoid the pitfalls of both Eastern and Western ecclesiologies. The West can learn much from the East's rich use of the doctrine of the Trinity for all aspects of church life; similarly Orthodox congregations could learn a lot from the Western churches' christological emphasis, along with their understanding of soteriology when it rests upon the doctrine of justification by faith. Many of the church metaphors in the NT are christological, such as God's building (1 Cor 3:9–14), and Christ should be our theological starting point, but the ultimate goal is the worship of the Triune God. The imagery of God's temple (1 Cor 3:16–17) is something identified by Origen and Maximus as a rich metaphor. It is the church as God's temple, by the help of the Holy Spirit that should magnify God as Trinity, in its

48. Calvin, *Commentary on Psalms*, vol. 3, Ps 76:2, 194–95, and vol. 4, Ps 111:5, 315.
49. John Calvin, "Name of God," 17–19.

worship, preaching, and the content of its faith, prayer, and the administration of the sacraments.

Gus George Christo helps us to conclude with his summary in *The Church's Identity*, which is the result of his research on the ecclesiology of John Chrysostom (349–407). He states that: "[Chrysostom's] christocentric conception of the church presupposes a certain kind of Christology. Christ the Second Person of the Trinity."[50] We must always consider Christ in unbreakable union with the Triune God to provide a Trinitarian context and background to everything about Christ's person and work. Similarly we should always contemplate the Triune God, at least initially, through the lens of the revelation of the Father's only begotten Son (John 1:14, 1:18).

VOLF'S PROPOSAL: "THE ECCLESIALITY OF THE CHURCH"

A Summary of This Proposal

Chapter 3 in *AOL* explores the question "what makes the church, the church?" and asks "what does it mean for the church to call itself a church in the first place?"[51] Volf puts forward a series of successive propositions before he culminates in his final definition for what he believes are the marks of a holy, catholic, and apostolic church.

The Presence of the Spirit of Christ Makes the Church

Volf suggests that "since ecumenical consensus holds that the presence of the Spirit of Christ makes a church a church, it is precisely questions concerning the external conditions of this presence that become ecumenically significant for the identity of the church."[52] A natural question arises: how does he arrive at this conclusion? Volf's starting point is eschatological, and he writes that the "all-embracing framework for an appropriate understanding of the church is God's eschatological new creation (Rev. 21:1—22:5)."[53] He summarizes that the church's "future

---

50. Christo, *Church's Identity*, 402. It is interesting to note that Christo, writing as an Orthodox pastor, makes no mention as to the role of preaching in Chrysostom's ecclesiology, even though he rightly explains that John is remembered as "the golden mouth" for his exceptional oratorical skill (1–2).

51. Volf, *AOL*, 127.

52. Ibid., 130.

53. Ibid., 128, 128n3; Volf explains that he shares this eschatological perspective with Moltmann, *Church in the Power*, and Pannenberg, *Reich Gottes*.

participation in the communion of the Triune God, however, is not only an object of hope for the church but also its present experience" and the "final answer" to Jesus' high priestly prayer ("that they may all be one, just as you, Father are in me, and I in you, that they also may be in us," John 17:21).[54]

The future indwelling of the Triune God among the glorified saints becomes, for Volf, the blueprint for the church's present experience, and he makes specific appeal to two second-century church fathers: Ignatius of Antioch (?35–?107) and Irenaeus of Lyons (?130–?200). Volf asserts that ever since the time when Ignatius taught that "wherever Jesus Christ is, there is the universal church," that sufficient grounds were established to ground the presence of Christ or the Spirit with the presence of the church.[55] He assumes that thereafter any future constitution of a church along these lines became a settled issue, and he quotes a statement by Irenaeus that says "where the Spirit of God is, there is the church, and every kind of grace," to buttress this claim.[56]

Matthew 18:20 Determines the Constitution of a Church

This proposal by Volf for the constitution of a church is taken a step further when he writes:

> I will join this long tradition by taking Matthew 18:20 as the foundation not only for determining what the church is, but also for how it manifests itself externally as a church. Where two or three are gathered in Christ's name, not only is Christ present among them but a Christian church is there as well, perhaps a bad church, a church that may well transgress against love and truth, but a church nonetheless.[57]

According to Volf this "long tradition" that bases its definition of a church on Matt 18:20 includes the Free Church theologians such as John Smyth, but he claims that this idea actually stretches back to the works of Ignatius, Tertullian (?160–?225), and Cyprian of Carthage (?200–258).

Adding to the previous quotation from the work of Ignatius that states "wherever Jesus Christ is, there is the universal church," Volf

---

54. Volf, *AOL*, 128–29. Volf also appeals to the work of Gundry, "New Jerusalem," 254–64.

55. Ignatius, "The Epistle of Ignatius to the Smyrnæns," *ANF*, vol. 1, 89–90.

56. Irenaeus, "Irenaeus Against Heresies," *ANF*, vol. 1, 3.24.1, 458.

57. Volf, *AOL*, 136.

believes that this thought was adopted by Tertullian who wrote "where there are three, there is the church."[58] Volf introduces Cyprian into his argument to buttress his ecclesial presupposition that Matt 18:20 is of central significance for ecclesiology.[59] A rather surprising admission is made by Volf, who explains that his proposition for ecclesiology based on Matt 18:20 is one that is based on theological reflection and not purely exegetical studies.[60] He elaborates this thought in a footnote, and he concedes that the exegetical conclusion that "two or three" refers to the church (*ekklēsia*) is uncertain.[61] Despite this admission that the exegetical grounds for his assertions are tenuous he still stresses:

> Here I follow the early church in construing Matt. 18:20 theologically as a statement not only about spirituality, but also about the church itself. Whether this possesses ecclesiological cogency depends less on the exegetical determination of the identity of the "two or three" than on the persuasive power of my overall reading of the New Testament and of my ecclesiological-systematic outline.[62]

This concession is startling. Volf sanctions his own approach to reinterpret the generally agreed upon exegesis of the passage in Matt 18:15–20, which is based on his "overall reading of the NT" and his systematic outline. Is that preconceived? It is certainly individualistic.

The Church Is First of All an Assembly

The next stage in Volf's developing argument for his understanding of a church is the recommendation of his idea that the "church is first of all an assembly."[63] This metaphor is chosen by Volf to describe the local church in preference to many other possibilities, but he does not restrict the life of the church to the work of the assembly. He endorses Otto Weber's designation that the church is a "visible assembly of visible

---

58. Ibid., 136, 136nn34, 33; Ignatius, "The Epistle of Ignatius to the Smyrnæns," *ANF*, vol. 1, 8, 89–90. Tertullian, "Baptism, VI," *ANF*, vol. 3, 672.

59. Cyprian, "On the Unity of the Church, 12."

60. Volf, *AOL*, 136–37.

61. Ibid., 137n37.

62. Ibid. Volf suggests that Gundry perceives that the "two or three" in Matt 18:20 may be the assembled congregation, but he concedes that this may not be the case. Gundry, *Matthew*, 370.

63. Volf, *AOL*, 137.

persons at a specific place for specific action," and Volf insists that the primary sense of the NT's use of *ekklēsia* is that of a "concrete assembly of Christians at a specific place."[64]

Volf, however, does not limit his understanding of *ekklēsia* to that of a local assembly of Christians. He recognizes that in the letters to the Ephesians (Eph 1:22, 2:22, 3:10, 5:22–33) and to the Colossians (Col 1:18) that there is a second sense, that being the universal church. Volf understands that this does not mean all "Christians dispersed through the world" but that instead it refers to "a heavenly and simultaneously eschatological entity."[65] This enables Volf to put forward a fresh and dynamic thesis, and he explains:

> It is precisely as partially overlapping entities that both the local church and the universal church are constituted into the church through the common relation to the Spirit of Christ, who makes them both into the anticipation of the eschatological gathering of the entire people of God. This is why every local church can also be *completely* the church even though it encompasses only a part of the universal church.[66]

This eschatological vision for the local church he supports by his understanding of the NT use of term for the body of Christ (*soma Christou*). Volf states that he agrees with Heon-Wook Park who conceives that *soma Christou* refers not to the body organically as of one person, but rather communally, as the body of several persons.[67] Volf also agrees with Gundry, who espouses that Paul's notion of the "body of Christ" must be understood in a nonphysical manner where the "Christian is 'one spirit with' the Lord (1 Cor. 6:17)."[68]

This position means that Volf categorically rejects the Catholic and Orthodox view of the church as a collective subject as the whole Christ, in preference for a metaphorical "communion of persons."[69] The outworking of this notion is that "Christ cannot be identical with the church," and the connection between Christ and the church, and

---

64. Weber, *Versammelte Gemeinde*, 32; Volf, *AOL*, 137.
65. Volf, *AOL*, 138–39.
66. Ibid., 141.
67. Ibid., 141–42; Park, "Die Vorstellung."
68. Gundry, "Soma in Biblical Theology," 223–44.
69. Volf, *AOL*, 141–42.

between different churches, is through the same Holy Spirit.[70] It is the presence of Christ manifested by the Holy Spirit that dynamically works in the church as an assembly that then "connects every local church with all [the] other churches of God," and this makes for an "eschatological gathering of the entire people of God."[71]

The Public Confession of Christ Is the Central Constitutive Mark of the Church

Volf does not confuse his thinking of the church by limiting it just to an assembly, and he qualifies his proposal by stating that it is when "people assemble in the name of Christ," that apparently marks the "precondition for the presence of Christ in the Holy Spirit, which is itself constitutive for the church."[72] This understanding of the church is founded upon Volf's conclusion of the significance of Matt 18:20 as the basis for constituting a local assembly; while he does not dismiss the importance of "sound doctrine" or the "content of faith" he prefers to suggest two other conditions for a basis of a church. These are firstly "faith in Jesus Christ as Saviour" and secondly a "commitment of those assembled to allow their lives to be determined by Jesus Christ." This second point Volf claims is a point of departure that the Free Churches took from the Calvinist tradition.[73] It is through the public confession of faith about the work and person of Jesus Christ that Volf's definition comes to expression, and he explains: "The public confession of faith in Christ through the pluriform speaking of the word is the central constitutive mark of the church."[74]

He provides a footnote reference to Luther to undergird his own definition, but it would appear that an emphasis on a communal confession of faith does not accurately reflect Luther's own understanding of the church.[75] Volf's intention is revealed as he asserts that we need to

70. Ibid., 142–45.
71. Ibid., 145.
72. Ibid.
73. Ibid., 148–49.
74. Ibid., 150.
75. Ibid., 150n94: Luther, *Works*, 50.629.28–30, "Wherever you hear such words and see preaching, believing, confessing and commensurate behaviour, you can be sure that a proper ecclesia sancta catholica must be there." Volf seems to ignore Luther's stress on preaching, and he only focuses on believing and confessing. For Luther the preaching of pure doctrine was an indispensable condition for any church, as Clowney

think of church as a "multi-dimensional confession of the whole church" and not think of it through the "narrow portals of ordained office."[76] Volf rejects the view of Ignatius who insisted that "without [deacons, presbyters and bishops] no [group] can be called a church" because he contends that ordained office belongs to the well-being (*ben esse*) and not the essence (*esse*) of the church.[77]

There Is No Church without the Sacraments of Baptism and the Lord's Supper

"Without baptism and the Lord's Supper, there is no church" insists Volf, who then states that that these two sacraments belong to the *esse* of the church.[78] He presents them as "indispensable conditions of ecclesiality, only if they are a form of the confession of faith."[79] This brings into question Volf's soteriology, and unfortunately he repeatedly makes bold assertions without offering any detailed explanations. He states:

> Through baptism a person becomes a Christian, and through the Lord's Supper a person lives as a Christian; through these two sacraments, a person gains access to salvific grace grounded in Christ's death and resurrection, salvific grace anticipating the eschatological new creation. Insofar as baptism and the Lord's Supper mediate salvific grace, they are constitutive for the church.[80]

Volf links the faith of an individual to the sacraments, but it remains unclear as to his intention behind this somewhat oblique phrase "salvific grace."

Volf's Definition of a Holy, Catholic, and Apostolic Church

Interchurch relations are a sincere concern for Volf, and this is to be expected because of his desire for ecumenism. However it has to be pointed out that he often expresses himself with the use of convoluted

---

makes clear: Clowney, *Church*, 92, 101.

76. Volf, *AOL*, 152.

77. Ibid., 152, 152n103; Ignatius, "The Epistle of Ignatius to the Trallians," *ANF*, vol. 1, 3.1, 67.

78. Volf, *AOL*, 152.

79. Ibid., 152–53. Volf claims that he prefers Luther's supposed stronger view of the sacraments to Calvin's, but he does not explain further (153n106–7).

80. Ibid.

language that would be hard for ordinary church people to understand. Here is an example as he writes that "the openness to all other churches is the interecclesial minimum of the concrete ecclesial proleptic experience of the eschatological gathering of the whole people of God."[81] Volf commonly uses this kind of complex language to express his views, and it would strengthen his thesis further if he were to employ clearer sentences to express his theological thought.

Volf concludes chapter 3 with a definition of the church, and he uses strong language to condemn those who do not manifest the same principle of "openness to all other churches,"[82] and he alleges:

> A discriminatory church [is] not merely a bad church, but no church at all; it is unable to do justice to the catholicity of the eschatological people of God. Even if such a church were to assemble in the name of Christ and profess faith in him with its lips, it could expect only rejection from its alleged Lord: "I never knew you" (Matt. 7:21–23).[83]

This statement seems to be a circular argument that leads to an inbuilt contradiction to his case because in his attempt to formulate a synthesis of different theological contributions he concludes with a definition of the church that is itself discriminatory. In effect he condemns all churches and theologians who do not agree with his own description of a church. He defines the ecclesiality of the church as follows:

> *Every congregation that assembles around the one Jesus Christ as Saviour and Lord in order to profess faith in him publicly in pluriform fashion, including through baptism and the Lord's Supper, and which is open to all churches of God and to all human beings, is a church in the full sense of the word, since Christ promised to be present in it through his Spirit as the first fruits of the gathering of the whole people of God in the eschatological reign of God. Such a congregation is a holy, catholic, and apostolic church.*[84]

There are a number of presuppositions displayed in Volf's definition for a holy, catholic, and apostolic church that deserve critical evaluation; this now forms the basis around which our discussion follows.

81. Ibid., 157.
82. Ibid.
83. Ibid., 158.
84. Ibid.

A Critical Evaluation of Proposal 1

A Critical Evaluation of Volf's Methodology to Define a Local Assembly

The ecclesiological paradigm that Volf endorses sits comfortably within a Free Church model, and his case revolves around the significance of Matt 18:20 to define a local assembly. Chapter 5 of this monograph critically analyzes the theological impulses that he receives from the writings of Smyth, and this matter is not repeated here. Our concern is to examine the sources that he draws upon, in order to assess the validity and strength of his argument.

Volf makes an appeal to a range of patristic writings to buttress his presentation that Matt 18:20 forms a sufficient basis to develop a doctrine of the church. During a first reading of *AOL* the integration of such highly esteemed church fathers as Ignatius, Irenaeus, and Tertullian appears impressive. However, a close inspection of the quotations he uses leads us to conclude that he cherry-picks material from their writings, and he also takes their sayings out of context.

Ignatius is an early patristic writer, and because of his close proximity to the first apostles, he furnishes us with potentially vital clues for ecclesiology. Volf selectively utilizes a single quotation from "The Epistle of Ignatius to the Smyrnæns" that states "wherever Jesus Christ is, there is the Catholic Church" in order to assert that the presence of Christ constitutes a church.[85] This inference was not Ignatius's aim because he actually wrote to clarify the significance of the office of bishop for the life of the church. This is the quotation in its wider setting, and Ignatius writes:

> Wherever the bishop shall appear, there let the multitude (of the people) also be; even as, wherever Jesus Christ is, there is the Catholic Church. It is not lawful without the bishop either to baptise or to celebrate a love-feast; but whatever he shall approve of, that is also pleasing to God, so that everything that is done may be secure and valid.[86]

Far from supporting Volf's ecclesial model, Ignatius firmly contradicts it, as he affirms: "let nothing be done without the bishop."[87]

---

85. Ibid., 136, 136n33; Ignatius, "The Epistle of Ignatius to the Smyrnæns," *ANF*, 90.
86. Ignatius, "The Epistle of Ignatius to the Smyrnæns," *ANF*, 90.
87. Ibid., 89.

Tertullian is similarly taken out of context to claim a correspondence between the "two or three" (Matt 18:20) and the constitution of a church. Volf inserts Tertullian into *AOL* to affirm that "where three are, the church is."[88] This is extremely tenuous, and it finds little basis from the work of Tertullian. While expounding on baptism Tertullian actually writes: "Inasmuch as, wherever there are three (that is, the Father, the Son, and the Holy Spirit), there is the Church, which is the body of three."[89] Far from dealing with two or three persons constituting the minimum number for a church, this quote is referring to the presence of the Triune God at baptism. A further veiled reference is given by a supposed piece of work by Tertullian; however this is an extremely obscure reference, one that was probably unfinished and written during his Montanist period.[90]

Sadly the few patristic sources that Volf includes in this section of *AOL* are handled irresponsibly, and they are taken out of context to support a markedly different construction for the church. Additionally, Volf does not engage in exegetical work to determine the context of Matt 18:20; this passage deals with church discipline, forgiveness, and reconciliation, and not the formation of a local assembly.[91] Christ introduces the concept for *ekklēsia* in relation to the assembling of Christians that are recorded in two pericopes, found only in Matthew's Gospel: 16:13–20 and 18:15–20. Volf fails to interact with the overall explanation that Christ gives for the church; he ignores the connection between these two passages and the christological introduction by Christ for the whole framework for the church.

Volf creatively introduces eschatology as a potentially informative goal for the church's development, on the basis of Rev 21:1–22:5. While an eschatological viewpoint offers a fresh approach and an end point or vision for the church, it cannot be used as the theological starting point in the manner that Volf suggests for his ecclesial model.[92] The prototype

---

88. Volf, *AOL*, 136.

89. Tertullian, "On Baptism," *ANF*, vol. 3, 6, 672.

90. Tertullian, "De pudicitia" [On Modesty], an unfinished work of Tertullian, trans. from Latin to English, last section, 16, http://www.tertullian.org/articles/claesson_pudicitia_translation.htm; this is an extremely obscure reference by Tertullian, probably unfinished and written during his "Montanist Period" (Volf, *AOL*, 197).

91. Calvin, *Harmony of Matthew, Mark and Luke*, vol. 16, 351–62; Hendriksen, *Gospel of Matthew*, 697–703; Carson, "Matthew," 368.

92. Volf, *AOL*, 128–30.

A Critical Evaluation of "The Ecclesiality of the Church" 181

for the Free Church that Volf envisages is one that is constructed upon subjective assumptions with eschatological assertions that seem to provide a "blank check" for his thesis. The absence of biblical exegesis, the misuse of patristic sources, and the oversight of a connectional and collegial model (the relation between the "one" and the "many," 1 Cor 10:17) for local congregations makes this doctrine of the church flimsy.

Can Matthew 18:20 Be Used as a Basis to Constitute a Church?

It is everywhere evident that Volf's ecclesiology hinges upon the significance of Matt 18:20 "to determine the foundation of a church."[93] Can this one Bible verse provide sufficient grounds for the development of an ecclesiology? This particular verse provides a closing promise to a composite passage (Matt 18:15–20) where Jesus handles the matter of church discipline and reconciliation.[94] Jesus begins this particular teaching by announcing that: "If your brother sins against you, go and tell him his fault (18:15)." William Hendriksen correctly points out that this passage lays down a logical progression for the "steps in discipline," and its connection to a familiar OT principle: "Only on the evidence of two witnesses or of three witnesses shall a charge be established" (Deut 19:15).[95] The twin statements, "if two of you agree" (Matt 18:19) and "where two or three are gathered in my name, there am I among them" (Matt 18:20) actually relates to the two or three people who are appointed by the church to resolve disputes.

W. D. Davies and Dale C. Allison comment that the paragraph (Matt 18:15–20) "sets down the community rules for dealing with trouble between Christians," and they remark that "in church history Matthew 18:20 has been employed in sundry ways . . . as a justification of Free Churches (the church is present for any two or three gathered in his name; no institution is required)."[96] Eduard Schweizer observes the connection between the rabbinic saying "but if two sit together and words of the law (are spoken) between them, the Divine presence rests between them" and the promise of Christ; Davies and Allison put

---

93. Volf, *AOL*, 136.

94. Davies and Allison, *Matthew*, 304–7; Schweizer, *According to Matthew*, 374–75; Hagner, *Word Biblical Commentary*, 528–34; Morris, *According to Matthew*, 466–70.

95. Hendriksen, *Matthew*, 697, 699–700.

96. Davies and Allison, *Matthew*, 304, 306.

forward that Christ replaces "torah" by "in my name" (Matt 18:20).[97] Donald A. Hagner makes the vital link between this promise of Christ and Matt 28:20.[98]

Calvin writes extensively on the doctrine of the church, and book 4 of the *Institutes of the Christian Religion* is dedicated solely to that purpose.[99] He links the promise of Matt 18:20 to the visible marks of the church, and he writes:

> From this the face of the church comes forth and becomes visible to our eyes. Wherever we see the Word of God purely preached and heard, and the sacraments administered according to Christ's institution, there, it is not to be doubted, a church of God exists (cf. Eph 2:20). For his promise cannot fail: "Wherever two or three are gathered in my name, there I am in the midst of them (Mt. 18:20)."[100]

Calvin teaches every theologian some valuable lessons, because he establishes his doctrinal framework for the church by drawing on the whole panorama of the teaching of Scripture. He carefully introduces the works of the church fathers to anchor his arguments historically. It would be incomprehensible to think that Calvin would be persuaded by Volf"'s proposal in *AOL*, where a church constitution is built around one Bible verse, alongside a persistent mishandling of patristic sources. Calvin's theology cannot be ignored because his teaching exerted significant influence across Western Europe during the time of Smyth's Free Church experiments; the resultant Baptist practices emerged from what was initially a Calvinistic stable.

Rather astutely, Calvin is ahead of his time because he preempts the misuse of the covenant promise for the presence of God in the church, as taught in Mat 18:20. He warns:

> Let us therefore define what that means [those gathered in His name]. I deny that they are gathered in His name who, casting aside God's commandment that forbids anything to be added or taken away from his Word (Deut. 4:2; cf. Deut. 12:32; Prov. 30:6; Rev. 22:18–19), ordain anything according to their own decision;

---

97. Schweizer, *According to Matthew*, 374–75; Davies and Allison, *Matthew*, 307.

98. Hagner, *Word Biblical Commentary*, 528–34.

99. Calvin, "Book Four: The External Means or Aids by which God Invites us Into the Society of Christ and Holds us Therein," in *Institutes*, vol. 2, 4.1.1, 1009.

100. Calvin, *Institutes*, 4.1.9, 1023.

who not content with the oracles of Scripture, that is, the sole rule of perfect wisdom, concoct some novelty out of their own heads.[101]

Using the plain speech of Calvin, it is not unreasonable to assert that he would judge Volf (and Smyth) as having "concocted some novelty out of his head" regarding his doctrine of the church—a doctrine that Calvin would reject as containing insufficient evidence for us to take seriously. R. T. France similarly undermines the Free Church argument where a disproportionate amount of weight is often placed on Matt 18:20 for the doctrine of the church. He concludes that Matthew is not primarily "an 'ecclesiastical' gospel . . . ecclesiology is subordinate to Christology" and that Matt 18:15–20 teaches that the church is to be a "community of unlimited forgiveness."[102]

---

101. Ibid., 4.9.2, 1166–67.
102. France, *Matthew*, 250–52, 312.

11

A Critical Evaluation of "Faith, Person, and Church"

A SUMMARY OF THIS PROPOSAL

IN THIS PROPOSAL, "THE Ecclesiality of the Church" (chapter 4 in *AOL*), Volf attempts to forge a way between what he describes as two incompatible models for the church; those that tend toward "individualism" or alternatively "holism" (or collectivism).[1] He perceptively observes that significant overlap exists between ecclesiology, soteriology, and the way a church understands that faith is mediated. Friedrich Schleiermacher famously distinguished between these two forms of Christian communion by asserting that "Protestantism makes the individual's relation to the Church dependent on his relation to Christ" while Catholicism "makes the individual's relation to Christ dependent on his relation to the church."[2] Volf endorses this view, while advancing his own Free Church model that attempts to avoid both extremes.

Faith and the Church

There is a communal character to the mediation of faith according to Volf. He takes his understanding of the church from Matt 18:20 and the apparent promise for the presence of Christ to the entire congregation, not just an individual. He validates this view by putting forward a notion

---
1. Volf, *AOL*, 159–60.
2. Schleiermacher, *Christian Faith*, 24.

for "the motherhood of the church" while carefully guarding his own opinion that while the church may lead one to "entrust one's life to God in faith," it cannot give a person "this all-decisive faith."[3] Volf clarifies this by stating that "one must insist that the church is not the subject of salvific activity with Christ; rather Christ is the only subject of such salvific activity."[4]

There is a consistency in Volf's appeal here because in chapter 3 of *AOL* he likewise focuses on the "multidimensional confession of faith" that the whole church plays in conjunction with the "word of God that creates faith."[5] This moves the locus of the mediation of faith, in Volf's mind, away from the centrality of public preaching or ordained ministry and places this instead into the midst of the whole church. Volf summarizes:

> Understood in this way, the mother church does *not* stand *over against* individual Christians; rather, Christians *are* the mother church; the mother church is the communion of brothers and sisters that has always existed vis-à-vis the individual Christian. The universal priesthood of believers implies the "universal motherhood of believers."[6]

Volf walks on a tightrope regarding the individualism of faith, to co-equally maintain that while "faith is a gift of God; yet God does not bypass human will when giving faith to a person."[7]

Potential questions concerning the necessity for preaching and the hearing of the gospel message are creatively preempted by Volf as he proposes that "faith always arises by hearing" but that faith is not restricted to being mediated by the spoken or written word.[8] He suggests that during Paul's missionary work, faith came by seeing (Gal 3:1) and experiencing it on a believer's own body (1 Cor 2:4, 4:20; Rom 15:19; 1 Thess 1:5). This concept is stretched even further, to the point where

---

3. Volf, *AOL*, 163.

4. Ibid., 164.

5. Ibid., 166. Volf also appeals (Volf, *AOL*, 162n20) to Otto Weber who emphasized that we cannot have Christ "at all outside the congregation": Weber, *Versammelte Gemeinde*, 36; Bonhoeffer, *Sanctorum Communio*, 101.

6. Volf, *AOL*, 166: Volf quotes Jüngel to support this view that "Christians are the mother church": Jüngel, "Die Kirche als Sakrament?" 329, 335–45.

7. Volf, *AOL*, 171.

8. Ibid., 170.

Volf insists that the "non-verbal presentation of the gospel must always be accompanied by the verbal proclamation of it."[9] Volf asserts that faith is a gift of the Holy Spirit, and in principle he agrees with C. K. Barrett's remark that "Christ is the agent and the Gospel is the means by which men are brought to new life."[10] However, Volf interprets the way the gospel is mediated by the community with a much wider-angled lens than Barrett, and this deserves scrutiny.

The Ecclesial Character of Salvation

"Salvation and the church cannot be separated" declares Volf.[11] This inspiring proclamation underscores a commitment by Volf to the local church as the place where those who are reborn by the Spirit of God enjoy communion with the Triune God. He gives no foothold for individuals to think that they can experience fellowship with God apart from the church or for any weakened ecclesiology that simply views the church as an external aid to salvation.[12] Volf explores the inestimable value of church membership among the Free Churches in order for him to fuse together the pneumatological presence of God and the role of the human will, as two constitutive elements of the church. He writes:

> The Spirit of God, acting through the word of God and the sacraments ("from above"), is the real subject of the genesis of the church. It is *the Spirit* who constitutes the church ... holding fast to the notion of "from below." ... [It is] the human will to come together and to abide together as a concrete church [that] must be viewed as a constitutive element of the being of the church.[13]

On the matter of "human will," Volf claims that Free Church theologians have given insufficient attention to reflect on this indispensable element to a concrete church.[14]

His social model for the church builds on Dietrich Bonhoeffer's *Sanctorum Communio*, Cyprian's use of the social metaphor of "mother" in *De Unitate*, and Moltmann's vision for a church as an "open

---

9. Ibid.
10. Ibid., 163, 167; Barrett, *Epistle to the Corinthians*, 115.
11. Volf, *AOL*, 174.
12. Ibid., 172–75.
13. Ibid., 176–77; Bonhoeffer, *Sanctorum Communio*, 178, 186.
14. Volf, *AOL*, 176–77.

fellowship"; Volf puts forward an organic and associative understanding of the church.[15] Volf takes these ideas a stage further with the use of the NT metaphors of "brothers/sisters" and "friends" to synthesize his own social definition for the church. He makes clear that he is pursuing an ideal where "the church is an 'open' fellowship of friends and siblings, who are called to summon enemies and strangers to become friends and children of God and to accept each other as friends and siblings."[16]

Personhood in the Ecclesial Community

At this point in *AOL*, Volf turns his attention to matters that have anthropological significance, and he does so in the light of Trinitarian reflection. He concludes that a human being "is addressed by God equiprimally with regard to both God and to himself," which therefore "grounds common humanity" with the "equal dignity of every human being"[17] who does not stand isolated from other human beings or the environment.[18] It is precisely Volf's interpretation of Gen 1:27 ("So God created man in his own image, in the image of God he created him; male and female he created them") that leads him to deduce that a "person's inner 'makeup' is still that of a social and natural being."[19] Hence the title: *After Our Likeness*. Volf persistently pursues anthropology from his doctrine of the Trinity, which he believes is to be reflected to some degree by humanity, society, and the church.

In agreement with Pannenberg, Volf is careful to balance his thesis, in that humanity is socially determined where humanity is able to encounter society and nature in freedom. This impacts the proposal in *AOL* regarding the "way one becomes a person (anthropology)" and the "way one becomes a Christian (soteriology)." Volf states: "Hence as a person and as a Christian, one is indeed an independent, and yet simultaneously a socially conditioned entity."[20]

---

15. Ibid., 180–81, 180n109; Bonhoeffer, *Sanctorum Communio*, 185, 180n110; Cyprian, *De Unitate*, 23, cited in Volf, *AOL*, 180n110; Moltmann, *Church in the Power*, 119.

16. Volf, *AOL*, 181.

17. Ibid., 182.

18. Volf uses two articles to support his overall argument, and these are: Dalferth and Jüngel, "Person und Gottebenbildlichkeit," 70; Welker, *Gottes Geist*, 230.

19. Volf, *AOL*, 183.

20. Ibid., 184–85; Pannenberg, *Anthropology in Theological Perspective*, 224–42.

A clear distinction is upheld in this thesis between anthropology, soteriology, and ecclesiology. The aspect of the doctrine of the Trinity that is of most interest to Volf is that of the mutual indwelling of the three persons (perichoresis) and the preferred term that is utilized in *AOL*, personal interiority. Volf applies this notion to what he believes is one of the NT's basic soteriological texts (Gal 2:20) to demonstrate the paradox that this doctrine apparently presents. He highlights the difference between a free person's individuality ("I live by faith") and a Christian's constitution through a relationship with God ("Christ who lives in me").[21] With respect to ecclesiology, Volf moves this perichoretic notion forward as he explains that this same principle works in relation to a prophet speaking to a congregation (1 Cor 12:4–11, 14:3, 14:26–33) where the "prophet speaks in the Spirit" and simultaneously the "Spirit is speaking in him."[22]

Personal interiority is applied to the personal indwelling of the Holy Spirit, and Volf maintains that "the Spirit present in Christians is a person different from them, just as they are persons different from the Spirit."[23] The impulse for this emphasis on the Holy Spirit within the church is Moltmann's *The Church in the Power of the Spirit*. Volf agrees with his mentor that through the indwelling of the Holy Spirit through faith in the hearts of Christians, the church similarly enters into a "Trinitarian fellowship" of the mutual indwelling with God and among each other, one that upholds unity and the distinction of persons.[24]

A CRITICAL EVALUATION OF PROPOSAL 2: FAITH, PERSON, AND CHURCH

It is quite difficult to know which direction to take in critically evaluating the work of Volf in *AOL*. He persistently builds his case in each chapter by taking Bible verses out of their immediate context, he demonstrates no obvious regard for the authorial intent of those chosen texts, and he imports his own reading into passages at will. If we examine Volf's assertions from this chapter concerning "how faith is mediated in the

---

21. Volf, *AOL*, 186–87.
22. Ibid., 187–88.
23. Ibid., 189.
24. Ibid,; Moltmann, *Church in the Power*, 218, 289.

church," we will see his irregular practices, which make for an unstable argument throughout.[25]

Volf eliminates the necessity for ministerial officers or the proclamation of the Word of God as requisite for the mediation of faith. He declares that the "character of faith as a gift does not require a priestly office [as] fundamentally different from the general priesthood of believers through which God gives faith to individuals."[26] But how does he arrive at this conclusion? He makes the confession by all the Christians in a congregation as the central constitutive mark of the church and the means by which faith is mediated to individuals, and he tries to substantiate this from Rom 10:8–10.[27] He bases the flow of his argument on what the apostle Paul teaches here in Romans, a passage which is immediately followed by Paul's own explanation as to the way faith is transmitted to the world and the church. Paul states:

> How then will they call on him in whom they have not believed? And how are they to believe in him of whom they have never heard? And how are they to hear without someone preaching? And how are they to preach unless they are sent? As it is written, "How beautiful are the feet of those who preach the good news!" But they have not all obeyed the gospel. For Isaiah says, "Lord, who has believed what he has heard from us?" So faith comes from hearing, and hearing through the word of Christ. (Rom 10:14–17)

It is clear that Volf's appeal to Rom 10:8–10 for the negation of the necessity of preaching to produce faith is firmly refuted by Paul himself, who affirms that "faith comes from hearing . . . the word of Christ" (10:17). Paul highlights that the single human sense that God uses to produce faith is that of "hearing" and the means by which God does this is "preaching." Volf contends that this "preaching" is done by the whole congregation collectively, but is this the teaching of the Book of Romans?

---

25. Edgar, "Justification and Violence," 139. Edgar critiques Volf's teaching on the atonement and justification, and he concludes that Volf "omits, or at least dramatically downplays, the idea of a God whose justice needs to be satisfied, and whose wrath needs to be deflected onto Christ."

26. Volf, *AOL*, 166.

27. Ibid., 150, 166.

G. K. Beale, D. A. Carson, and Mark A. Siefrid conduct a serious exegetical study of Rom 10:1–13 and 10:14–21 to determine the NT's use of the OT.[28] Their conclusions are deduced after a thorough examination of the texts in Hebrew and Greek, with reference to the Septuagint (LXX), textual analysis, and painstaking details support their critical analysis. Their findings totally undermine Volf's assertions. Siefrid explains that Rom 10:8–10 is not concerned with the mediation of faith but the fruit that results from a changed life. He writes:

> Salvation transforms us in the most radical and fundamental way: the human lie that denies the Creator, and that issues in cursing and bitterness, is now replaced by the confession of Christ as Lord and faith in God's work in him. The acts of "confessing" and "believing" arise from the "heart" and "mouth" in which the "word" is now present.[29]

Furthermore he concludes that preaching is not a congregational act in Rom 10:14–17, and he summarizes:

> Both the prophet in the past and the apostle in the present bear "a report" (*akoē*), a message that is announced and proclaimed. The term also appears in Isa. 52:7 LXX ("good news of a report of peace"; the Hiphil *mašmîa* is read as the noun *mišma*), which is thematically linked to Isa. 53:1 (see also 1 Thess. 2:13; Gal. 3:2, 5). Paul thus grounds his mission in the pattern of God's dealings with Israel in the past. A report however must have content.[30]

Douglas J. Moo explains that Rom 10:15 provides "scriptural confirmation of the necessary role of preaching" and that the "use of the verb 'preach good news' in the Isaiah text" suggests an allusion that preaching is to be through "authorised messengers" that are "sent out by God."[31] C. K. Barrett agrees that the force of this Scripture is that "God did not fail to send out authorised preachers," and he assumes that "the verb 'sent' (ἀποσταλῶσιν) is cognate with the noun 'apostle' (ἀπόστολος)."[32] On the basis of Rom 10:8–10, Volf puts forward that this substantiates his notion for the mediation of faith through the congregation. Moo, Barrett,

---

28. Beale and Carson, *Commentary*. The particular chapter of interest is Siefrid, "Romans."

29. Siefrid., "Romans," 659.

30. Ibid., 662.

31. Moo, *Epistle to the Romans*, 664.

32. Barrett, *Epistle to the Romans*, 190.

A Critical Evaluation of "Faith, Person, and Church" 191

and James D. G. Dunn disagree, and they place the accent for the phrase "the word of faith" (Rom 10:8) upon the necessity for the proclamation of the gospel message by specially commissioned, ordained, and accredited messengers in an ongoing sense.[33]

This brief analysis of the way Volf handles these particular Scripture references could be pursued time and again from *AOL* to demonstrate that he displays a range of exegetical, hermeneutical, and textual errors. He does not utilize biblical theological tools, and he does not furnish his readers with explanations to support his conclusions from the "proof-texts" he cites.

In this chapter of *AOL*, Volf advances the notion that in Paul's missionary work that faith was mediated not only by what people heard but also by "seeing something with one's eyes" (Gal 3:1) and experiencing it "on one's body" (1 Cor 2:4, 4:20; Rom 15:19; 1 Thess 1:5).[34] Galatians 2:20 Volf interprets as "one of the NT's basic soteriological texts" to undergird his idea that "personhood is not reduced to pure relation in the experience of salvation."[35] These assumptions are questionable: F. F. Bruce and Dunn, in commentating on Galatians, do not support Volf's explanation of Gal 2:20 and 3:1;[36] Beale suggests that 1 Thess 1:5 teaches that "if there is no true message delivered by authentic and legitimate divine spokesmen, there could be no genuine faith on the part of those who hear."[37] This line of interpretation by Beale contradicts Volf's rationale for the mediation of faith by experiencing it "on one's body." This proof-texting methodology is repeated successively by Volf, which renders his doctrine of church and the relationship between "Faith, Person and Church" (chapter 3, *AOL*) as indefensible.

---

33. Moo, *Epistle to the Romans*, 656–66; Barrett, *Epistle to the Romans*, 186; Dunn, *Word Biblical Commentary*, 613–30.

34. Volf, *AOL*, 170.

35. Ibid., 187.

36. Bruce, *Epistle of Paul*, 144, 147, 148; Dunn, *Epistle to the Galatians*, 145–46, 150–52.

37. Beale, *1–2 Thessalonians*, 55.

12

A Critical Evaluation of "Trinity and Church"

A SUMMARY OF THIS PROPOSAL

Correspondences and Their Limits

THIS IS THE FIRST chapter in *AOL* where Volf presents his model to link the church and the Trinity together, and he makes an a priori assumption that this stance should be taken. He states that "today, the thesis that ecclesial communion should correspond to Trinitarian communion enjoys the status of an almost self-evident proposition."[1] His own aim in this chapter is to "sketch out the Trinitarian foundation of a non-individualistic Protestant ecclesiology" in order to "make a contribution to the Trinitarian reshaping of Free Church ecclesiology."[2]

Volf freely admits that there is some measure of opposition to his desired thesis, but he believes that Erik Peterson oversteps the mark in condemning to failure any and every attempt to shape the church in the light of the Trinity.[3] At the same time Volf demonstrates restraint as he explains that a theologian should not "overestimate the influence of Trinitarian thinking on political and ecclesial reality" because there are "limits to the analogy."[4] He writes that "it does not seem that the conceptualisation process proceeds simply in a straight line from above

---

1. Volf, *AOL*, 191.
2. Ibid., 191, 197.
3. Peterson, "Der Monotheismus," 47, 104–5; Volf, *AOL*, 192.
4. Volf, *AOL*, 194.

(Trinity) to below (church and society)."[5] So, how does Volf envisage a correspondence between the Trinity and the church?

He states that his analogy is "grounded in Christian baptism" (in the name of the Father, and of the Son, and of the Holy Spirit), but that the church's experience is "rendered possible by the Spirit" between the Triune God and the church as it moves toward its eschatological consummation (1 John 1:3-4; Rev 21-22).[6] He agrees with Arthur W. Wainwright and Alistair I. McFadyen that the church's experience of the Triune God arose from God's redemptive revelation in Christ, and Volf puts forward three passages that he believes determined this reality (1 Cor 12:4-6; 2 Cor 13:14; Eph 4:4-6).[7] It is the high priestly prayer of Jesus for his disciples that enables the church, according to Volf, to "presuppose the communion of the church with the Triune God."[8] We could say that metaphorically speaking, there are two bookends that support Volf's thesis for a correspondence between the church and the Trinity: baptism (Matt 28:19b) and eschatological consummation (John 17:21: "that they may all be one, just as you, Father, are in me, and I in you, that they also may be in us").

The unrelenting pursuit of a Free Church in the image of the Trinity, Volf spells out: "I will try to show how those assembled in the name of Christ, even if they number only three, can be an εἰχών (image) of the Trinity."[9] He draws on the evidence of Origen who said that "the church is full of the Holy Trinity" and Cyprian, but most especially Tertullian.[10] Tertullian is the father whom Volf believes "brought in to correspondence the ecclesial and Trinitarian three" especially where he writes:

> For the church itself, properly and principally, the Spirit Himself, in whom there is a Trinity of one divinity, Father, Son and Holy Spirit. He unites in one congregation that church which the Lord

---

5. Ibid., 194-96, 194nn18, 19: Volf observes that for Smyth it was Christology that shaped his ecclesiology, not the Trinity (Smyth, *Works*, 274, 733, 740), and also that Zizioulas understands it was ecclesial experience that shaped the development of the patristic doctrine of the Trinity (Zizioulas, *BAC*, 16).

6. Volf, *AOL*, 195.

7. Ibid,; Wainwright, *Trinity*, 266; McFadyen, "Trinity and Human Individuality," 14.

8. Volf, *AOL*, 195.

9. Ibid., 195-97.

10. Origen, "Selections of the Psalms," 12.1265b; Cyprian, "Liber de Oratione Dominica," 4.553; Bobrinskoy, *Le Mystère*; Volf notes in *AOL* 195n23 that Bobrinskoy bases his study on the principle that "the church is full of the Trinity," 147-97.

> said consists of three persons. And so, from that time on, any number of persons at all, joined in this faith, has been recognised as the church by Him who founded and consecrated it.[11]

For Volf this means that "Tertullian's allusion to Matt. 18:20 is unmistakable," and therefore he asserts that it is a congregation assembling in the name of Christ that realizes the church as an image of the Trinity.[12]

Volf builds his unfolding thesis upon three key texts. These are Matt 18:20 in chapter 3 for his understanding of "the ecclesiality of the church," Gal 2:20 as a building block for the "mediation of faith" in chapter 4, and for "the structure of the church" in chapter 6 he applies 1 Cor 14:26. His intention is then to relate these three "proof-texts" to John 17:21, eschatologically.[13]

A statement given by Volf deserves to be quoted in full because this discloses to his readers in *AOL* the source of his doctrine of the Trinity. He writes:

> Although any consideration of the relationship between the Trinity and the church presupposes a complete doctrine of the Trinity, a comprehensive Trinitarian reflection of this sort is not possible within the framework of this chapter. Instead, I will adopt the general features of the social model of the Trinitarian relations as proposed especially by Moltmann (though also by Pannenberg), developing only certain aspects of this model, especially where required by consideration of the correspondence between the Trinity and the church.[14]

It must be clarified that where Volf says that "a comprehensive Trinitarian reflection of this sort is not possible within the framework of this chapter," he actually extends this idea to the whole book. In *AOL*, Volf does not offer a detailed explanation of what he means by "the social model of Trinitarian relations."[15] This is surprising, especially when he devotes so much time to critiquing the notions of the Trinity and the church

---

11. Tertullian, "De pudicitia" [On Modesty], 16; this is an extremely obscure reference by Tertullian, probably unfinished and written during his "Montanist Period" (Volf, *AOL*, 197).

12. Volf, *AOL*, 197.

13. Ibid.

14. Ibid., 198.

15. Ibid., 204–13; this section represents the only brief summary of his doctrine of the Trinity, and there is little supporting evidence as to the reasons for his conclusions. His doctrine of the Trinity simply assumes Moltmann's doctrine of the Trinity to be valid.

from the writings of Ratzinger and Zizioulas. He expends much effort in defining his doctrine for a Free Church in chapters 3 and 4, when his overall goal is actually "Trinity and Communion." Is it unreasonable to suggest that his starting point in *AOL* should have been to lay down a clear and systematic outline of his doctrine of the Triune God, before anything else?

Trinitarian Persons and Church

It must be remembered that when Volf contemplates the church, he always does so by starting from the local church. Volf's doctrine of the Trinity focuses exclusively on the communion that exists between the divine persons and not on the divine unity of essence. This becomes his model for a correspondence of relationships in the church to those of the Trinity on the basis of the inner-Trinitarian perichoretic relationship between the divine persons. He states that the "Trinity indwells in the local churches in no other way than through its presence within the persons constituting those churches, since the church is those who gather in the name of Christ."[16] There are three sides to his social doctrine of the Trinity that he applies to his social doctrine of the church; these are relational personhood, perichoretic personhood, and the nonhierarchical relations of the persons.

Relational Personhood

God's Being, Essence, and Unity Is Derived from the Communion of the Three Persons

Volf endorses Moltmann's view of the Trinity that the "Persons themselves constitute both their differences and their unity" so that "there are no persons without relations; but there are no relations without persons either. Person and relation are complementary."[17] This theological move by Volf ensures that the idea of person and relation are conceived simultaneously, and he sets down a marker to differentiate what he believes is a different and radically flawed conception of the Trinity by Ratzinger and Zizioulas. Volf rejects Ratzinger's Trinitarian unity of the persons based on the dominance of the one substance of God and Zizioulas's

---

16. Ibid., 203.
17. Moltmann, *Trinity and the Kingdom*, 175, 174.

unity of God grounded in the monarchy of the Father.[18] "God's being coincides with the communion of the Three Divine Persons" according to Volf, and he asserts that the concrete relations of the three persons are sufficient for maintaining a doctrine of divine unity.[19]

God as One Substance Is Dispensed with Entirely

This premise by Volf insists on a theological focus on the Three Persons at the expense of the traditional doctrine of monotheism. He explicitly asserts that "it is advisable to dispense entirely with the one numerically identical divine nature and instead to conceive the unity of God perichoretically."

The Trinity Is an Open and Inviting Communion

"The Trinity is precisely an open and inviting communion" writes Volf, and it is for this reason that he expects churches that correspond to the Trinity to be "open to other churches."[20] Volf's desire for unity across the one universal church, constituted by many local churches, is rooted in his eschatological vision, and he states:

> If a church is open to other churches . . . it already corresponds partially to the Triune God . . . [because] it corresponds to the eschatological gathering of the entire people of God in communion with the Triune God, and in so doing is actually a church in the first place. Hence the minimum of interecclesial correspondence to the Trinity seems to consist not in actual "being with all others," but rather in "being from others" and "seeking toward all others."[21]

Perichoretic Personhood

Perichoresis Refers to the Reciprocal Interiority of the Persons of the Trinity

The Johannine Jesus is probably the wellspring for this ancient theological conception that relates to the doctrine of the Trinity (John 10:38, 14:10–11, 17:21), and Volf adopts G. L. Prestige's definition that perichoresis is "co-inherence in one another without any coalescence

---

18. Volf, *AOL*, 201.
19. Ibid., 202–4.
20. Volf, *AOL*, 208.
21. Ibid.

or commixture."²² Volf is particularly concerned to uphold the paradox between "mine" and "not mine" in John 7:16 (Jesus answered them "My teaching is not mine") while "emphasising both equally."²³ Therefore the three persons can indwell each other without losing their identity as distinct persons, and this is what Volf terms, along with Dimitru Staniloae, the "reciprocal interiority of the Persons of the Trinity."²⁴

From the Interiority of the Divine Persons Emerges the Catholicity of Persons

Volf prefers to utilize the phrase "catholicity," but he uses this in reference to the mutual unity of the Father, Son, and Holy Spirit. He believes that the doctrine of perichoresis is of utmost help because it is this doctrine that can uphold the unity and distinction of persons simultaneously. For example, we can speak uniquely of the Son, but this mutual interiority means that to do so carries at the same time reference to the Father and the Son through their mutual indwelling (John 10:38: "the Father is in me and I am in the Father").²⁵

The Unity of the Trinity Is Grounded upon Perichoresis, Instead of the One Substance

"It is often assumed that perichoresis and the oneness of the divine substance are two complementary ways of conceiving the unity of God" writes Volf, who then inserts doubt concerning this idea when he then writes that it is "questionable, however, whether the two ideas are compatible."²⁶ Volf advances his idea that "the unity of the divine essence is the obverse of the interiority and catholicity of the divine Persons," and he "presupposes that one abandons the numerical identity of the divine substance."²⁷ (The key supporting quote by Pannenberg, that Volf adopts, is that the Trinitarian persons are "living realisations of separate centres of action").²⁸

It is correctly put forward by Volf that "in a strict sense, there can be no correspondence to the interiority of the divine Persons at the human

---

22. Ibid., 209n84; Prestige, *God in Patristic Thought*, 298.
23. Volf, *AOL*, 209.
24. Ibid.; Staniloae, "Trinitarian Relations," 38.
25. Volf, *AOL*, 209.
26. Ibid., 210n87.
27. Ibid., 210, 210n87.
28. Ibid., 215: Pannenberg, *Systematic Theology*, 1.319.

level."²⁹ However, he does ground his proposal for the unity of the church in the interiority, or indwelling, of the Holy Spirit in Christians, and his vision for the fulfillment of John 17:21, alongside an anticipation of the "eschatological gathering of the entire people of God."³⁰ He concludes:

> It is not the mutual perichoresis of human beings, but rather the indwelling of the Spirit common to everyone that makes the church into a communion corresponding to the Trinity, a communion in which personhood and sociality are equiprimal.³¹

Nonhierarchical Relations of the Persons

Volf is very aware (along with Moltmann) that if the relations of the persons of the Trinity are only conceived in terms of the generation of the Son and the procession of the Holy Spirit (the constitution of the persons) then there is a very real danger that this can foster hierarchical relations. Volf supports Moltmann's proposal that a distinction should be clearly made between the inner-Trinitarian relations at a constitutional level (hypostatic divinity) and the relational level (inner-Trinitarian form) so that "unilinear hierarchical relations can disappear from the Trinitarian communion."³² "A community of perfect love between the Persons who share all the divine attributes" is the conclusion that Volf arrives at, and this is a communion where any "notion of hierarchy or subordination is inconceivable."³³

It appears that Volf's doctrine of the Trinity in *AOL* only considers the single divine attribute of perfect love, and in this respect he agrees with Moltmann again, in that it is by the power of the eternal love that the persons of the Trinity constitute themselves in complete union.³⁴ The implications of Volf's doctrine of the Trinity shapes the anticipation in *AOL* of what a church shaped by the Trinity should look like. This has implications for Trinitarian and ecclesial structures, and Volf writes:

---

29. Volf, *AOL*, 210.
30. Ibid., 213.
31. Ibid.
32. Ibid., 217; Moltmann, *Trinity and the Kingdom*, 165, 175; Moltmann, *Geist des Lebens*, 321–23.
33. Volf, *AOL*, 217.
34. Moltmann, *Trinity and the Kingdom*, 174; Moltmann, "Die einlande Einheit," 124; Volf, *AOL*, 210, 217, 219–20.

> The structure of the Trinitarian relations is characterised neither by a pyramidal dominance of the one (so Ratzinger) nor by a hierarchical bipolarity between the one and the many (so Zizioulas), but rather by a polycentric and symmetrical reciprocity of the many . . . the symmetrical reciprocity of the relations of the Trinitarian Persons finds its correspondence in the image of the church in which *all* members serve one another with their specific gifts of the Spirit in imitation of the Lord and through the power of the Father. Like the divine persons, they all stand in a relation of mutual giving and receiving.[35]

We may not agree with Volf's construction of his doctrine of the Trinity, but *AOL* demonstrates that a theologian's doctrine of the Trinity exerts much influence upon ecclesiology and especially with the ordering of the ecclesial communion.

A CRITICAL EVALUATION OF VOLF'S SOCIAL DOCTRINE OF THE TRINITY FOR THE CHURCH

Can We Develop a Doctrine of the Church from the Trinity?

This broad question is an attempt to investigate the validity of making connections between the doctrine of the Trinity and ecclesiology. When we consider that the Triune God is the God of the church it would be strange if there were to be no meaningful links between these two subjects, so perhaps our question should ask, in what way should we expect our doctrine of the Trinity to inform our doctrine of the church?

In consideration of these kinds of questions a range of critics are emerging.[36] Stephen R. Holmes rejects Volf's social model for the Trinity and concludes:

> Finding our basis for our ecclesiology in the doctrine of the Trinity has no support in Scripture or tradition; there is good reason to suppose that it cannot work, and even if it can work, it results in an oppressive and unhappy account of the life of the church. I wonder why it has been so popular?[37]

While Holmes raises some valuable criticisms concerning Volf's revised Trinity, he sadly gives the impression that we should write off all

---

35. Volf, *AOL*, 217, 219.
36. Holmes, "Three Versus One?" 73–89; Kilby, "Perichoresis and Projection."
37. Holmes, "Bad Systematics."

attempts toward a Trinitarian ecclesiology. Maybe Holmes has overreacted against Volf's thesis in *AOL* and failed to see how a renewed appreciation of the Trinity can enrich the church's worship and sharpen our missionary message in a pluralistic world.

In *AOL*, Volf rightly addresses some of the issues surrounding the correspondences and the limits of the analogy between the Trinity and the church.[38] While he acknowledges that there are limits, he does not apply any restraint to his own application of his social Trinity for a social church model. So, how does he couple these two themes together? In an article written in 2002, Volf reveals in a condensed format the whole thrust of his thesis in *AOL*, and the title is: "Community Formation as an Image of the Triune God: A Congregational Model of Church Order and Life." Community and structural formation is Volf's goal throughout *AOL* while he simultaneously advocates a congregational model as the best image of the Trinity; this aim represents a glaring omission. Volf moves the discussion in a direction that is somewhat alien to historical theology with respect to the Trinity, and he makes a sparse contribution in connecting the Triune God to the church's worship, faith, piety, preaching, right administration of the sacraments, and liturgy.

The doctrine of the church is a huge theological undertaking, and we cannot hastily sweep away the significance of the church's doctrine of God as something peripheral to ecclesial life. However, Volf's innovative proposals teach us a number of valuable lessons. Firstly, he projects his particular conception of the Trinity to suggest community remodeling. This moves the church into hazardous waters. Gunton rightly cautions against the perils of using the doctrine of the immanent Trinity to validate principles of ethics, in the manner of Volf. Gunton observes that "moves from the immanent Trinity to the created world are not obvious and are fraught with dangers of idealising and projection,"[39] and instead he appeals that "the doctrine of the Trinity must not be abstracted from the doctrine of the atonement."[40] Consequently it is the Trinity revealed in the economy of salvation that should guide our theology and eccle-

---

38. Volf, *AOL*, 192–200.

39. Gunton, *Father, Son and Holy Spirit*, 25.

40. Ibid., 24. The whole essay by Gunton "The God of Jesus Christ" is helpful, and 21–25 especially upholds the need for an ontological Trinity to serve as "a foundation for the relative independence and so integrity of worldly reality also, and thus for human freedom" (24).

siology, yet this assertion in no way denies the necessity of belief in an ontological Trinity (which is also called the immanent Trinity).

Secondly, Volf teaches us the danger of failing to make a clear distinction between the ontological and economic Trinity. Not only does this stance reduce the apophatic and transcendent element of theology but it wrongly assumes that conclusions can be drawn from an aspect of God that is "wholly other"; Thomas G. Weinandy brilliantly argues against such developments.[41] Torrance helpfully employs the terms "God for us" and "God in himself" to distinguish between the economic and immanent Trinity.[42] Paul D. Molnar agrees, and he warns that when "there is no distinction between the immanent and economic Trinity" then there is "no God independent of the World."[43] There are not two Trinities, but these two dimensions of the doctrine of the Triune God form a guardrail, to prevent hasty moves in drawing lines directly from the ontological Trinity to the church. The great Augustine in contemplating the Trinity warns us: "In no other subject is error more dangerous or inquiry more laborious, or the discovery of truth more profitable."[44]

Thirdly, Volf does not do justice to the richest of all lines related to this enquiry.[45] This is the process of learning from the various sections of Christendom as to how the doctrine of the Trinity is to be applied to the church's worship, piety, and missionary message. It is in this field of ecclesiology that we should seek to develop a doctrine of the church from the Trinity.

Is Volf's Social Doctrine of the Trinity an Inverted Pyramid?

The two primary sources that supply an understanding of Volf's social doctrine of the Trinity are *AOL* and his article "The Trinity Is Our Social Program." Volf claims in *AOL* that there are two theologians who have particularly influenced his own Trinitarian paradigm; he writes that "he will adopt the general features of the social model of the Trinitarian relations as proposed especially by Moltmann (though also

---

41. Weinandy, "Yahweh"; Weinandy, *Does God Change?* xxi–xxxii; Murphy, *Consuming Glory*, 185–88.
42. Torrance, *Christian Doctrine of God*, 7.
43. Molnar, *Divine Freedom*, 221.
44. Augustine, "On the Trinity," *NPNF*, vol. 3, 1.3.5, 19.
45. Fox, *God as Communion*. Here Fox makes plain that the doctrine of the Trinity is used to support different agendas including feminism.

by Pannenberg)."[46] In chapter 3 of this monograph we observe that there are marked structural dissimilarities for the Trinity between Moltmann and Pannenberg. In fact Pannenberg, with his emphasis on the monarchy of the Father fits comfortably within the Zizioulas school (chapter 9 of this monograph).[47] Zizioulas comes under sustained criticism by Volf, and therefore for him to claim that he adopts the general features of Pannenberg's Trinity is a contradictory statement. In reality, it is in fact Moltmann who impacts Volf's Trinitarian theology most strongly, and this will now be highlighted as we consider the four pillars of Volf's social doctrine of the Trinity.

Our aim is to investigate the theological support for each of these four pillars in order to critically evaluate the weight that we can place on the application of this Trinitarian construct for ecclesiology.

The Rejection of Monotheism and the One Substance of God

He appeals to two sources for his "clarion call" to abandon the historic doctrine of monotheism: these are Schwartz and Moltmann.[48] In Volf's attempt to employ the Trinity as a blueprint for a social program, he appeals to Schwartz, and he quotes her in his article to undermine the doctrine of monotheism. The quotes are:

> Belief in the One God "forges identities antithetically" . . . . "violent practices stem from such a conception of identity" . . . . we should "free ourselves from the tentacles of the injunction 'you shall have no other gods before me'" . . . and instead "embrace the vision of a world in which everyone walks 'in the name of his god.'"[49]

How does Volf respond to these arguments in his article? He states:

> I doubt the adequacy of her analysis [but] she rightly claims that any understanding of divinity centring on the singleness of an omnipotent subject will tend to forge "hard identities and foster violence." I want to argue here that a viable alternative to such an

---

46. Volf, *AOL*, 198.

47. O'Donnell, "Pannenberg's Doctrine of God," 73–97. This article confirms that Pannenberg has no problem with monotheism, and he handles the Trinity in a theologically responsible way.

48. Schwartz, *Curse of Cain*, x, 16, 38, 63, 69, 88 (Volf quotes her in "The Trinity Is Our Social Program," 408); Moltmann, *Trinity and the Kingdom* (in Volf, *AOL*, 203).

49. Volf, "Trinity Is Our Social Program," 408; Schwartz, *Curse of Cain*, 16, 88, 69, 38, respectively.

understanding of monotheism is available. It is enshrined in the doctrine of the Trinity.[50]

Schwartz, when writing this book, was the professor of literature, religion, and law at Northwestern University, USA. She does not claim to be writing as part of the community of the Christian faith, and she rejects the authority and integrity of biblical narratives wholesale. She states that the accounts of original sin and the stories of Cain and Abel in the book of Genesis are foundational myths, and she rejects their authenticity.[51] Incessantly she repeats while commenting on different OT narratives that they are nothing more than a collection of myths. This includes her interpretation of Exod 20:5–6, a projection in her view of "the myth of monotheism."[52] Her conclusion at the end of the book sums up her attitude to the Bible: she writes that "the old 'monotheistic' Book must be closed so that the new books may be fruitful and multiply. After all, that was the first commandment."[53]

The second source that Volf appeals to, this time in *AOL*, in order to do away with monotheistic theology is the work of Moltmann in *The Trinity and the Kingdom*. In chapter 4 of this monograph we conclude that Volf's doctrine of the Trinity is virtually a mirror image of Moltmann's work in *The Trinity and the Kingdom*, and they both make perichoresis the central Trinitarian concept. Moltmann similarly offers little explanation as to how and why he dispenses of the necessity to uphold the one substance of God. Moltmann proposes:

> The unity of the Trinity must be understood in a Trinitarian sense, not monadically . . . if the doctrine of God is built up in two parts [One substance—Three Persons] like this, then God's unity has to be dealt with twice.[54]

Moltmann not only drives a wedge between God's oneness and threeness but he rejects any thinking in terms of God's one substance (*ousia*) altogether.

There are a number of criticisms that need to be leveled at Moltmann's overall theological approach. Firstly, Moltmann offers little supporting

50. Volf, "Trinity Is Our Social Program," 408.
51. Schwartz, *Curse of Cain*, ix–xi, 1–13.
52. Ibid., 15, 42.
53. Schwartz, *Curse of Cain*, 176.
54. Moltmann, *Trinity and the Kingdom*, 177.

evidence for his many assertions, and though Richard Bauckham is sympathetic to the notion of a social Trinity, he accuses Moltmann of engaging in "undisciplined" and "unfounded speculation."[55] Bauckham cites evidence of this with respect to Moltmann's handling of the *filioque* question and the use of female imagery for God. Regarding the *filioque* question, Bauckham believes that Moltmann is guilty of "hermeneutical irresponsibility in the service of speculation which, whatever its value for ecumenical politics, surely lacks any theological interest."[56] Concerning Moltmann's response to any supposed connections between feminism, the Trinity, and the Holy Spirit, Bauckham summarizes: "Whether the Spirit as an impersonal female principle is a desirable way of introducing feminine language into Trinitarian terminology, I doubt."[57]

According to Bauckham, "Moltmann freely employs inferences from biblical phrases and metaphors which he sometimes admits (e.g., *God in Creation*, 218) cannot be warranted by historical-critical exegesis."[58] Letham agrees that Moltmann engages in "unbridled speculation"[59] and Kärkkäinen concurs that this "is especially true of the way he constructs his Trinitarian understanding of creation or his vision of eschatology as the 'homecoming' of the Triune God."[60]

The most concerning accusation of this social doctrine of the Trinity, one that excludes monotheism, is the charge of Tritheism. Ted Peters comments that Moltmann's doctrine of the Trinity may:

> Unnecessarily take him too far toward sacrificing divine unity. His emphasis on the three separate subjects or centres of action risks a final plurality. . . . It appears that we end up with a divine nominalism.[61]

While Peters is relatively polite, Richard Neuhaus declares that Moltmann "fails seriously to treat the foundational statement of biblical faith, 'shema Israel.' . . . We are, if you will, Trinitarian monotheists and monotheistic Trinitarians. Our belief is not against monotheism; our belief is that One

---

55. Bauckham, *Theology of Jürgen Moltmann*, 167.
56. Ibid., 168.
57. Ibid., 170.
58. Ibid., 167.
59. Letham, *Holy Trinity*, 306.
60. Kärkkäinen, *Trinity*, 122.
61. Peters, *God as Trinity*, 109.

God is Father, Son and Spirit."⁶² Moltmann is recognized to be one of a number of people who reject monotheism, according to Schwöbel, who ably defends his own position and declares: "Only a radically monotheistic theology can be a proper Trinitarian theology, and only a proper Trinitarian theology can be a radically monotheistic theology."⁶³ George Hunsinger delivers a devastating analysis of Moltmann's suggestion that there has never been a Christian tritheist,⁶⁴ and he remarks:

> If this is true then one can only conclude that Moltmann is vying to be the first. Despite the evident scorn with which he anticipates such a charge, *The Trinity and the Kingdom* is about the closest thing to tritheism that any of us are ever likely to see.⁶⁵

All of these criticisms can be equally leveled at Volf's handling of the doctrine of the Trinity, and this leads us to suggest that on the evidence so far, Volf has developed a Trinitarian construct that is an inverted pyramid—large conclusions that are established on a very narrow base of evidence. What is more, the radical assertion to reject monotheism by Moltmann and Volf has indirectly resulted in their developing a nonecumenical thesis.

Perichoresis

Regarding Volf's definition of the doctrine of divine perichoresis he stands within the historic Christian tradition to maintain that this principle means "co-inherence in one another, without any coalescence or commixture."⁶⁶ However the way he applies this doctrine causes him to make a significant departure from creedal and confessional Christian traditions. He makes perichoresis the single Trinitarian concept for his doctrine of God, he uses perichoresis to overcome grounding the unity of the Trinity that includes the one substance of God, and he takes his model for a perichoretic Trinity to establish a model for human identity and human relationships within the church.⁶⁷

---

62. Neuhaus, "Moltmann Versus Monotheism," 241.
63. Schwöbel, "Radical Monotheism," 57–59, 74.
64. Moltmann, *Trinity and the Kingdom*, 144, 144n43.
65. Hunsinger, "Review of Jürgen Moltmann," 129–39, 131.
66. Volf, *AOL*, 209; he quotes Prestige, *God in Patristic Thought*, 298, and Stanilaoe, "Trinitarian Relations," 38.
67. Volf, *AOL*, 208–13.

He selectively quotes from the writings of John of Damascus, Gunton, and Zizioulas,[68] but none of these authors could subscribe to the way Volf adapts and revises this ancient doctrine. John of Damascus's "Exposition of the Orthodox Faith" is a theological masterpiece, and many credit him for coining the phrase "co-inherence" in relation to the Trinity; it had already been used in Christology.[69] However we must underline that John's purpose for developing this concept was to preserve the unity of God. Volf's handling of perichoresis would probably mystify John because he sat firmly within the theological tradition of the NCC. Gunton and Zizioulas include perichoresis as part of their doctrine of God, but they assert that God's oneness is preserved in the monarchy of the Father; therefore to appeal to authors in support of his own thesis, while engaging in open disagreement with them on the Trinity, as Volf does, seems perplexing. Classically perichoresis accompanied other co-ordinates—homoousios, the indivisible divine essence, and so forth—which in Volf's case are not there or are not properly safeguarded.

In chapter 9 of this monograph we concluded that Volf's doctrine of the Trinity represents a departure from Eastern and Western theological traditions. The reasons for this can probably be explained as we evaluate the hermeneutical principles that Volf employs. Thus far we have established that *AOL* does not present a case that rests on detailed biblical exegesis or thorough appeals to church tradition, councils, creeds, or confessions. Letham identifies that "in the case of Orthodoxy, strong ecclesial and doctrinal anchors have largely spared them from the turmoil over critical scholarship that has engulfed the Western church."[70] So, what are the anchors for Volf's theological method?

The patristic sources represent one of the richest deposits concerning teaching on the Holy Trinity, and if we compare the writings of Augustine, Athanasius, Hilary of Poitiers, Gregory of Nyssa, Basil of Caesarea, Gregory of Nazianzus, and John of Damascus with Volf's proposal we see significant divergence. There are nuanced differences between the patristic writers on the Trinity, but there is an obvious unity on the major themes that undergird this doctrine. None of them places

---

68. Volf, "Trinity Is Our Social Program," 408–9.

69. John of Damascus, "Exposition of the Orthodox Faith," *NPNF*, vol. 9, 11: Perichoresis had already been used in connection with the *communicatio idiomatum*; John of Damascus was the first to apply it to the Trinity.

70. Letham, *Through Western Eyes*, 191.

the relations between the Trinitarian persons as the central and exclusive concept through which God is to be understood.

In the West there are three common approaches to the relationship between Scripture and tradition, and Letham clarifies:

> Later developments in the West placed tradition over Scripture (as in medieval Rome), or pitted Scripture against tradition (the Anabaptists and many contemporary evangelicals), or put Scripture over tradition without rejecting it (the Reformation).[71] With Orthodoxy, Scripture is a primary part of the organic nature of tradition.[72]

In the light of our preceding discussion, we conclude that Volf does not fit any of these schemes, and in fact, both Moltmann and he utilize a subjective approach to their theological narratives. Volf's doctrine of the Trinity provides only a narrow base of supporting evidence where there is the absence of standards that are to be judged on quantitative data, in favor of subjective theological opinions. Subjectivity is the hermeneutical principle that guides Volf's approach throughout *AOL*. A valuable lesson from historical theology is that the development of the church's comprehension of the Triune God emerged steadily over many centuries. We need to exercise great caution whenever revisions for the monumental teaching of the Trinity arise with claims contrary to sound ecclesial acceptance. In closing this section, there is an important learning point from the ministry of John of Damascus, something which S. D. F. Salmond highlights:

> For his aim was, not to strike out views of his own or anything novel, but rather to collect into one single theological work the opinions of the ancients which were scattered through various volumes ... [this was] the method of this most careful teacher.[73]

---

71. Lane, "Scripture, Tradition and Church," 37–55.

72. Letham, *Through Western Eyes*, 282.

73. Salmond, "Prologue," *NPNF*, vol. 9, vii. Louth and Letham observe the same pattern in John's method; John was not concerned to produce original (new) material, as in a Western sense, but originality for him meant going back to the original sources and therefore being faithful to those sources. Louth, *St. John Damascene*; Letham, *Through Western Eyes*, 108–9.

Nonhierarchical Trinitarian Relations

Volf proposes two reasons for his adoption of the idea that the relations between the three persons of the Trinity are nonhierarchical; his quest for a blueprint of anthropological identity[74] and the distinction he makes between the inner-Trinitarian relations at a constitutional level (hypostatic divinity) and the relational level (inner-Trinitarian form).[75] This egalitarian quest manifests itself at every level of Volf's critical theory that he then applies to the Trinity, the church, and society. Stanley Grenz unequivocally sets forth that a social view of God aims to move from "the one subject to the Three Persons" while engaging in the task of "theological anthropology" to "set forth the Christian understanding of what it means to be human."[76] He believes that "over the last hundred years, none has more far-reaching implications for anthropology than the rediscovery of the doctrine of the Trinity,"[77] but we should clarify that this relates only to the social Trinity that is obviously motivated by anthropological concerns.[78] Mark Husbands refutes Volf's theory as he irrevocably insists that the "Trinity is not our social program."[79]

The chosen headings that Volf makes use of to outline his Trinitarian frame in *AOL* reveal this prevalent theological pursuit: they are "Relational Personhood" and "Perichoretic Personhood."[80] Without qualification Volf maintains: "I will not pursue it here further [discussion concerning hierarchy and equality in the Trinity]. Having sided with the egalitarians, I will instead explore . . . identity . . . and self-donation."[81] A similar example arises when he states: "I do not specifically address the ordination of women; I simply assume it."[82] A drive toward feminism seems to similarly explain his favor of egalitarianism.

---

74. Volf, "Trinity Is Our Social Program," 409–12.
75. Volf, *AOL*, 216–17.
76. Grenz, "From the One Subject," 43.
77. Ibid., 3–4.
78. Holmes, *Trinity in Human Community*, 134–63; Holmes, like Volf, places anthropological communities at the heart of a local church instead of theology and doxology.
79. Husbands, "Trinity Is Not," 120–41.
80. Volf, *AOL*, 204, 208.
81. Volf, "Trinity Is Our Social Program," 407–8.
82. Volf, *AOL*, 2.

Volf makes Moltmann his single reference to buttress this argument, and Volf adopts Moltmann's negation of the constitutional relations (of begetting and procession) in order to form a blueprint for nonhierarchical ecclesial relations.[83] There appears to be a convenient use of the distinction between the immanent and economic Trinity in an attempt to sidestep potential objections regarding the plain order that exists between the Trinitarian persons in the economic Trinity, as revealed in the NT (Matt 28:19; John 1:1–18, 13:31—17:23; 1 Cor 11:2–3; Eph 1:3–14, 5:20–33).

Olson is quick to point out this mistake by Moltmann (which is mirrored by Volf), and he describes:

> This dynamic interpretation seems weakened however, by his assertion that this "inner-life" of the Trinity is to be distinguished from the "constitution" of the Trinity. The implied split between the ontological order and the functional, historical order threatens to reintroduce what Moltmann so firmly rejects.[84]

This begs the question, what motivation lies behind the introduction of this split in the "inner-Trinitarian life"? Letham observes that Moltmann's "almost pathological abhorrence of power is everywhere evident,"[85] and concerning the impact of feminism upon his development of antihierarchical concepts he writes:

> Moltmann's Christian society is a feminized society of persons in relationship, devoid of authority. One might call it a castrated theology. It is a mixture of Christian teaching and paganism. Whatever else one might say, it is certainly "politically correct."[86]

Volf projects his egalitarian agenda in two primary directions; upon the Trinity and onto the church to similarly adopt a politically correct stance. Whatever else we may learn from this, an anthropological enquiry is unwarranted as a starting point for theology and ecclesiology.

---

83. Ibid., 216–17; Moltmann, *Trinity and the Kingdom*, 165, 175; Moltmann, *Spirit of Life*, 289–95. Moltmann calls his revised Trinity that collapses the immanent and economic Trinity together "the Primordial Trinity" (293–94).

84. Olson, "Trinity and Eschatology," 225.

85. Letham, *Holy Trinity*, 311.

86. Ibid., 312.

A Single Divine Attribute: Love

A single divine attribute, namely "a community of perfect love" is the only one that Volf identifies for the Trinity and for the church to reflect.[87] This is unfortunate because he misses an opportunity to explore a fruitful line of enquiry for the Trinity and also for the church—that being an understanding of the divine attributes within a Trinitarian framework. Perfect love is supposedly something for the church to copy by the removal of all notions of hierarchy and subordination and the expression of mutual giving and receiving, which includes the giving up of the "practice of claiming goods."[88] Volf concludes chapter 5 ("Trinity and Church") in *AOL* by pointing the church, now, to the eschatological vision for the new creation where "human beings in communion with the Triune God will reflect perfect divine love."[89]

This social Trinity with a strong emphasis on the single divine attribute of love as mutual self-giving is fast gaining momentum in the contemporary evangelical world. Timothy Keller's influential book *The Reason for God*[90] advocates a similar view of the Trinity to Volf. What are we to make of the suggestion that perfect love, in the context of community is the single attribute for the church to pursue?

Our first impression is that Volf's development of the Trinitarian attributes is disappointingly threadbare, and it leaves a subjective imprint as to what it means to foster this characteristic within church communities. It would have been helpful if Volf had developed a clear systematic framework with supporting evidence from Scripture and tradition, for the being of the Triune God (who is God?) followed by a detailed summary of the attributes of the Trinity (what is God like?). For how can the church reflect something that is not clearly presented? Volf's eschatological thrust indicates that the church should be actively working towards manifesting the end goal, here and now. There is a very real danger that the social Trinitarian emphases on openness and perfect love may pave the way for "open theism," and this is something that Clark Pinnock, an advocate for "the openness of God," commends Moltmann and others

---

87. Volf, *AOL*, 217; Lock, "Space of Hospitality." Lock connects hospitality to perichoresis from this icon, and he states that this concept "involves 'making room' which is the very heart of hospitality" (51).

88. Volf, *AOL*, 217, 219–20; Volf, "Trinity, Unity, Primacy," 177–80.

89. Volf, *AOL*, 217, 219–20.

90. Keller, *Reason for God*, 213–26.

for.⁹¹ Volf's idea for the love of God is seen in abstraction from all else, and it does not cohere with the love of God as seen in the Bible and the history of the church's interpretation, as mutually defining with God's power, holiness, and goodness.

A viable approach is the proposal for a Trinitarian approach towards systematizing the divine attributes that builds on the Corinthian Benediction (2 Cor 13:14) where love is ascribed to the Father, grace to the Son, and fellowship to the Holy Spirit. The Father's love can be envisaged as "outward moving and dynamic love"; the Son's grace as self-giving action that is manifested in Christ's incarnation, perfect life of obedience, and atonement; and the Holy Spirit's fellowship (*koinōnia*) as the "dynamic creation of communion and community and the latter could be illustrated by the phrase 'Comm-Unity' building."⁹²

This quest for a Trinitarian theology for the divine attributes based initially on the benedictory formulation can probably be developed much further through a biblical theological study of 2 Corinthians. Under the umbrella of "the Father's love" there are some other characteristics that are directly ascribed to God the Father by Paul in this letter. These are mercy ("the Father of mercies," 1:3), comfort ("the God of all comfort," 1:3–4), and peace ("the God of love and peace will be with you," 2 Cor 13:11). There are additional insights into other attributes distinctly revealed by the Son, and these are generosity (Paul encourages a generosity in the church's giving by connecting this to the example of Christ's grace in his atoning work, 8:1—9:15), and meekness-gentleness ("the meekness and gentleness of Christ," 10:1). The Spirit is specifically connected to holiness (the only person of the Trinity whose name includes an attribute) alongside fellowship, which appears as something that is jointly shared within the divine and ecclesial communion.

Any theology of the Trinity requires the maintenance of an undivided Trinity. Even though further research is merited to move systematic theology and the doctrine of God along Trinitarian lines, this in no way signifies a distinction of essence within the Triune God. Owen rightly insists that "all the works of the Trinity *ad extra* are indivisible,"⁹³ and this sustains the simplicity of God; all the Trinitarian actions and attributes are equally ultimate and mutually interconnected. Regarding the

91. Pinnock, "Systematic Theology," 107–9.
92. Bidwell, "Church's Diaconal Ministry," 25–36.
93. Owen, *Works*, vol. 2, 269.

inner-Trinitarian relations there are not three wills, and the three persons are not individuals in a postmodern Western sense, as Pannenberg implies (and Volf endorses) with the phrase "living realisations of separate centres of action."[94]

Our investigation of Volf's social doctrine of the Trinity unmasks a model that has a narrow base, built upon subjective presuppositions, speculations, and anthropological concerns for human identity and equality. This leads Volf to ignore patristic and historical sources of theology, to abandon the theological anchor of monotheism, and to compress all of his Trinity into a tritheistic mould called perichoretic relations and personhood. Volf"s presentation in *AOL* may well provide support for politically correct or feminist agendas; however this imaginative construct for the Trinity remains remarkably isolated from the theological consensus across East and West, and across the centuries, spanning back to the first Council of Nicea in 325. It is not unreasonable, therefore, to assert that Volf has indeed developed a framework for the doctrine of the Trinity that is an inverted theological pyramid.

---

94. Volf, *AOL*, 215: Pannenberg, *Systematic Theology*, 1.319.

13

A Critical Evaluation of "Structures of the Church"

A SUMMARY OF THIS PROPOSAL

ECCLESIOLOGY IS OFTEN DEFINED by a particular understanding of office as the title of the ecumenical document *Baptism, Eucharist and Ministry*[1] indicates. This presents a problem in Volf's thinking because he believes that "God as communion" should impact our understanding of the communion of the church and address a particular problem—the lack of church member participation. Similarly he perceives the Catholic and Orthodox ecclesiologies to be fundamentally flawed with their respective ideas on the "whole Christ" and episcopacy-centered structures.[2] Instead Volf proposes a participative and charismatic model for the Free Church in chapter 6 of *AOL*.

A Polycentric–Participative Model of Church Life

Volf argues for a church that is not a single subject but a "communion of interdependent subjects," where salvation is mediated through the "communal confession" of all the church members, so that it is constituted by the Holy Spirit rather than through office bearers.[3] It is from these

---

1. British Council of Churches, *Churches Respond to BEM*; Lazareth, *Baptism, Eucharist and Ministry*.
2. Volf, *AOL*, 223.
3. Ibid., 224.

three theological tenets that Volf proposes that a church is a "polycentric community" with a "participative structure." This pattern is based on his understanding of 1 Cor 12–14, and especially Paul's teaching that says "when you come together, each one has a hymn, a lesson, a revelation, a tongue, or an interpretation" (1 Cor 14:26).[4]

The outworking of this model means that the life of the church is ordered around the exercise of charismatic gifts by the whole church, expressed as a polycentric–participative church model, and not around officeholders (though Volf believes they are still indispensable). He appeals to the early Pentecostal pioneer Donald Gee who spoke of "open" worship services characterized by "general liberty for all to take part as the Spirit moved upon the members of the congregation."[5]

A Charismatic Church

This blueprint is a pneumatological structure, and Volf describes that "the church is constituted by the Spirit of God through charismatic activity."[6] He aims to move the locus of activity from the church's leaders to the midst of the gathered congregation. He states that "all members have *charismata* (Acts 2:17–21; 1 Pet. 4:10)," that the "members of the body of Christ have different gifts (Rom. 12:6; 1 Cor. 12:7–11)," and that this represents a church community of mutual giving and receiving (Phil 4:15).[7]

This charismatic church model does not negate the need for church officers; instead they take on a quite different function to avoid ministerial bottlenecks for church activity. Volf declares that the task of leaders is to coordinate the church to engage in charismatic activities and to be responsible for testing the manifestations of the Spirit (1 Thess 5:21). It is in this way that the church serves each other "in anticipation of God's new creation."[8]

---

4. Ibid., 224–25.

5. Ibid., 225n17; Gee, *Concerning Spiritual Gifts*, 15; Volf, *AOL*, 225n11, 17; Volf here also appeals to Fee, *First Epistle*, 690; and Lim, *Spiritual Gifts*, 34.

6. Volf, *AOL*, 229.

7. Ibid., 230–31.

8. Ibid.

The Trinity as a Model for the Church

There are four specific ways that the charismatic–participative church presented by Volf reflects his proposed model for the Trinity. He states that "the church reflects in a broken fashion the eschatological communion of the entire people of God with the Triune God in God's new creation."[9] Firstly, Volf puts forward that the church is institutionalized through Christians "confessing Jesus Christ as Lord and Saviour, through baptism in the Triune God" and through the "eucharist, which celebrates communion with the Triune God."[10] The church has an essentially social dimension in Volf's ecclesiology where salvation is profoundly christological but the sacraments are Trinitarian.

Secondly the charismatic structure for the church presented in *AOL* is seen to correspond to the Trinitarian relations, as proposed by Paul in 1 Cor 12:4–6.[11] This decisively Trinitarian passage stands at the head of the biblical pericope (1 Cor 12–14) that Volf particularly draws on for his thesis for a NT charismatic church. The apostle Paul states:

> Now there are varieties of gifts, but the same Spirit; and there are varieties of service, but the same Lord; and there are varieties of activities, but it is the same God who empowers them all in everyone. (1 Cor 12:4–6)

Thirdly, a nonhierarchical and freely constituted cohesion among the church members is seen by Volf to best represent the Triune God, or at least to reflect his own doctrine of the Trinity. Volf consistently engages in polemic against the hierarchical Trinities consisting of asymmetrical relations held by Ratzinger and Zizioulas, and he insists that this leads to the maintenance of the hierarchical church structures in the Catholic and Orthodox churches. Volf's antithesis affirms that he follows the Trinitarian and ecclesial models proposed by Moltmann, and he states:

> In following Moltmann,[12] I by contrast take as my premise the symmetrical relations within the Trinity.[13] This yields the ecclesial principle that the more a church is characterised by symmetrical and decentralised distribution of power and freely affirmed in-

---

9. Ibid., 235.
10. Ibid., 234–25.
11. Ibid., 235.
12. Ibid., 236.
13. Moltmann, *Trinity and the Kingdom*, 174.

teraction, the more will it correspond to the Trinitarian communion. Relations between charismata, modelled after the Trinity, are reciprocal and symmetrical; all members of the church have charismata, and all are to engage their charismata for the good of all others.[14]

This brings into focus the influence of not only Moltmann's doctrine of the Trinity but also his ecclesiology that is outlined in *The Church in the Power of the Spirit*. Moltmann formulates a charismatic and pneumatological doctrine of the church akin to Volf's prototype for a church that is supposed to reflect the Trinity.

Fourthly, a church that mirrors the eschatological goal of the new creation should be "a church of love and the church of law."[15] These twin principles should govern the church that endeavors to be shaped in the image of the Trinity to ensure that the work of the Holy Spirit among its members takes place with peace and order, without confusion (1 Cor 14:29, 14:33).

Church Officers, Ordination, and Their Election

"Offices are a particular type of charismata" according to Volf; therefore "there can be no difference in principle between officeholders and other members of the church." On the basis of the universal priesthood of all believers Volf maintains that there are not "two groups" of priests among the church on the basis that there is the "equality of all ministries." Volf states that "by contrast [to Ratzinger and Zizioulas], I have advocated a symmetrical understanding of the relations between the Trinitarian persons, which yields a basically collegial understanding of ecclesiastical office of the sort attested by the New Testament writings (Phil. 1:1; 1 Tim. 3:1–4:8, 5:17; Titus 1:5–7; 1 Pet. 5:1)." In agreement with the *BEM* document, Volf agrees with their threefold understanding of office under the titles of "bishop" (ἐπίσκοποι), "presbyters" (πρεσβύτεροι), and "deacons" (διαχονοι).[16]

While offices are not viewed as necessary for a church, Volf does nonetheless uphold the need for officeholders to secure a church's confession of faith in Christ and for the celebration of the sacraments.

---

14. Moltmann, *Church in the Power*, 305.

15. Volf, *AOL*, 237–44.

16. Ibid., 247–48; Association of Evangelical Lutheran Churches, *Baptism, Eucharist and Ministry*, 22.

Ordination is seen to be a "divine–human act" of the "entire local church led by the Spirit of God," and the exercise of democratic election by members in full communion is recommended by Volf.[17]

The reorganization of church structures alone is not seen as the sole answer to overcome hierarchical expressions of church government, and Volf recognizes that without the presence of the Spirit, "even a church with a decentralized participative structure and culture will become sterile, and perhaps even more sterile even than a hierarchical church."[18] He suggests that a successful participative church life must be sustained by "deep spirituality" and that only the "members who live from the Spirit of communion (2 Cor. 13:14) can participate authentically."[19] These statements raise many questions as to the viability of such a model, besides which no recommendations are given by Volf as to how the presence of the Spirit can be secured among a church or how its members should sustain a "deep spirituality."

A CRITICAL EVALUATION OF THIS PROPOSAL

Volf does not give us sufficient information for us to get a handle on his argument so that we can thoroughly critique it. We may ask, does Volf's doctrine of the Trinity inform his doctrine of the church or vice versa? Volf systematically projects his egalitarian worldview upon everything; this includes his biblical exegesis, his doctrine of the church, and his doctrine of the Trinity. Therefore it appears that unsubstantiated assumptions of democratic and antihierarchical principles inform his theology and ecclesiology.

Furthermore Volf maintains a liberal approach to Scripture, and he is quite content to override its authority or its content when it clashes with his own presuppositions. For example in handling the doctrine of the church, Volf asserts that the NT "does not contain any unified, theologically reflected view of church organisation," rather he believes that it simply provides a collection of witnesses as to how "early churches regulated their own lives within various cultural spheres."[20] In contemplating

---

17. Volf, *AOL*, 249–56.
18. Ibid., 257; Gee, *Concerning Spiritual Gifts*, 15.
19. Volf, *AOL*, 257.
20. Ibid., 245.

the interpretation of the apparently subordinationist passages of Gen 1 and 2, 1 Cor 11:2–16, and Eph 5:21–33 he states:

> I will simply disregard the subordinationism as culturally conditioned and interpret the statements from within the framework of an egalitarian understanding of the Trinitarian relations and from the egalitarian thrust of such central biblical assertions as the one found in Galatians 3:28: "There is neither male nor female, for you are all one in Christ Jesus."[21]

This approach to tradition, authority, and the sufficiency of the biblical record compounds our difficulty to critically evaluate Volf's ecclesiology. In effect he places himself as a subjective interpreter of biblical revelation with unshackled assumptions. This postmodern literary position that Volf espouses places his theology on a slippery slope because his own ecclesiology is culturally conditioned by politically correct, egalitarian, and feminist motives that are superimposed upon the biblical record.

Despite the recognition of these difficulties to analyze Volf's doctrine of the church, a range of valuable opportunities are presented in using this ecclesial blueprint in *AOL* to think through ecclesiology. This we will do by comparing the church practice of first-century Corinth with Volf's model.

Did the New Testament Church at Corinth Practice Volf's Polycentric–Participative Church Model?

A persistent concern is upheld by Volf in all of his writings that manifests itself as a persistent dislike of hierarchy, and the rejection of hierarchal church structures. There does not appear to be an appreciation that a clearly ordered church constitution where "all things should be done decently and in order" (1 Cor 14:40) can be possible unless the church officers are reduced to be little more than coordinators and testers of charismatic activity by its members.[22] This produces flattened structures where charismatic participation by the members is the main activity of the church. Any prior organization of a church meeting by the leadership seems to be negated by this participative model.

Was this model of leadership practiced in the church at Corinth? Most commentators do not take this passage (1 Cor 12–14) as an

---

21. Volf, *EE*, 182–83.
22. Volf, *AOL*, 230–31.

exclusive starting point for understanding the role of leaders and certainly not to assert the kind of ministerial functions that Volf proposes. Additionally Volf does not qualify his assertions, but he merely assumes that the Corinthian church practiced spontaneous charismatic participation. Perhaps it will be helpful to concentrate the issues in view by considering the differing interpretations of 1 Cor 14:29–33, which reads:

> Let two or three prophets speak, and let the others weigh what is said. If a revelation is made to another sitting there, let the first be silent. For you can all prophesy one by one, so that all may learn and all be encouraged, and the spirits of prophets are subject to prophets. For God is not a God of confusion but of peace.

Here Paul seems to address the role of one office at least, that of prophet, and he appears to encourage the universal church participation by members in the gift of prophecy.

There are at least five main (Protestant) ways of interpreting this passage in relation to the nature of prophecy and that of prophets, and the conclusions that are reached on these matters shape any particular church model significantly. Therefore we cannot sidestep this somewhat prickly issue, and we must be aware that there is not scholarly consensus on this somewhat controversial passage (1 Cor 12–14) upon which Volf chooses to base his ecclesiology. Dunn subdivides 1 Corinthians into three main sections, and he assumes that chapters 11–16 form a single unit where Paul deals with the "problems of worship and belief."[23] Anthony C. Thiselton similarly subdivides 1 Corinthians to suggest that 11:2—14:40 forms a unit in this book that he believes relates to "mutual respect in matters of public worship."[24]

If we accept the broad divisions suggested by Dunn and Thiselton we observe that our pericope (1 Cor 14:29–33) is sandwiched between two apparently contradictory passages: one that appears to permit women to prophesy (1 Cor 11:2–16) and one that forbids it (1 Cor 14:34–5). This makes our exegetical problem even more demanding, and therefore our conclusion on these matters inevitably overflows into the role of women in the church.

---

23. Dunn, *1 Corinthians*, 69–89.
24. Thiselton, *1 Corinthians*, 169–250.

The advocates of Volf's charismatic/Pentecostal position are most notably Moltmann and Gordon D. Fee.[25] Moltmann does not engage in an exegetical study of our chosen passage, but he extensively writes on the pneumatological dimension of the church, which involves the free-flowing use of charismatic prophecy (and other gifts) with a nonhierarchical "presbyterial leadership."[26] Fee meticulously writes with great detail, and he defines prophecy as consisting of "spontaneous, Spirit-inspired, intelligible messages, orally delivered in the gathered assembly, intended for the edification or encouragement of the people."[27] Thus it is not the delivery of a previously prepared sermon."[28] He explains that the ordering where "two or three prophets speak" does not "mean that in any given gathering there must be a limit of two or three prophecies," and he remarks that the phrase "you can all prophesy" means that "all have the opportunity to participate" in the congregation.[29] This leads Fee to insist in participation in the assembly by men and women, and he removes the prohibition by Paul for "women to be silent" (1 Cor 14:34–35), by asserting on textual grounds, that: "the exegesis of the text itself leads to the conclusion that it is not authentic. If so, then it is certainly not binding for Christians."[30] This may conveniently solve Fee's exegetical problem, but Carson irrefutably objects to such moves, and he argues:

> I confess I am always surprised by the amount of energy and ingenuity expended to rescue Paul from himself and conform him to our image. In any case, from a purely text-critical point of view, the evidence that these verses are original and in their original location (and not, as in some manuscripts, with verses 34–35 placed after 14:40), is substantial.[31]

Dunn echoes this view and specifically rejects Fee's (and Hans Conzelmann's[32]) postulation. He states that the "text-critical case is so

---

25. Moltmann, *Church in the Power*, 291–300; Fee, *First Epistle*.
26. Moltmann, *Church in the Power*, 291–336; especially 294–302, 310.
27. Fee, *First Epistle*, 595.
28. Ibid., 595n73.
29. Ibid., 693. Fee rejects the opinion that "prophets are a special group of authorised persons in the [church] community (694)."
30. Ibid., 709.
31. Carson, *Showing the Spirit*, 124.
32. Conzelmann, *1 Corinthians*, 246.

strongly in favour of its authenticity" and that it is "better to take the text as it stands and see what sense it makes."[33]

A second stance is that held by Grudem who draws a distinction between the office and ministry of teaching from the office of prophet and prophesying.[34] Grudem succinctly summarizes his view and asserts:

> Prophecy, not only in 1 Corinthians but in the entire NT, has two distinctive features. First, it must be based on a "revelation": If there is no revelation, there is no prophecy. Second, it must include a public proclamation. The mere reception of a revelation does not constitute a prophecy until it has been publicly proclaimed.
>
> Teaching, on the other hand, is always based on an explanation and/or application of Scripture or received apostolic doctrine; it is never said to be based on revelation. That is why teaching has so much more authority for governing the congregatio, and it also explains why Paul was perfectly willing to have women as well as men prophesy in the assembled congregation, while he restricted the authoritative teaching functions to men only.[35]

Grudem contends that prophecy is a permanent gift for the church, one that includes the participation of men and women, even though the individuals who exercise the gift do not permanently possess the actual gift of prophecy because the Holy Spirit distributes "as he wills" (1 Cor 12:11).[36] Carson comments that he is "generally sympathetic" to Grudem's thesis and that he agrees with him, that prophecy is "revelational," as opposed to an "informational base" built upon study.[37]

Dunn represents a third position, one that advocates a feminist rereading of the NT, rejects the patriarchal household codes as also taught by Schüssler-Fiorenza,[38] and refuses to permit a subjective view of prophecy. He states:

> The need for such evaluation [the testing of prophecy] as a hermeneutical principle, in effect the answer to the danger of false prophecy as recognised throughout the history of biblical prophecy (e.g. Deut. 13:1–3; Jer. 28; Mic. 5:4–8; 1 Jn. 4:1–3), is also

33. Dunn, *1 Corinthians*, 74.

34. Note that "prophecy" is the noun and "prophesy" is the verb, and both of these are connected in the NT.

35. Grudem, *Gift of Prophecy*, 123.

36. Ibid., 173–74.

37. Carson, *Showing the Spirit*, 94, 119, 162.

38. Schüssler-Fiorenza, "Women," 153–66; Schüssler-Fiorenza, *Bread Not Stone*.

subverted by Grudem with his arbitrary distinction between primary (canonical) prophecy ("authority of general content") and Corinthian prophecy as a secondary type of prophecy ("authority of actual words").[39]

This means that he is content with the notion that women have a role in public worship while he does not accept the "Volf–Moltmann–Fee," or "Grudem–Carson" paradigms on prophecy and prophets. Thiselton offers very similar conclusions to Dunn in his commentary on 1 Corinthians.[40]

A fourth posture is found in the works of Calvin, William Perkins, and Geerhardus Vos. Perkins simply states: "There are two parts to prophecy: preaching the word and public prayer" and that the "prophet has two public duties: One is preaching the Word and the other is praying to God in the name of the people."[41] Calvin likewise in commenting on 1 Cor 11–14 explains that prophets are "first of all, eminent interpreters of Scripture" and prophecy is "unfolding the secret will of God," and he equates the gift of prophecy to the office of teacher.[42] This implies a degree of permanence of these gifts in our own day and a measure of continuity with the OT ministries, and also that public ministry is only open to men.

Vos condemns the type of prophecy that Grudem proposes as "mystical revelation."[43] Carson, aware of this criticism, attempts to sweep away this opinion by claiming that such a "view of revelation" by Vos is "narrower than that employed in Scripture."[44] Additionally Vos supports his conclusion with an etymological study of the Greek word *prophētēs*, which he says means "an interpreter" rather than a communicator of fresh revelation.[45]

A fifth posture is the cessationist argument, one that is cogently defended by Robert L. Reymond[46] and O. Palmer Robertson. They

---

39. Dunn, *1 Corinthians*, 83. Dunn, *Jesus and the Spirit*; here he puts forward that *charisma* (1 Cor 12:4–11) is the embodiment and manifestation of grace.
40. Thiselton, *1 Corinthians*, 201–2, 250–51.
41. William Perkins, *Art of Prophesying*, xi.
42. Calvin, *Commentary on 1 Corinthians*, 402, 415, 417.
43. Vos, *Biblical Theology*, 304.
44. Carson, *Showing the Spirit*, 161–63.
45. Vos, "Conception of a Prophet," 191–97.
46. Reymond, *What about Continuing Revelations*, 1977.

propose that the continuation of prophecy and supernatural signs is erroneous because these gifts ceased at the end of the apostolic era and canonical closure. Robertson defines NT prophecy (in relation to 1 Cor 14:29–33) as the "forthtelling of a revelation" and that the "new covenant prophet fits the OT pattern"[47] of a prophet. While he accepts that there was a revelational dynamic at work in the church at Corinth, he contends that "in Jesus Christ, revelation from God . . . has reached its climax," therefore the era of special revelation has ceased since God's word is found in the Bible.[48]

A theologian's conclusions on prophecy and the meaning of prophet in the church at Corinth has significant impact upon their doctrine of the church, the mediation of faith, the worship of God, and the image of God in the church. Our brief survey of the way 1 Cor 11–14 is interpreted by different theological streams highlights the dangers in making this biblical passage prescriptive for ecclesiology.

It would be extremely tenuous to insist that the Corinthian Christians practiced a polycentric, participative model as Volf proposes. Even if revelatory prophecy was at work in the congregation at Corinth, it seems very unlikely that it was participatory without the office of preacher and teacher in conjunction with these charismatic gifts. Furthermore Volf offers no evidence to validate his opinion that the Corinthian church leaders were simply coordinators of a polycentric and charismatic church meeting.

DID THE POST-APOSTOLIC CHURCH AT CORINTH CORRESPOND WITH VOLF'S ECCLESIAL MODEL?

A rich source of theological material is found in the writings of the church fathers, and the three men who were closest to the apostolic witness are Clement of Rome (flourished c. 96), Polycarp of Smyrna (c. 69–c. 155, but possibly slightly later), and Ignatius of Antioch. A study of these early bishops' writings should enable us to reconstruct a doctrine of the church that was established within decades of the deaths of the apostles Peter, Paul, and John and also provide clues as to how they connected the Triune God to the church's worship. Our main concern here

---

47. Robertson, *Final Word*, 4, 12–13.
48. Ibid., 53–59.

is a letter by Clement to advise the post-apostolic church at Corinth on some weighty church matters.

Clement of Rome is mainly remembered for his *Epistle to the Corinthians*, which makes him of particular interest for our evaluation of Volf's doctrine of the Church that is fashioned upon 1 Cor 12–14. Dunn believes that Clement's epistle settles the matter concerning the Pauline authorship of 1 Corinthians, and he writes:

> 1 Corinthians has the kind of attestation of which most students of ancient texts can only dream. One of the earliest post-NT writings, *1 Clement* (usually dated to the late first century), is addressed to the same church, and explicitly calls upon its readers to "Take up the epistle of the blessed Paul the apostle.... With true inspiration he charged you concerning himself and Cephas and Apollos, because even then you had made yourselves partisans (*1 Clem.* 47:1–3)." The reference to One Corinthians is beyond dispute; to have such a clear cross reference within about 40 years of the first letter is highly unusual.[49]

A. Cleveland Coxe explains that Clement is probably the man referred to by the same name in Paul's Letter to the Philippians (4:3), and he states that Clement's "epistle was held in very great esteem by the early church."[50] The church historian Eusebius of Caesarea (c. 260–c. 340) remarks that this epistle is "acknowledged to be genuine and is of considerable length and of remarkable merit. He wrote it in the name of the church of Rome to the church of Corinth, when a sedition had arisen in the latter church."[51] Eusebius adds that Clement was the third bishop of the church in Rome, and that "he had seen and conversed with the blessed apostles, and their preaching was still sounding in his ears, and their tradition was still before his eyes."[52] There is a second epistle to the Corinthians supposedly written by Clement, but its authorship is seriously doubted, and therefore we will only consider his *First Epistle to the Corinthians*.[53]

---

49. Dunn, *1 Corinthians*, 13.

50. Coxe, "Introductory Note," 1–2.

51. Eusebius, "The Church History of Eusebius," *NPNF*, vol. 1, 3.16, 147. There is a second epistle to Corinthians, but Clement's authorship is seriously doubted: Keith, "Epistles of Clement," 249.

52. Eusebius, "The Church History of Eusebius," 5.6, 221.

53. Keith, "Epistles of Clement," 249.

The whole theme of Clement's letter is his attempt to deal with the "sedition, and disagreement and schisms"[54] that had arisen among them in the church. What is immediately striking is the method that he employs as a Bible expositor; he persistently appeals to the Scriptures (OT and NT), and he does not write as an inspired prophet or apostle, but rather as a pastor–teacher. Clement accepts the authority of the biblical record, and he urges the Corinthian Christians by writing: "You understand, beloved, you understand well the sacred Scriptures, and you have looked very earnestly into the oracles of God. Call then these things to remembrance."[55] There is not the slightest mention of any words that may have been given by prophets or through prophecies of the kind advocated by Volf in his charismatic church model.

Clement makes an unmistakable reference to the church offices that were established in Corinth: presbyters, bishops, and deacons.[56] He takes for granted that clear authority structures existed in the congregation and that the office-bearers were to represent a servant–leadership model. However, Clement anticipates a congregational response, and he exhorts:

> For you did all things without respect of persons, and walked in the commandments of God, being obedient to those who had the rule over you, and giving all fitting honour to the presbyters among you.[57]

Furthermore he endorses the primacy of preaching for ministry, and he elucidates that this is the main vehicle for the mediation of faith and doctrine. He explains:

> The apostles have preached the gospel to us from the Lord Jesus Christ; Jesus Christ (has done so) from God. Christ therefore was sent forth by God, and the apostles by Christ. Both these appointments, then, were made in an orderly way, according to the will of God. Having therefore received their orders and being fully assured by the resurrection of our Lord Jesus Christ, and established in the word of God, with full assurance of the Holy Spirit, they went forth proclaiming that the kingdom of God was at hand. And thus preaching through countries and cities, they

---

54. Clement of Rome, "First Epistle of Clement," iii, liv, 5–6, 19.
55. Ibid., liii, 19.
56. Ibid., i, xlii, xliv, lvii, 1, 5, 16, 20.
57. Ibid., i, 5.

> appointed the first-fruits (of their labours), having first proved them by the Spirit, to the bishops and deacons of those who should afterwards believe.[58]

There also appears to have been a pattern in place for the installment of new presbyters, and Clement elucidates:

> When these [ministers] should fall asleep, other approved men should succeed them in their ministry. We are of the opinion therefore, that those appointed by them [the apostles], or afterwards by other eminent men, with the consent of the whole church, and who have blamelessly served the flock of Christ in a humble, peaceable, and disinterested spirit, and have for a long time possessed the good opinion of all, cannot be justly dismissed from the ministry.[59]

This last statement seems to pinpoint the root of the sedition as something that involved the congregation's attempt to exercise an internal authority to dismiss a minister of the gospel. Such congregational decision making is ruled out by Clement himself who writes to the church as a bishop (pastor–teacher) to the congregation in Corinth; his approach to the problem indicates the existence of a connection between some of the different NT churches.

The overall church pattern that existed in Corinth, as portrayed by Clement, appears to be at some variance with Volf's ecclesiology. Firstly the mediation of faith is understood by Clement to primarily take place through the preaching of the bishops, though this may be also through deacons, as opposed to confession of faith of the whole congregation as Volf suggests. The notion of leaders being facilitators of charismatic activity with flattened structures is overturned by Clement's assertions that church members are to be obedient to those presbyters who had the rule over them. Nowhere does Clement suggest that egalitarianism is the answer to any pastoral problems, and neither does he put forward that the doctrine of God is to be seen as the blueprint for ministerial structures. The ministerial plan is patterned after Christ, along with the instructions given by the apostles for churches; this seems to indicate a presbyterian scheme where the locus of authority does not rest solely in the midst of the congregation,

---

58. Ibid., xliii, 16.
59. Ibid., xliv, 17.

and the election of officers is not based solely on democratic church elections (as Volf suggests[60]), but the process included the oversight of eminent men for the appointment of new presbyters.

Some final comments on this letter concern Clement's didactical method, one that is redemptive-historical, systematic, and intensely pastoral. He is not writing as an academic but as a pastor of "the church which sojourns at Rome" to the "church of God sojourning at Corinth."[61] His use of language reflects his audience; it is a well-taught church that appears to be extremely familiar with the panorama of salvation history. He does not utilize convoluted, hypothetical, or academic language or metaphors (as does Volf in *AOL*). This seems to contrast highly with the majority of Western theological writings, which usually arise from professional theologians, as opposed to church pastors. This observation is worthy of further critical reflection to ensure that Western theology does not become distant and isolated from the reality of local church life.

Clement attempts to resolve the sedition, divisions, and disorder in the life of the church, and he chooses to take a whole range of biblical narratives to bring his teaching for humility, unity, and reconciliation to the Christians. He begins by exposing the sin of envy, and he does so by beginning with Cain and Abel, then Jacob fleeing from Esau, followed by Joseph being sold into slavery by his brothers, and so on.[62] He continues this method throughout the letter as he introduces the danger of envy from the narratives of events that surrounded the lives of Abraham, Moses, Aaron, David, Elijah, and Elisha, the martyrdom of Peter and Paul and so on. The crowning example that Clement uses is the sufferings of the Lord Jesus Christ and a call for humility that follows Christ's example.[63]

One final observation is that Clement is not concerned with teaching a mere moralism or exhortation to good works only, but his letter is filled with gospel doctrine anchored in the doctrine of justification by faith apart from works.[64] He commends them in that they were carefully attending to God's words and that they were "inwardly filled with His [God's] doctrine and His [Christ's] sufferings were before your

60. Volf, *AOL*, 252–57.
61. Clement, "First Epistle of Clement," i, 5.
62. Ibid., iv–x, 6–8.
63. Ibid., xvi, xxiii, 9, 15.
64. Ibid., xxxii, 13.

eyes"; even though their "sedition against its presbyters" makes their "recent discord worse than that which took place in the times of Paul."[65] Clement's solution is for the authors of the sedition to submit themselves "to the presbyters and receive correction so as to repent, bending the knees of [their] hearts."[66] It would be unthinkable to find this approach to church structures from Volf's theology, and we conclude that the doctrine of the church that was in operation in first-century Corinth is fundamentally different to Volf's congregational church that envisages egalitarian and symmetrical ecclesial relations.

---

65. Ibid., ii, xlvii, 5, 18.
66. Ibid., lvii.

14

A Critical Evaluation of "The Catholicity of the Church"

VOLF ASTUTELY RECOGNIZES THAT much of the contemporary debate with respect to catholicity is static and often built around sterile theological impasses that hinder further theological development. He is not afraid to critique the common Free Church position, one that he perceives to be uncatholic because "they lack forms of communion with all other churches, that is, with the whole church," because their holiness is exclusive, and because their apostolicity "lacks connection to the whole church in its history."[1] Similarly he asserts that the "unity of the Catholic Church is uncatholic because the Pope (or bishop), to use Luther's words, 'declares that his court alone is the Christian church.'"[2]

CATHOLICITY AND NEW CREATION

An alternative understanding of the catholicity of the local church is sought by Volf, and he attempts to apply his eschatological vision, which is incidentally a consistent thread throughout *AOL*, to this particular ecumenical problem. His vision springs from Rev 21–22 where in the "new creation is the mutual indwelling of the Triune God and the glorified people in a new heaven and new earth."[3] Volf fosters the concept of "anticipation" among churches that acknowledge that they possess the

---

1. Volf, *AOL*, 259–60.
2. Ibid., 260, 260n2; Luther, *Works*, 50, 283.
3. Volf, *AOL*, 266.

presence of the Spirit of Christ (which he believes constitutes a church), and Volf states: "The church is catholic because the Spirit of the new creation present within it anticipates in it the eschatological gathering of the whole people of God."[4] This, he believes, forges a new path through exclusive claims that a single branch of the church alone represents the original apostolic pattern and approval.

THE CATHOLICITY OF THE LOCAL CHURCH AND PERSON

The uppermost concern for Volf is firstly to consider the local congregation, and this leads him to propose a definition of a church. He states: "Every church has the whole Christ, along with all the means of salvation and is for that reason not part of the church, but rather is a whole church and is in this sense catholic."[5] He proposes that the way forward is openness to all other churches of God as the "minimum of catholicity" and that this is the "identifying feature of catholicity."[6] In turn this should lead to a universal openness toward all human beings who confess faith in Christ without distinction. Volf finishes *AOL* with a fairly abrupt end as he defines his understanding of the catholicity of individual persons, and he concludes:

> The Spirit of communion opens up every person to others, so that every person can reflect something of the eschatological communion of the entire people of God with the Triune God in a unique way through the relations in which that person lives.[7]

HOW CATHOLIC AND ECUMENICAL IS VOLF'S THEOLOGY?

One of Volf's chief aims in *AOL* is an ecumenical thesis, and he explains that today, a renewed "evaluation of the church is meaningful only as an ecumenical project."[8] Furthermore he rejects claims that there is "but one correct ecclesiology,"[9] and he does not restrict himself to his own Free Church tradition. He summarizes his intent: "I focus on the local church

---

4. Ibid., 268.
5. Ibid., 271.
6. Ibid., 274–75.
7. Ibid., 282; Volf, *EE*, 50.
8. Volf, *AOL*, 19.
9. Ibid., 21.

itself in this ecumenical study of the ecclesial community as an icon of the Trinitarian community."[10] Our question remains: how ecumenical is Volf's theology? This we shall consider in two parts: firstly in relation to his doctrine of the Trinity, and secondly with reference to his ecclesiology.

One of the main stumbling blocks to ecumenism relates to the *filioque* clause, and this is a major cause of concern for the Eastern churches, yet Volf makes no attempt to resolve this theological impasse. Our conclusion in chapter 9 of this monograph is that Volf correctly acknowledges that there remain differences in the conception of the Trinity between East and West, but his own social doctrine of the Trinity represents a departure from both of these traditions. Volf's Trinitarian construal rejects monotheism and many other creedal formulations for the Trinity,[11] and this means that his social Trinity remains remarkably isolated from the majority of Christendom. Therefore his ecumenical goal for theology and ecclesiology becomes quickly lost because his proposal for the doctrine of the Trinity is unlikely to be accepted by most theologians as a credible alternative to historically agreed upon Trinitarian dogma.

With respect to Volf's ecclesiology, he demonstrates an intense dislike to both the RCC and the OC, as chapter 6 to 9 of this monograph discusses. Within Protestantism, Volf's Free Church model remains also quite isolated, with his charismatic, antihierarchical model, one that some church leaders could read to be a recipe for ecclesial anarchy. In chapter 5 of this monograph we observed that Volf distances himself from his chosen church representative Smyth, whom he believes exhibits "sectarian narrow-mindedness and arrogance."[12] This accusation is because Smyth denied ecclesiality to episcopal churches, and while Volf does not openly deny ecclesiality to all other churches he effectually condemns every local church that has any vestige of hierarchical leadership. Even though Volf does not intend to pursue a single ecclesial blueprint, his own thesis desires universal obedience to his revisionist view of the Trinity and the church. Sadly Volf's thesis attempts to get local churches to be conformed not to the image of the Trinity as explained in the NCC, but as "charismatic Free Churches in the image of Volf's reconstructed

10. Ibid., 25.

11. Young, *The Shack*; this book attempts to popularize a politically correct version of a feminist Trinity, similar to those espoused by Moltmann and Volf.

12. Volf, *AOL*, 134.

Trinity." This understandably lacks ecumenical persuasion in terms of the one and the many. Volf seems to privilege the many, both in his Trinitarianism and ecclesiology. Is this a form of nominalism, in which reality exists exclusively in the particular?

AN ESCHATOLOGICAL HERMENEUTIC FOR ECCLESIOLOGY

A consistent and dynamic thread throughout *AOL* is Volf's fascination to connect ecclesiology to the church's eschatological goal in the new creation.[13] The theological impulse for this forward-looking vision for the church is probably Moltmann's ground-breaking thesis,[14] *Theology of Hope*. The biblical theologian Vos is keen to point out that the "Old Testament dispensation is a forward-stretching and forward-looking dispensation."[15] Volf does all theologians a great service to remind us that the NT dispensation is also forward stretching and forward looking in what is a neglected posture in some strands of contemporary theology.

This whole theme of an eschatological hermeneutic is beyond our scope of study, but Bauckham offers a valuable caution, in that theology must provide "politically and pastorally responsible eschatology."[16] Volf commonly uses the church's final eschatological goal as a motivating force for local churches to reform themselves now, in the image of Volf's nonhierarchical Trinity. This theological use of eschatology is tenuous because it can be loaded with subjective, postmodern interpretations, so that each local church ends up modeling itself after its own favorite theologian's particular emphases. However a forward-moving eschatological perspective can ensure that public worship and theology has a hope-filled future that is centered upon fellowship with the Triune God.

CONCLUSION

Our aim in the preceding chapters of this monograph has been to provide far more than a survey of Volf's five proposals in *AOL*, for the church to be contemplated as an image of the Trinity. In-depth theological analysis is offered at crucial junctures of each thesis put forward by Volf in an attempt to critically assess the validity of his proposal and the

---

13. Ibid., 100–102, 104, 128, 138–40, 181, 195–99, 203, 235, 266–69.
14. Volf, "After Moltmann," 233–57.
15. Vos, *Biblical Theology*, 299.
16. Bauckham, "Eschatology," 33–34.

methodology that he employs. The first conclusion reached is that the church needs to recover the ecclesial symbol for "the church as an image of Christ and the Trinity." The danger in *AOL* is that Volf's proposal tends to magnify the Trinity, which could be at the expense of Christ, with Volf's metaphor for the church in relation to the Trinity only. Therefore we suggest the adoption of a Christo-Trinitarian hermeneutic that seeks to ensure that Christ is the theological starting point, but the ultimate goal is the worship of the Triune God.

The first proposal that Volf suggests is for "The Ecclesiality of the Church," and he puts forward that Free Church ecclesiology revolves around the significance of Matt 18:20. Indeed this single Bible verse was pivotal in the theology of Smyth and the English Separatists; however Volf's construct of the church based primarily on this single text causes him to endorse an extremely fragile ecclesiology. Additionally his construct for the church is built upon subjective assumptions, a notable absence of biblical exegesis, and the misuse of patristic sources. This chapter in *AOL* provides the springboard for the succeeding arguments in the rest of the thesis, and because the doctrine of the church is weak with limited supporting evidence it destabilizes the remainder of Volf's monograph.

Volf's second thesis, "Faith, Person and Church" handles the question, how is faith mediated in the church? He makes the corporate testimony of individuals in a local congregation the principal means by which faith is mediated, but he does not exclude other unusual means, such as charismatic experiences. Our analysis centers upon Paul's missionary method in Rom 10, and we conclude that the apostles placed the weight of responsibility upon the heralds of the gospel as the primary means of mediating faith. This does not minimize a dependence upon the direct work of the Holy Spirit, but it does minimize the way in which this is to happen through the church. This means that preaching is an oral event that is the preeminent designated method for the reception of faith, which is through the sense of hearing: "Faith comes by hearing . . . the Word of Christ" (Rom 10:17).

The next proposal "Trinity and Church" is most likely the crux of Volf's overall thesis. In this section, chapter 5 in *AOL* is where Volf's doctrine of the Trinity comes to its clearest expression, and it is found to rest upon three pillars: relational personhood, perichoretic personhood, and nonhierarchical relations among the persons. Upon close inspection it becomes apparent that Volf's social doctrine of the Trinity is an inverted pyramid: a mushroom of conclusions established on a narrow base of subjective presuppositions, speculations, and anthropological concerns for human identity and equality. Our conclusion is that the doctrine of the Trinity should be primarily applied to the church's worship, piety, and missionary message, not church structures, and it is in this field of ecclesiology that we should seek to develop a doctrine of the church from the Trinity.

This contrasts with the way that Volf applies the Trinity to the church, which he uses to buttress his template for a polycentric-participative charismatic church. This church model is founded upon Volf's interpretation of the charismatic activity supposedly at work in the Corinthian church, especially in relation to 1 Cor 12–14. There exists a rainbow of explanations among theologians to justify different meanings of spiritual gifts, and this element alone makes Volf's case difficult to establish. The exercise of charismatic gifts continues to be a controversial subject, and Volf's important attempt to design a "church as the image of the Trinity" becomes somewhat lost in the plethora of debate surrounding Corinthian disorder in public worship.

Exegetical and historical studies do not justify Volf's flattened participative model for public worship, but this should not discourage other attempts to connect the Trinity to the activity that takes place in the public worship of local churches. Walter Kasper agrees, and he writes:

> Thus the doctrine of God and the Trinity gives rise to perspectives which by no means have yet been taken to their logical, ontological, ecclesiological and practical conclusion. Thought on the doctrine of God and the Trinity as the sum of all theology still represents a big challenge and an unfulfilled and rewarding task.
>
> So it is time to speak of God, to testify and think about God. If theology wishes to gain a hearing among the contemporary pluralist Babel of voices and opinions, it must fully and above all know what it is. It can only have relevance, if it steadfastly maintains its own identity.[17]

Similarly Johannes Hoff points ecclesiologists in the right direction as he asserts that our vision of God is to be considered in "doxological and liturgical terms."[18]

---

17. Kasper, "Timeliness of Speaking," 310–11.
18. Hoff, "Self-Revelation as Hermeneutic Principle."

15

Conclusion

A RESURGENCE OF TRINITARIAN interest gained momentum in the twentieth century, and it is showing little sign of abating in the twenty-first century. This research endeavors to critically evaluate Volf's ecclesial model for "the church as the image of the Trinity," which he presents with the English title, *After Our Likeness*. This work is a translation of his original German thesis called *Trinität und Gemeinschaft: Eine ökumenische Ekklesiologie* (Trinity and Communion: An Ecumenical Ecclesiology), and this title probably more accurately reflects Volf's intention in his thesis, as compared with the publisher's title in English for *AOL*.

We have sought in chapter 4 to define the theological paradigm of Volf in specific relation to *AOL*. This yields a series of significant conclusions. Moltmann's theology is quite clearly seen to be the primary influence upon Volf's thinking, and there are eight presuppositions that undergird Volf's Trinitarian and ecclesial paradigm. These are: a nonhierarchical doctrine of the Trinity, a communal and egalitarian ecclesiology, the existence of a direct relationship between the Trinity and the church, a rejection of ecclesial individualism and hierarchical holism in favor of ecclesial sociality, the endorsement of feminist ecclesiologies and women's ordination, an ecumenical approach, the missiological value of his study, and a perceived need for a model that engages with the catholicity of the church.

The starting point and foundation for Volf's theological modeling is an anthropological concern for identity. This pursuit for human identity becomes an all-controlling interpretive window through which all of his theology is projected. His particular understanding of a social Trinity informs his conception for a nonhierarchical Free Church, and he anticipates an ecclesial reconstruction that is moving towards the eschatological goal of an egalitarian new creation.

The theology and work of John Smyth is his chosen ecclesial representative, and "Smyth's voice" is a thread that runs throughout *AOL*. This research has attempted the arduous task of examining the English Separatist movement, out of which Smyth came, to see if he can be described as the predominant Free Church father, which Volf assumes that he is. While Smyth displays continuity with his fellow English Separatist leaders on a number of fronts, he also demonstrates significant discontinuity with that movement. If there is one consistent mark of Smyth's theology and ecclesiology, it is an evolutionary development in his doctrine and practice.

It has been advanced that the Achilles' heel of Volf's use of Smyth is that he makes no reference to these evolutionary changes that occurred in most aspects of his theology and ecclesiology. Smyth becomes a launching pad to support Volf's own proposals, but the theological snapshots that he presents of his chosen ecclesial representative fail to capture the whole panorama of Smyth's ever-changing theology. However there are many valuable lessons on the doctrine of the church that can be gleaned from Smyth's life and his writings. Additionally, any researcher that desires to comprehend the ecclesiology of Volf and indeed the Free Church would benefit in a myriad of ways by grasping the theological reasoning employed by this unusual and indeed radical Baptist pioneer.

In chapter 6, 7, 8, and 9 we switch gears to engage directly with part 1 of *AOL*; this is a critical evaluation of Volf's dialogue with Ratzinger and Zizioulas. Volf consciously and persistently rejects every vestige of hierarchy in the doctrines of the Trinity and the ecclesiologies of these two dialogue partners. In many ways Volf handles his assessment with Ratzinger more intensely than with Zizioulas, and it becomes evident that he disagrees with the former on almost every point.

Volf fails to recognize that Ratzinger gives equal priority to the one substance of God and the relatedness of persons; this leads Volf to overemphasize the priority that Ratzinger gives to the one substance in God. Similarly Volf does not seem to pick up that Ratzinger's ecclesiology and especially the RCC pattern for ministry is driven primarily by

Christology. Volf repeatedly insists that the Trinity holds explanatory significance for Ratzinger's ecclesiology. While this is true for Zizioulas and Volf, the same cannot be said of Ratzinger; however Ratzinger's theology is a united and consistent whole, and the doctrine of the Trinity forms part of this harmonious whole. There is an additional oversight by Volf because he does not actively seek to bring out a range of valuable lessons from Ratzinger's theology in order that we can all better understand how "the church is the image of the Trinity."

As for Zizioulas, his neopatristic synthesis makes much for explicit connections between the church and the Trinity, and along the same vein as Volf, Zizioulas sees that the Trinity is the interpretative lens to understand the church. Zizioulas's Orthodox ecclesiology is eucharistic with an apostolic succession based on all the apostles and not just Peter as in the RCC. This doctrine of the Trinity is founded upon the concepts for monarchy, communion, and hierarchical order among the three persons. This leads him to openly rebut the Moltmann theological school of thought (of which Volf belongs) because they reject any notion for hierarchy in God, the church, or society.

Volf's own ecclesiology deals almost exclusively with the notion of the local church, and he fails to adequately respond to the clear framework offered by Zizioulas, where equal ultimacy is upheld for the universal and local church. There is a larger measure of agreement between Volf and Zizioulas than there is between Volf and Ratzinger. The areas of agreement include their mutual appreciation for the ecclesial metaphor for "the church as the image of the Trinity," their consent that there exists clear paradigmatic differences between Eastern and Western constructions of the Trinity, and their anticipation that the doctrine of the Trinity always has explanatory significance for ecclesiology.

While Volf freely acknowledges that there is a difference between the construal of the Trinity between East and West, we investigate a key question: is Volf's "social trinity" a departure from both the Eastern and Western conceptions of the trinity? We conclude that Volf's (and Moltmann's) social doctrine of the Trinity exhibits a departure from both Eastern and Western understandings of the Trinity, the Reformers, historic creeds, and the church fathers. The consequent result is that Volf's newly conceived doctrine of the Trinity remains remarkably isolated from the majority of Christendom, and it is still far from being compatible with the broader scholarly consent.

Our research continues in chapter 10 to 14 by interacting directly with Volf's presentation of his five theses for the church that are presented in *AOL* (chapters 3 to 7). One conclusion reached is that the church needs to recover the ecclesial symbol for "the church as an image of Christ and the Trinity." The danger in *AOL* is that Volf's proposal tends to magnify the Trinity, which could be at the expense of Christ, with his metaphor for the church in relation to the Trinity only. Therefore we suggest the adoption of a Christo-Trinitarian hermeneutic that seeks to ensure that Christ is the theological starting point, but the ultimate goal is the worship of the Triune God.

The first proposal that Volf suggests is for "The Ecclesiality of the Church," and he puts forward a Free Church ecclesiology that revolves around the significance of Matt 18:20. However Volf's construct of the church based primarily on this single text causes him to endorse an extremely fragile ecclesiology. Additionally his construct for the church is built upon subjective assumptions, a notable absence of biblical exegesis, and the misuse of patristic sources. This chapter in *AOL* provides the springboard for the succeeding arguments in the rest of Volf's thesis, and because the doctrine of the church is weak with limited supporting evidence it destabilizes the remainder of Volf's monograph.

Volf's second thesis, "Faith, Person and Church" handles the question, how is faith mediated in the church? He makes the corporate testimony of individuals in a local congregation to be the principal means by which faith is mediated, but he does not exclude other unusual means, such as charismatic experiences. Our analysis centers upon Paul's missionary method in Rom 10, and we conclude that the apostle placed the weight of responsibility upon authorized heralds of the gospel as the primary means of communicating the content of the faith and not the whole congregation as Volf suggests. This pattern and method exemplified and taught by the apostle Paul differs markedly from the way Volf envisages that faith is to be mediated.

Volf's next proposal "Trinity and Church" is most likely the crux of his overall monograph. This section (chapter 5 in *AOL*) is where Volf's doctrine of the Trinity comes to its clearest expression, and it is found to rest upon three pillars: relational personhood, perichoretic personhood, and nonhierarchical relations among the Trinitarian persons. Upon close inspection it becomes apparent that Volf's social doctrine of the Trinity is an inverted pyramid: a mushroom of conclusions established on a narrow base of subjective presuppositions, speculations, and anthropological concerns for human identity and equality. Our conclusion is that the doctrine of the Trinity is to be applied to the church's worship, piety, and missionary message, and it is in this field of ecclesiology that we should seek to develop a doctrine of the church from the Trinity.

This contrasts with the way that Volf applies the Trinity to the church, which is used largely to buttress his template for a polycentric-participative charismatic church. This church model is founded upon Volf's interpretation of the charismatic activity supposedly at work in the Corinthian church, especially in relation to 1 Cor 12–14. There exists a rainbow of explanations among theologians to justify different meanings of spiritual gifts, and this element alone makes Volf's case difficult to establish.

It is here put forward that the new covenant name of God is "the Father, the Son and the Holy Spirit," and that this is revealed by Jesus in Matt 28:19. This Trinitarian motif should inform everything that the church says, and does, in relation to God. A Christo-Trinitarian hermeneutic is needed, and there should be a circular movement between the doctrine of God and the doctrine of Christ as mediator. A Trinitarian-christological motif is therefore understood to be the guiding principle for every stage of the church's liturgy and public worship.

The church's public worship is the arena that should be most obviously enriched and informed by our suggested Trinity–Christ as mediator connective. Letham emphatically contends that the Trinity has been neglected in the Western church and that this has led to a spiritual impoverishment because he states: "Since theology and worship are integrally connected, as the Fathers taught, this is a serious problem."[1] This Trinitarian neglect means that there is the need for an ongoing task to ground the church in its ontological foundation—the Triune God—while guarding against this doctrine being wrongly applied to political theology, economics, or the affirmation of nonhierarchical church models.

The Trinity should be expounded as something that is central to the church's faith and worship because God is revealed as Triune through Christ's incarnation. This is an established dogma approved by the church fathers and the creeds because the whole divine economy is the work of the three divine persons. Gregory of Nazianzus agrees, and he

---

1. Letham, Holy Trinity, 407–24, 410, 410n9.

declares: "One God; one in diversity, diverse in unity."[2] Therefore the divine work is understood as a Trinitarian mission from beginning to end. Gregory of Nazianzus confirms this teaching on the Trinity, where he proclaims:

> Above all guard for me this great deposit of faith for which I live and fight, which I want to take with me as a companion, and which makes me bear all evils and despise all pleasures: I mean the profession of faith in the Father and the Son and the Holy Spirit. I entrust it to you today.[3]

In all of the enthusiasm to recover the much neglected doctrine of the Trinity, Volf provides a timely and valuable caution because he loses sight of Christology in his pursuit of a church to reflect the Trinity. Molnar succinctly describes this contemporary phenomena, and he writes:

> Theology needs to begin and end its task with Jesus Christ as the revelation of God in history. Any other starting point will mean a self-chosen one and thus one that stands in conflict with God's freedom for us exercised in Christ. This is where Trinitarian theology is important. A theology of the Trinity recognises who God is who meets us in Christ and then thinks about various contemporary issues and problems in the light of the relation between creator and creatures reconciled by God in Christ . . . Jesus Christ himself . . . the starting point and norm for theology.[4]

Paul reminded Timothy that "there is one mediator between God and men, the man Christ Jesus" (1 Tim 2:5). Let us ensure that any fresh appreciation of the Trinity does not obscure the glory of Christ, the Second Person of the Trinity.

---

2. Gregory of Nazianzus, "Orations: Against the Eunomians," NPNF, 2.28.1, 288.
3. Gregory of Nazianzus, "Orations," 40–41, NPNF, vol. 3, 417; CCC, 1.2.1.2.4, 61.
4. Molnar, Divine Freedom, 25.

Appendix

Suggested Reading

BIOGRAPHICAL INFORMATION ON MAXIMUS THE CONFESSOR

Letham, Robert. *Through Western Eyes: Eastern Orthodoxy; A Reformed Perspective*. Fearn, Ross-shire, UK: Christian Focus, 2007.

Louth, Andrew. *Maximus the Confessor*. Abingdon, UK: Routledge, 2006.

BIOGRAPHICAL INFORMATION ON JOHN SMYTH

Brachlow, Stephen. *The Communion of Saints: Radical Puritan and Separatist Ecclesiology, 1570–1625*. Oxford: Oxford University Press, 1988.

Burgess, Walter H. *John Smyth the Se-Baptist, Thomas Helwys and the First Baptist Church in England*. London: James Clarke, 1911.

Dexter, Henry Martyn. *The True Story of John Smyth: The Se-Baptist*. Boston: Lee and Shepard, 1881.

Lee, Jason K. *The Theology of John Smyth: Puritan, Separatist, Baptist, Mennonite*. Macon, GA: Mercer University Press, 2003.

White, B. R. "John Smyth's Re-Modelled Separatism." In *The English Baptists of the Seventeenth Century*. Didcot: Baptist Historical Society, 1996.

Whitely, W. T. "Biography of John Smyth." In *The Works of John Smyth*, vol. 1 and 2. Cambridge: Cambridge University Press, 1915.

ENGLISH CHURCH REFORM

Bremer, Francis J. *The Puritan Experiment: New England Society from Bradford to Edwards*. Basingstoke, UK: Palgrave Macmillan, 1976.

Collinson, Patrick. *The Elizabethan Puritan Movement*. Wotton-Under-Edge, UK: Clarendon, 1967. Reprinted in 1990.

Hall, Basil. "Puritanism: The Problem of Definition." In *Studies in Church History*, vol. 2, edited by G. J. Cunning. Nashville: Nelson, 1965.

Lunn, Nick. "Laurence Chadderton: Puritan, Scholar, and Bible Translator." *Banner Magazine*, June 2008.

Packer, J. I. *Among God's Giants*. Eastbourne, UK: Kingsway, 1991. Reprinted in 2000.

Pearse, Meic. *The Great Restoration*. Carlisle: Paternoster, 1998.

MIROSLAV VOLF'S REFERENCES TO JOSEPH RATZINGER ON THE TRINITY AND THE CHURCH

Ratzinger, Joseph. *Church, Ecumenism and Politics: New Endeavours in Ecclesiology*. Translated by Michael J. Miller et al. San Francisco: Ignatius, 2008.

———. *Die Christliche Bruderlichkeit*. Munich: Kösel, 1960.

———. *Introduction to Christianity*. Translated by J. R. Foster. London: Search Press, 1971.

———. "Kirche II, III." *Lexikon für Theologie und Kirche*, 6 (1957–67) 172–83.

———. *Theologische Prinzipienlehre: Bausteine zur Fundamentaltheologie*. Munich: Erich Wewel, 1982.

JOSEPH RATZINGER'S REFERENCES TO AUGUSTINE ON THE TRINITY

Augustine. *Homilies on the Gospel of John*. Edited by Philip Schaff. Vol. 7 of *Nicene and Post-Nicene Fathers*. Peabody, MA: Hendrickson, 1995.

Augustine. *On the Holy Trinity: Doctrinal Treatises, Moral Treatises*. Edited by Philip Schaff. Vol 3. of *Nicene and Post-Nicene Fathers*. Peabody, MA: Hendrickson, 1995.

Augustine. "Psalm 69." In *Expositions on the Book of Psalms*. Edited by Philip Schaff. Vol. 8 of *Nicene and Post-Nicene Fathers*. Peabody, MA: Hendrickson, 1995.

HEIRARCHY, ORDER, AND SUBORDINATION IN THE TRINITY

Giles, Kevin. "The Evangelical Theological Society and the Doctrine of the Trinity" and "Rejoinder to Robert Letham." *Evangelical Quarterly* 80, no. 4 (2008) 323–38, 347–48.

———. *Jesus and the Father: Modern Evangelicals Reinvent the Doctrine of the Trinity*. Grand Rapids, MI: Zondervan, 2006.

———. *The Trinity and Subordinationism: The Doctrine of God and the Contemporary Gender Debate*. Downers Grove, IL: IVP, 2002.

Letham, Robert. "Kevin Giles on Subordinationism." In *The Holy Trinity: In Scripture, History, Theology and Worship*, pp. 489–96. Phillipsburg: P&R, 2004.

———. "Reply to Kevin Giles" and "Surrejoinder to Kevin Giles." *Evangelical Quarterly* 80, no. 4 (2008) 339–45, 348.

THE ZIZIOULAS SCHOOL

Gunton, Colin E. *Act and Being*. London: SCM, 2002.

———. "The Church: John Owen and John Zizioulas on the Church." In *Theology through the Theologians: Selected Essays, 1972–1995*. Edinburgh: T&T Clark, 1996.

———. "Eastern and Western Trinities: Being and Person in T. F. Torrance's Doctrine of God." In *Father, Son and Holy Spirit: Essays toward a Fully Trinitarian Theology*. London: T&T Clark, 2003.

———. "God, Grace and Freedom." In *God and Freedom: Essays in Historical and Systematic Theology*, Edinburgh: T&T Clark, 1995.

———. "Immanence and Otherness: Divine Sovereignty and Human Freedom in the Theology of Robert W. Jenson." In *Promise of Trinitarian Theology*, pp. 122–41. Edinburgh: T&T Clark, 1991.

———. *Promise of Trinitarian Theology*. Edinburgh: T&T Clark, 1991.

———. "Trinity, Ontology and Anthropology: Towards a Renewal of the Doctrine of *Imago Dei*." In *Persons, Divine and Human: King's College Essays in Theological Anthropology*, edited by Christoph Schwöbel and Colin E. Gunton. Edinburgh: T&T Clark, 1991.

Jenson, Robert W. "An Ontology of Freedom in the *De Servo Arbitrio* of Luther." *Modern Theology*, 10 (1994) 247–52.

———. *Triune God*. Vol. 1 of *Systematic Theology*. Oxford: Oxford University Press, 2001.

Schwöbel, Christoph. "The Quest for Communion: Reasons, Reflections and Recommendations." In *The Church as Communion: Lutheran*

Contributions to Ecclesiology (LWF Documentation No. 42), edited by H. Holze. Geneva: Lutheran World Foundation, 1997.

———. *Trinitarian Theology Today: Essays in Divine Being and Act*. Edinburgh: T&T Clark, 1995.

Bibliography

Abbott, Walter M., ed. *The Documents of Vatican II*. Translated by Joseph Gallagher. London: Geoffrey Chapman, 1965. Reprinted in 1967.
Afanasiev (Afanassieff), Nicholas. "The Church Which Presides in Love." In *The Primacy of Peter*, edited by John Meyendorff et al. London: Faith Press, 1963.
———. "L'Eglise de Dieu dans Le Christ." In *La Pensée Orthodoxe*, vol. 13. Paris: Le CNRS, 1968.
———. "Statio Orbis." *Irénikon* 35 (1962) 65–75.
Ainsworth, Henry, and Johnson, Francis. "An Apology or Defence of Such True Christians as Are Commonly (but Unjustly) Called Brownists," Amsterdam, 1604. In *The Communion of Saints: Radical Puritan and Separatist Ecclesiology, 1570–1625*, by Stephen Brachlow. Oxford: Oxford University Press, 1988.
Alighieri, Dante. *The Divine Comedy: Paradiso*. Translated by Allen Mandelbaum. New York: Knopf, 1995.
Anglican Consultative Council. *The Church of the Triune God: The Cyprus Statement Agreed by the International Commission for Anglican–Orthodox Theological Dialogue 2006*. London: Anglican Communion Office, 2006.
Antiochian Orthodox Christian Archdiocese of North America. *Service Book of the Holy Eastern Orthodox Catholic and Apostolic Church*. 9th edition. Englewood, NJ: Antiochian Orthodox Christian Archdiocese of North America, 1971.
Argyle, A. W. *The Gospel according to Matthew*. Cambridge: Cambridge University Press, 1963. Reprinted in 1973.
Association of Evangelical Lutheran Churches. *Baptism, Eucharist and Ministry*. St. Louis: Association of Evangelical Lutheran Churches, 1982.
Athanasius. *Select Writings and Letters*. Edited by Philip Schaff and Henry Wace. Vol. 4 of *Nicene and Post-Nicene Fathers*. Peabody, MA: Hendrickson, 1995.
Augustine. *Nicene and Post-Nicene Fathers*, vol. 2, 3, 4, 7, 8. Edited by Philip Schaff. Peabody, MA: Hendrickson, 1995.
Ayres, Lewis. *Nicaea and Its Legacy: An Approach to Fourth-Century Trinitarian Theology*. Oxford: Oxford University Press, 2006.
Balthasar, Hans Urs von. *Credo: Meditations on the Apostles' Creed*. Translated by David Kepp. San Francisco: Ignatius, 1990.
———. *Epilogue*. Translated by Edward T. Oakes. San Francisco: Ignatius, 2004.
———. *Mysterium Pascale: The Mystery of Easter*. San Francisco: Ignatius, 2000.
———. *Theo-Drama*, vol. 1–4. San Francisco: Ignatius, 1988.

Bannerman, James. *The Church of Christ: A Treatise on the Nature, Powers, Ordinances, Discipline and Government of the Christian Church.* Vol. 1. Edinburgh: Banner of Truth, 1869. Reprinted in 1974.

Barnes, Michel René. "De Régnon Reconsidered." *Augustinian Studies* 26 (1995) 51–79.

———. "Rereading Augustine on the Trinity." In *The Trinity: An Interdisciplinary Symposium on the Trinity*, edited by Stephen T. Davies, Daniel Kendall, and Gerald O'Collins. Oxford: Oxford University Press, 1999.

Barrett, C. K. *Commentary on the First Epistle to the Corinthians.* London: Black, 1968.

———. *The Epistle to the Romans.* 2nd edition. London: Black, 1991.

Barth, Karl. *Church Dogmatics.* Edited by G. W. Bromiley and T. F. Torrance. Edinburgh: T&T Clark, 1975.

Basil of Caesarea. *Letters and Selected Works.* Edited by Philip Schaff and Henry Wace. Vol. 8 of *Nicene and Post-Nicene Fathers.* Peabody, MA: Hendrickson, 1995.

Bauckham, Richard. "Eschatology in the Coming of God." In *God Will Be All in All: The Eschatology of Jürgen Moltmann*, edited by Richard Bauckham. Edinburgh: T&T Clark, 1999.

———. *The Theology of Jürgen Moltmann.* Edinburgh: T&T Clark, 1995.

Bavinck, Herman. *Holy Spirit, Church, and New Creation.* Vol. 4 of *Reformed Dogmatics.* Edited by John Bolt. Grand Rapids, MI: Baker, 2008.

Beale, G. K. *1–2 Thessalonians.* Leicester: IVP, 2003.

Beale, G. K., and Carson, D. A., eds. *Commentary on the New Testament Use of the Old Testament.* Grand Rapids, MI: Baker, 2007.

Behr, John. "The Trinitarian Being of the Church." *St. Vladimir's Theological Quarterly* 48, no. 1 (2003) 67–88.

Benedict XVI. "The Eucharistic Celebration, the Work of 'Christus Totus.'" In *Post-Synodal Exhortation On the Eucharist as the Source and Summit of the Church's Life and Mission. Sacramentum Caritatis.* March 13, 2007. Catholic Liturgical Library. http://www.catholicliturgy.com/index.cfm/FuseAction/documentText/Index/14/SubIndex/o/ContentIndex/573/Start/557

Berkhof, Louis. *Systematic Theology.* Edinburgh: Banner of Truth, 1958. Reprinted in 2005.

Berkouwer, G. C. *The Church.* Grand Rapids, MI: Eerdmans, 1976.

Bidwell, Kevin J. "The Church's Diaconal Ministry and the Triune God." MTh dissertation, Wales Evangelical School of Theology, 2007.

Bobrinskoy, Boris. *Le Mystère de la Trinité: Cours de Théologie orthodoxe.* Paris: Cerf, 1986.

———. "Le Saint-Esprit dans la liturgie." *Studia Liturgia* 1, no. 1 (1962) 47–60.

Bonhoeffer, Dietrich. *Sanctorum Communio: A Theological Study of the Sociology of the Church.* Edited by Clifford J. Green. Minneapolis: Augsburg Fortress, 2009.

Brachlow, Stephen. *The Communion of Saints: Radical Puritan and Separatist Ecclesiology, 1570–1625.* Oxford: Oxford University Press, 1988.

———. "John Smyth and the Ghost of Anabaptism: A Rejoinder." *Baptist Quarterly* 30, no. 7 (1984) 296–300.

———. "More Light on John Robinson and the Separatist Tradition." *Fides et Historia* 13 (1980) 6–22.

Bray, Gerald. *The Doctrine of God.* Leicester: IVP, 1993.

British Council of Churches. *British and Irish Churches Respond to BEM.* London: British Council of Churches, 1988.

———. *The Forgotten Trinity: The Report of the BCC Study Commission on Trinitarian Doctrine Today*. London: British Council of Churches, 1989.
Bruce, F. F. *The Epistle of Paul to the Galatians: A Commentary on the Greek Text*. Exeter: Paternoster, 1982.
Burgess, Walter H. *John Smyth the Se-Baptist, Thomas Helwys and the First Baptist Church in England*. London: James Clarke, 1911.
Burrage, Champlin. *The Early English Dissenters (In the Light of Recent Research) 1550–1641*, vol. 1. Cambridge: Cambridge University Press, 1912.
Butin, Philip Walker. *Revelation, Redemption and Response: Calvin's Trinitarian Understanding of the Divine–Human Relationship*. New York: Oxford University Press, 1995.
Calvin, John. *Commentary on 1 and 2 Corinthians*. Vol. 20 of *Calvin's Commentaries*. Grand Rapids, MI: Baker, 2005.
———. *Commentary on the Book of Psalms*. Vol. 4, 5, 6 of *Calvin's Commentaries*. Grand Rapids, MI: Baker, 2005.
———. *Harmony of Matthew, Mark and Luke*. Vol. 16 of *Calvin's Commentaries*. Grand Rapids, MI: Baker, 2005.
———. *Institutes of the Christian Religion*, vol. 1 and 2. Edited by John T. McNeill. Louisville: Westminster John Knox Press, 1960. Reprinted in 2006.
———. "Regarding the Name of God and Its Use in Prayer." In *Calvin's Ecclesiastical Advice*, translated by Mary Beaty and Benjamin W. Farley. Edinburgh: T&T Clark, 1991.
———. "Reply by John Calvin to Letter by Cardinal Sadolet to the Senate and People of Geneva." In *John Calvin: Tracts and Letters*, vol. 1, edited and translated by Henry Beveridge. Edinburgh: Banner of Truth Trust, 2009.
———. *Tracts and Letters*, vol. 1 and 3, edited and translated by Henry Beveridge. Edinburgh: Banner of Truth, 2009.
Carson, D. A. "Matthew." In *The Expositors Bible Commentary*, edited by Frank E. Gæbelein. Grand Rapids, MI: Zondervan, 1984.
———. *Showing the Spirit: A Theological Exposition of 1 Corinthians 12–14*. Grand Rapids, MI: Baker, 1987.
Chandler, Russell. *Racing toward 2001: The Forces Shaping America's Religious Future*. Grand Rapids, MI: Zondervan, 1992.
Christenson, Torben. *A Study in F. D. Maurice's Theology*. Leiden, Netherlands: Brill, 1973.
Christo, Gus George. *The Church's Identity: Established through Images according to Saint John Chrysostom*. Rollinsford, NH: Orthodox Research Institute, 2006.
Clark, R. Scott. *Recovering the Reformed Confession: Our Theology, Piety and Practice*. Phillipsburg, NJ: P&R, 2008.
Clement of Rome. "The First Epistle of Clement to the Corinthians." In *Ante-Nicene Fathers*, vol. 1, edited by Alexander Roberts and James Donaldson. Peabody, MA: Hendrickson, 1995.
Clowney, Edmund P. *The Church*. Leicester: IVP, 1995.
Coakley, Sarah. "Introduction: Gender, Trinitarian Analogies, and the Pedagogy of the Song." In *Re-thinking Gregory of Nyssa*, edited by Sarah Coakley. Oxford: Blackwell, 2003.
Coffey, John. *John Goodwin and the Puritan Revolution: Religion and Intellectual Change in Seventeenth-Century England*. Woodbridge, UK: Boydell Press, 2006.

Coggins, James R. "The Theological Positions of John Smyth." *Baptist Quarterly* 30 (April 1984) 247–64.

Cole, Alan. *The Body of Christ: A New Testament Image of the Church.* London: Hodder and Stoughton, 1964.

Collinson, Patrick. "Towards a Broader Understanding of the Early Dissenting Tradition." In *Godly People: Essays in English Protestantism and Puritanism.* London: Hambledon, 1983.

Conzelmann, Hans. *1 Corinthians.* Minneapolis: Augsburg Fortress, 1975.

Cooper, Adam G. *The Body in St. Maximus the Confessor: Holy Flesh, Wholly Deified.* Oxford: Oxford University Press, 2005.

Coxe, A. Cleveland. "Introductory Note to the First Epistle of Clement to the Corinthians." In *Ante-Nicene Fathers*, vol. 1, edited by Philip Schaff and Henry Wace. Peabody, MA: Hendrickson, 1995.

Cyprian. *Fathers of the Third Century: Hippolytus, Cyprian, Caius, Novatian.* Edited by James Alexander and James Donaldson. Vol. 5 of *Ante-Nicene Fathers.* Peabody, MA: Hendrickson, 1995.

———. "On the Unity of the Church, 12." In *Fathers of the Third Century: Hippolytus, Cyprian, Caius, Novatian.* Vol. 5 of *Ante-Nicene Fathers.* Christian Classics Etheral Library. http://www.ccel.org/ccel/schaff/anf05.iv.v.i.html.

———. "Liber de Oratione Dominica," 23. In *Patrologia Latina*, edited by Jacques-Paul Migne. Patrologia Latina Database. http://pld.chadwyck.com/.

Dalferth, Ingolf U., and Jüngel, Eberhard. "Person und Gottebenbildlichkeit." In *Christlicher Glaube in moderner Gesellschaft*, vol. 24, edited by F. Bröckle et al. Freiburg: Herder, 1981.

Daly, Mary. *Beyond God the Father: Toward a Philosophy of Women's Liberation.* London: Women's Press, 1973. Reprinted in 1991.

Davies, Gwyn. *Covenanting with God.* Bryntirion: Evangelical Library of Wales, 1994.

Davies, W. D., and Allison, Dale C. *Matthew: A Shorter Commentary.* London: T&T Clark, 2004.

de Halleux, André. *Patrologie et Oeuménisme: Receuil D'Études.* Leuven: Leuven University Press, 1990.

de Lubac, Henri. *Christian Faith: The Structure of the Apostles Creed.* Translated by Illtyd Trethowan and John Saward. London: Geoffrey Chapman, 1986.

———. *Corpus Mysticum: The Eucharist and the Church in the Middle Ages.* Translated by Gemma Simonds. London: SCM, 2006.

Denzin, Norman K., and Lincoln, Yvonna S., eds. *The Sage Handbook of Qualitative Research.* 3rd edition. London: Sage, 2005.

de Régnon, Theodore. *Études de théologie positive sur la sainté Trinité.* Vol. 1. Paris: Victor Retaux et fils, 1892.

Dexter, Henry Martyn. *The Congregationalism of the Last Three Hundred Years.* London: Hodder and Stoughton, 1880.

———. *The True Story of John Smyth: The Se-Baptist.* Boston: Lee and Shepard, 1881.

Doney, Simon. "The Lordship of Christ in the Theology of the Elizabethan Separatists with Particular Reference to Henry Barrow." PhD thesis, Lampeter, University of Wales, 2005.

Dulles, Avery. *Models of the Church.* New York: Doubleday, 1978. Reprinted in 2002.

Dunn, James D. G. *1 Corinthians.* Sheffield: Sheffield Academic Press, 1995.

———. *Romans 9–16.* Vol. 38 of *Word Biblical Commentary.* Dallas: Word Books, 1988.

Edgar, William. "Justification and Violence: Reflections on Atonement and Contemporary Apologetics." In *Justified in Christ: God's Plan for Us in Justification*, edited by K. Scott Oliphint. Fearn, Ross-shire, UK: Christian Focus, 2007.
Eusebius. *Church History from A.D. 1–324, Life of Constantine the Great, Oration in Praise of Constantine*. Edited by Philip Schaff and Henry Wace. Vol. 1 of *Nicene and Post-Nicene Fathers*. Peabody, MA: Hendrickson, 1995.
Eyt, Pierre. "Überlegungen von Pierre Yet." In *Die Krise der Kathechese und ihre Überwindung*, by Joseph Ratzinger, translated by Hans Urs von Balthasar. Einsiedeln: Johannes, 1983.
Fee, Gordon D. *The First Epistle to the Corinthians*. Grand Rapids, MI: Eerdmans, 1987.
Fox, Patricia A. *God as Communion: John Zizioulas, Elizabeth Johnson, and the Retrieval of the Symbol of the Triune God*. Collegeville, MN: Liturgical Press, 2001.
France, R. T. *Matthew: Evangelist and Teacher*. Exeter: Paternoster, 1989.
Gee, Donald. *Concerning Spiritual Gifts*. Springfield: Gospel, 1972.
George, Timothy. *John Robinson and the English Separatist Tradition*. Macon, GA: Mercer University Press, 1982.
Giles, Kevin. "The Evangelical Theological Society and the Doctrine of the Trinity" and "Rejoinder to Robert Letham." *Evangelical Quarterly* 80, no. 4 (2008) 323–38, 347–48.
———. *Jesus and the Father: Modern Evangelicals Reinvent the Doctrine of the Trinity*. Grand Rapids, MI: Zondervan, 2006.
———. *The Trinity and Subordinationism: The Doctrine of God and the Contemporary Gender Debate*. Downers Grove, IL: IVP, 2002.
Gregory of Nazianzus. *Theodoret, Jerome and Gennadius, Rufinus and Jerome*. Edited by Philip Schaff and Henry Wace. Vol. 3 of *Nicene and Post-Nicene Fathers*. Peabody, MA: Hendrickson, 1995.
Gregory of Nyssa. *Dogmatic Treatises; Select Writings and Letters*. Edited by Philip Schaff and Henry Wace. Vol. 5 of *Nicene and Post-Nicene Fathers*. Peabody, MA: Hendrickson, 1995.
Grenz, Stanley. "Isaac Backus and the English Baptist Tradition." *Baptist Quarterly* 30, no. 5 (January 1984) 221–31.
———. *The Social God and the Relational Self*. Louisville: Westminster John Knox, 2007.
Grudem, Wayne. *Systematic Theology: An Introduction to Biblical Doctrine*. Leicester: IVP, 1994. Reprinted in 2005.
———. *The Gift of Prophecy in the New Testament Today*. Wheaton, IL: Crossway, 1988. Reprinted in 2000.
Guardini, Romano. *The Church and the Catholic, and the Spirit of the Liturgy*. London: Sheed and Ward, 1935.
Gutiérrez, Gustavo. *Theology of Liberation: History, Politics and Salvation*. Translated by Caridad Inda and John Eagelson. London: SCM, 1974. Reprinted in 2001.
Gundry, Robert, H. *Matthew: A Commentary on His Literary and Theological Art*. Grand Rapids, MI: Eerdmans, 1982.
———. "The New Jerusalem: People as Place, Not Place for People." *Novum Testamentum* 29 (1987) 54–64.
———. *Soma in Biblical Theology with Emphasis on Pauline Anthropology*. Society for New Testament Studies Monograph Series 29. Cambridge: Cambridge University Press, 1976.

Gundry-Volf, Judith M. "Gender and Creation in 1 Corinthians 11:2–16: A Study of Paul's Theological Method." In *Schriftauslegung—Evangelium—Kirche*, edited by Otfried Hofius et al. Göttingen: Vandenhoeck and Ruprecht, 1997.

———. "Gender Distinctives, Discrimination, and the Gospel." *Evangelical Review of Theology* 21, no. 1 (1997) 41–50.

———. Personal Profile. Yale Divinity School. http://www.yale.edu/divinity/faculty/Fac.JGundry-Volf.shtml.

———. "Spirit, Mercy and the Other." *Theology Today* 52 (1995) 508–523.

———. *To Tell the Mystery: Essays on New Testament Eschatology in Honour of Robert H. Gundry*. Edited by Moses Silva and Thomas E. Schmidt. Sheffield: JSOT, 1994.

———. *A Spacious Heart: Essays on Identity and Belonging*. Leominster: Gracewing, 1997.

Gunton, Colin E. *Act and Being*. London: SCM, 2002.

———. *Becoming and Being*. London: SCM, 1978. Reprinted in 2001.

———. *Father, Son and Holy Spirit: Essays toward a Fully Trinitarian Theology*. London: T&T Clark, 2003.

———. *God and Freedom: Essays in Historical and Systematic Theology*. Edinburgh: T&T Clark, 1995.

———. *The One, the Three and the Many: God, Creation and the Culture of Modernity*. Cambridge: Cambridge University Press, 1993. Reprinted in 1996.

———. *The Promise of Trinitarian Theology*. Edinburgh: T&T Clark, 1991.

———. *Theology through the Theologians: Selected Essays, 1972–1995*. Edinburgh: T&T Clark, 1996.

———. "Trinity, Ontology and Anthropology: Towards a Renewal of the Doctrine of *Imago Dei*." In *Persons, Divine and Human: King's College Essays in Theological Anthropology*, edited by Christoph Schwöbel and Colin E. Gunton. Edinburgh: T&T Clark, 1991.

Hagner, Donald A. *Matthew 14–28*. Vol. 33a and 33b of *Word Biblical Commentary*. Dallas: Word Books, 1995.

Hanson, R. P. C. *The Search for the Christian Doctrine of God: The Arian Controversy 318–81*. Edinburgh: T&T Clark, 1988.

Hart, David Bentley. "The Mirror of the Infinite: Gregory of Nyssa on the *Vestigia Trinitatis*." In *Re-thinking Gregory of Nyssa*, edited by Sarah Coakley. Oxford: Blackwell, 2003.

Hart, D. G., and Muether, John R. *With Reverence and Awe: Returning to the Basics of Reformed Worship*. Phillipsburg, PA: P&R, 2002.

Hayes, Zachery. Introduction to *Works of Saint Bonaventure III: Disputed Questions on the Mystery of the Trinity*. Ashland, OH: BookMasters, 1979.

Hendriksen, William. *The Gospel of Matthew*. Edinburgh: Banner of Truth, 1989.

Heppe, Heinrich. *Reformed Dogmatics: Set Out and Illustrated from the Sources*. Translated by G. T. Thompson. Grand Rapids, MI: Baker, 1950.

Hilary of Poitiers. *Hilary of Poitiers, John of Damascus*. Edited by Philip Schaff and Henry Wace. Vol. 9 of *Nicene and Post-Nicene Fathers*. Peabody, MA: Hendrickson, 1995.

Hill, William J. *The Three-Personed God: The Trinity as a Mystery of Salvation*. Washington DC: Catholic University of America Press, 1982.

Hodge, A. A. *Outlines of Theology*. Edinburgh: Banner of Truth, 1860. Reprinted in 1999.

Hoff, Johannes. "Self-revelation as Hermeneutic Principle? A Genealogical Analysis of the Rise and the Fall of the Kantian Paradigm of Modern Theology." In *The

Grandeur of Reason: Religion, Tradition and Universalism, edited by Connor Cunningham and Peter Candler. London: SCM, 2010.

Holmes, Peter R. *Trinity in Human Community: Exploring Congregational Life in the Image of the Social Trinity.* Carlisle: Paternoster, 2006.

Holmes, Stephen R. "Bad Systematics: Why Ecclesiology Should not be Derived from the Doctrine of the Trinity?" Paper presented at the *Rutherford Dogmatics Conference*, Rutherford House, Edinburgh, 2009.

———. "Three Versus One? Some Problems of Social Trinitarianism." *Journal of Reformed Theology* 3, no. 1 (2009) 77–89.

Hunsinger, George. "Review of Jürgen Moltmann: *The Trinity and the Kingdom of God.*" *Thomist* (1983) 129–39.

Husbands, Mark. "The Trinity Is Not Our Social Program: Volf, Gregory of Nyssa and Barth." In *Trinitarian Theology for the Church: Scripture, Community, Worship*, edited by Daniel J. Treier and David Lauber. Nottingham: IVP, 2009.

Ignatius. *The Apostolic Fathers with Justin Martyr and Irenaeus.* Edited by Alexander Roberts and James Donaldson. Vol. 1 of *Ante-Nicene Fathers*. Peabody, MA: Hendrickson, 1995.

Irenaeus. *The Apostolic Fathers with Justin Martyr and Irenaeus.* Edited by Alexander Roberts and James Donaldson. Vol. 1 of *Ante-Nicene Fathers*. Peabody, MA: Hendrickson, 1995.

Jansen, Henry. "Relationality and the Concept of God." Dissertation, Amsterdam, 1995, cited in *After Our Likeness: The Church as the Image of the Trinity*, by Miroslav Volf. Grand Rapids, MI: Eerdmans, 1998.

Jenson, Robert W. "Karl Barth." In *The Modern Theologians*, edited by D. F. Ford. Oxford: Blackwell, 1989, 1:42, cited in *Doctrines of the Trinity in Eastern and Western Theologies: A Study with Special Reference to K. Barth and V. Lossky*, by A. Laats. Frankfurt am Main: Peter Lang, 1999.

———. "An Ontology of Freedom in the *De Servo Arbitrio* of Luther." *Modern Theology* 10 (1994) 247–52.

———. *The Triune God.* Vol. 1 of *Systematic Theology*. Oxford: Oxford University Press, 2001.

———. *The Triune Identity: God according to the Gospel.* Philadelphia: Fortress, 1982.

Joest, Wilfried. *Ontologie der Person bei Luther.* Göttingen: Vandenhoeck and Ruprecht, 1967.

John of Damascus. *Hilary of Poitiers, John of Damascus.* Edited by Philip Schaff and Henry Wace. Vol. 9 of *Nicene and Post-Nicene Fathers*. Peabody, Massachusetts: Hendrickson, 1995.

Johnson, Elizabeth A. *She Who Is: The Mystery of God in Feminist Theological Discourse.* New York: Crossroad, 1993.

Jones, Serene. "The God Which Is Not One: Irigary and Barth on the Divine." In *Transfigurations: Theology and French Feminists*, edited by C. W. Maggie Kim et al. Minneapolis: Fortress, 1993.

Jue, Jeffrey K. "The Active Obedience of Christ and the Theology of the Westminster Standards: A Historical Investigation." In *Justified in Christ: God's Plan for Us in Justification*, edited by K. Scott Oliphint. Fearn, Ross-shire, UK: Christian Focus, 2007.

Jüngel, Eberhard. "Die Kirche als Sakrament?" In *Wertlose Wahrheit: Zur Identität und Relevanz des christlichen Glauben; Theologische Erörterungen III, Beiträge zur evangelischen Theologie*. Munich: Kaiser, 1990.

———. *God as the Mystery of the World*. Grand Rapids, MI: Eerdmans, 2008.

Kärkkäinen, Velli-Matti. *The Doctrine of God: A Global Introduction*. Grand Rapids, MI: Baker Academic, 2004.

———. *An Introduction to Ecclesiology: Ecumenical, Historical and Global Perspectives*. Downers Grove, IL: IVP, 2002.

———. *Trinity and Religious Pluralism: The Doctrine of the Trinity in Christian Theology of Religions*. Aldershot, UK: Ashgate, 2004.

———. *The Trinity: Global Perspectives*. Louisville: Westminster John Knox, 2007.

Kasper, Walter. "The Timeliness of Speaking of God's Freedom and Communion as Basic Concepts of Theology." *Worship* 83, no. 4 (2009) 293–311.

Kehl, Mehard. Introduction to *Credo: Meditations on the Apostles' Creed*, by Hans Urs von Balthasar, translated David Kepp. San Francisco: Ignatius, 1990.

Keith, John. "The Epistles of Clement." In *Ante-Nicene Fathers*, vol. 9, edited by Allan Menzies. Peabody, MA: Hendrickson, 1995.

Keller, Timothy. *The Reason for God: Belief in an Age of Scepticism*. London: Hodder and Stoughton, 2008.

Kelly, J. N. D. *Early Christian Creeds*. 3rd edition. London: Continuum, 2006.

———. *Early Christian Doctrines*. London: Black, 1962.

Kilby, Karen. "Perichoresis and Projection: Problems with Social Doctrines of the Trinity." *New Blackfriars* 81 (2000) 432–45.

Klaassen, Walter, ed. *Anabaptism in Outline: Selected Primary Sources*. Waterloo, Ontario: Herald, 1981.

Krieg, Robert A. "Kardinal Ratzinger, Max Scheler und eine Grundfrage der Christologie." In *Theologische Quartalschrift*. Tübingen: University of Tübingen Press, 1980.

Kuhn, Thomas S. *The Structure of Scientific Revolutions*. 3rd edition. Chicago: University of Chicago Press, 1996.

LaCugna, Catherine Mowry. "God in Communion with Us: The Trinity." In *Freeing Theology: The Essentials of Theology in Feminist Perspective*, edited Catherine Mowry LaCugna. San Francisco: Harper, 1993.

———. *God for Us: The Trinity and Christian Life*. Harper: San Francisco, 1991.

LaCugna, Catherine Mowry, and McDonnell, Killan. "Returning from 'The Far Country': Theses for a Contemporary Trinitarian Theology." *Scottish Journal of Theology* 41 (1988) 191–215.

Lake, Peter. *Moderate Puritans and the Elizabethan Church*. Cambridge: Cambridge University Press, 1982.

Lane, A. N. S. *John Calvin: Student of the Church Fathers*. Edinburgh: T&T Clark, 1999.

———. "Scripture, Tradition and Church: An Historical Survey." *Vox Evangelica* 9 (1975) 37–55.

Lapide, Pinchos, and Moltmann, Jürgen. *Jewish Monotheism and Christian Trinitarian Doctrine: A Dialogue by Pinchos Lapide and Jürgen Moltmann*. Translated by Leonard Swidler. Philadelphia: Fortress, 1981.

Lazareth, William H. *Growing Together in Baptism, Eucharist and Ministry: A Study Guide*. Geneva: World Council of Churches, 1984.

Ledegang, F. *Mysterium Ecclesiae: Image of the Church and Its Members in Origen*. Leuven: Leuven University Press, 2001.

Lee, Jason K. *The Theology of John Smyth: Puritan, Separatist, Baptist, Mennonite.* Macon, GA: Mercer University Press, 2003.
Letham, Robert. *The Holy Trinity: In Scripture, History, Theology, and Worship.* Phillipsburg, PA: P&R, 2004.
———. "John Owen's Doctrine of the Trinity and Its Significance for Today." In *Where Reason Fails: Papers Read at the 2006 Westminster Conference,* edited by John Harris. Mirfield: Westminster Conference, 2007.
———. "Reply to Kevin Giles" and "Surrejoinder to Kevin Giles." *Evangelical Quarterly* 80, no. 4 (2008) 339–45, 348.
———. *Through Western Eyes: Eastern Orthodoxy; A Reformed Perspective.* Fearn, Ross-shire, UK: Christian Focus, 2007.
———. "The Trinity between East and West." *Journal of Reformed Theology* 3, no. 1 (2009) 42–56.
———. *The Westminster Assembly: Reading Its Theology in Historical Context.* Phillipsburg, PA: P&R, 2009.
Lim, David. *Spiritual Gifts.* Springfield: Gospel Publishing, 1991.
Littell, Franklin. "The Periodisation of History." In *Continuity and Discontinuity in Church History,* edited by Timothy George and Francis Church. Leiden, 1979, cited in *The Communion of Saints: Radical Puritan and Separatist Ecclesiology, 1570–1625,* edited by Stephen Brachlow. Oxford: Oxford University Press, 1988.
Livingstone, E. A. *The Concise Oxford Dictionary of the Christian Church.* Oxford: Oxford University Press, 2000.
Lock, Charles. "The Space of Hospitality: On the Icon of the Trinity Ascribed to Andrei Rublev." *Sobornost* 30, no. 1 (2008) 21–53.
Lossky, Vladimir. *In the Image and Likeness of God.* Translated by John H. Erickson and Thomas E. Bird. London: Mowbrays, 1975.
———. *The Mystical Theology of the Eastern Church.* Translated by members of the Fellowship of St. Albans and St. Sergius. Cambridge: J. Clarke, 1957.
———. *Orthodox Theology: An Introduction.* New York: St. Vladimir's Seminary Press, 1980.
———. *The Vision of God.* Translated by Asheleigh Moorhouse. Clayton, WI: Faith Press, 1963.
Louth, Andrew. "The Ecclesiology of Saint Maximos the Confessor." *International Journal for the Study of the Christian Church* 4, no. 2 (2004) 109–120.
———. *Greek East and Latin West: The Church AD 681–1071.* New York: St. Valdimir's Press, 2008.
———. *St. John Damascene: Tradition and Originality in Byzantine Theology.* Oxford: Oxford University Press, 2002.
Luther, Martin. *Works of Luther.* Missouri: Concordia, 2002.
Mackennal, Alexander. *The Story of the English Separatists.* London: Congregational Union, 1893.
Macleod, Donald. *Priorities for the Church: Rediscovering Leadership and Vision in the Church.* Fearn, Ross-shire, UK: Christian Focus, 2003.
———. *Shared Life.* Fearn, Ross-shire, UK: Christian Focus, 1995. Reprinted in 2006.
Marshall, Bruce D. *Trinity and Truth.* Cambridge: Cambridge University Press, 2000.
Maximus the Confessor. *La Mystagogie.* Paris: Migne, 2005.
———. "Mystagogy." In *Selected Writings (Classics of Western Spirituality Series),* edited by George Berthold. Dublin: Paulist Press International, 2005.

McFadyen, Alistair I. "The Trinity and Human Individuality: The Conditions for Relevance." *Theology*. London: SPCK, 1992.
McGrath, Alistair E. *Reformation Thought: An Introduction*. 2nd edition. Oxford: Blackwell, 1993.
McNaspy, C. J. "Introduction to the Liturgy." In *The Documents of Vatican II*, edited by Walter M. Abbott, translated by Joseph Gallagher. London: Geoffrey Chapman, 1967.
McPartlan, Paul. *The Eucharist Makes the Church: Henri de Lubac and John Zizioulas in Dialogue*. Edinburgh: T&T Clark, 1993.
Menand, Louis. "The Culture Wars." *New York Review of Books*, October 6, 1994.
Meyendorff, John. Foreword to *Being As Communion: Studies in Personhood and the Church*, by John D. Zizioulas. London: Darton, Longman and Todd, 1985.
Milne, Bruce. *Know the Truth: A Handbook of Christian Belief*. 2nd edition. Nottingham: IVP, 1998. Reprinted in 2006.
Milton, Anthony. *Catholic and Reformed: The Roman and Protestant Churches in English Protestant Thought, 1600–1640*. Cambridge: Cambridge University Press, 1995.
Minear, Paul S. *Images of the Church in the New Testament*. London: Lutterworth Press, 1960.
Molnar, Paul D. *Divine Freedom and the Doctrine of the Immanent Trinity*. London: T&T Clark, 2002.
Moltmann, Jürgen. *The Church in the Power of the Spirit: A Contribution to Messianic Ecclesiology*. Translated by Margaret Kohl. London: SCM, 1977.
———. *The Crucified God: The Cross of Christ as the Foundation and Criticism of Christian Theology*. Translated by R. A. Wilson and John Bowden. London: SCM, 2001.
———. "Die einlande Einheit des dreieinigen Gottes." In *In der Geschichte des dreieinigen Gottes: Beiträge zur trinitarischen Theologie*. Munich: Kaiser, 1991, 11–21.
———. *Geist des Lebens: Ganzheitliche Pneumatologie* [The Spirit of Life]. Munich: Kaiser, 1991.
———. *God for a Secular Society: The Public Relevance of Theology*. Translated by Margaret Kohl. London: SCM, 1999.
———. *God in Creation: An Ecological Doctrine of Creation*. Translated by Margaret Kohl. London: SCM, 1985.
———. *History and the Triune God: Contributions to Trinitarian Theology*. Translated by John Bowden. London: SCM, 1991.
———. *The Spirit of Life: A Universal Affirmation*. Translated by Margaret Kohl. Minneapolis: Fortress, 1992.
———. *Theology and Joy*. Translated by Reinhard Ulrich. London: SCM, 1973.
———. *Theology of Hope*. Translated by James W. Leitch. London: SCM, 1967.
———. *The Trinity and the Kingdom: The Doctrine of God*. Translated by Margaret Kohl. Minneapolis: Fortress, 1993.
———. *The Way of Jesus Christ: Christology in Messianic Dimensions*. Translated by Margaret Kohl. London: SCM, 1990.
Moltmann-Wendel, Elisabeth, and Moltmann, Jürgen. *God—His and Hers*. Translated by John Bowden. London: SCM, 1991.
Moo, Douglas J. *The Epistle to the Romans*. Grand Rapids, MI: Eerdmans, 1996.
Morris, Leon. *The Gospel according to Matthew*. Leicester: IVP, 1995.

Müller, Christoph Gregor. *Gottes Pflanzug, Gottes Bau, Gottes Tempel: Die metaphorische Dimension paulinischer Gemeindetheologie in 1 Kor. 3, 5–17.* Frankfurt am Main: Verlag, 1995.
Muller, Richard A. *Post-Reformation Reformed Dogmatics*, vol. 3 and 4. Grand Rapids, MI: Baker, 2003. Reprinted in 2006.
Neuhaus, Richard John. "Moltmann Versus Monotheism." *Dialog* 20, no. 3 (1981) 239–43.
Newbigin, Lesslie. *The Household of God: Lectures on the Nature of the Church.* London: SCM, 1964.
———. *Trinitarian Doctrine for Today's Mission.* Eugene, OR: Wipf and Stock, 1988. Reprinted in 2006.
Nichols, Aidan. *The Thought of Pope Benedict XVI: An Introduction to the Theology of Joseph Ratzinger.* London: Burns and Oates, 2007.
Nicholls, David. "Divinity Analogy: The Theological Politics of John Donne." *Political Studies* 32, no. 4 (1984) 570–80.
———. "The Political Theology of John Donne." *Theological Studies* 49, no. 1 (1988) 45–66.
Nissiotis, Nikos. "The Importance of the Doctrine of the Trinity for Church Life and Theology." In *The Orthodox Ethos: Essays in Honour of the Centenary of the Greek Orthodox Archdiocese of North and South America*, edited by A. J. Philippou. Oxford: Holywell Press, 1964.
Oberman, Heiko A., "Quo vadis, Petre? Tradition from Irenæus to *Humani Generis*." In *The Dawn of the Reformation: Essays in Late Medieval and Early Reformation Thought.* Edinburgh: T&T Clark, 1986.
O'Donnell, John. "Pannenberg's Doctrine of God." *Gregorianum* 72 (1991) 73–98.
O'Leary, Paul Patrick. *The Triune Church: A Study in the Ecclesiology of A. S. Xomjakov.* Dublin: Dominican, 1982.
Olson, Roger. "Trinity and Eschatology: The Historical Being of God in Jürgen Moltmann and Wolfhart Pannenberg." *Scottish Journal of Theology* 36 (1983) 213–237.
Origen. *Commentary on the Epistle to the Romans, Book 6–10.* Vol. 104 of *The Fathers of the Church.* Translated by Thomas P. Scheck. Washington, DC: Catholic University of America Press, 2002.
———. "Selections of the Psalms." *The Fathers of the Church.* Washington DC: Catholic University of America Press, 2002.
———. Vol. 4 of *Ante-Nicene Fathers.* Edited by Alexander Roberts and James Donaldson. Peabody, MA: Hendrickson, 1995.
Owen, John. *Communion with God.* Edited by R. J. K Law. Edinburgh: Banner of Truth, 1991. Reprinted in 2000.
———. *The Works of John Owen*, vol. 2 and 6. Edited by William H. Goold. Edinburgh: Banner of Truth, 1965. Reprinted in 2004.
Pannenberg, Wolfhart. *Anthropology in Theological Perspective.* Translated by Matthew J. O'Connell. Edinburgh: T&T Clark, 1985.
———. *The Apostles' Creed: In the Light of Today's Questions.* Translated by Margaret Kohl. London: SCM, 1972.
———. *Christianity in a Secularized World.* Translated by John Bowden. London: SCM, 1989.
———. *Christian Spirituality and Sacramental Community.* London: Darton, Longman and Todd, 1984.

———. "Die Bedeutung der Eschatologie für das Verständnis der Apostolizität und Katholizität der Kirche." In *Katholizität und Apostolizität*, edited by R. Groscurth. Göttingen: Vandenhoeck and Ruprecht, 1971.

———. *An Introduction to Systematic Theology*. Edinburgh: T&T Clark, 1991.

———. *Jesus: God and Man*. Translated by Lewis L. Wilkins and Duane A. Priebe. London: SCM, 1968.

———. "Okumenisches Amtsverständnis." In *Ethik und Ekklesiologie*. Göttingen: Vandenhoeck and Ruprecht, 1977.

———. *Systematic Theology*, vol. 1-3. Translated by Geoffrey Bromiley. Edinburgh: T&T Clark, 1991.

———. "The Teaching Office and the Unity of the Church." In *The Future of Theology: Essays in Honour of Jürgen Moltmann*, edited by Miroslav Volf, Carmen Krieg, and Thomas Kucharz. Grand Rapids, MI: Eerdmans, 1996.

Park, Heon-Wook. "Die Vorstellung vom Leib Christi bei Paulus." Dissertation. Tübingen: University of Tübingen, 1988.

Paul, Robert S. "A Way to Wyn Them: Ecclesiology and Religion in the English Reformation." In *Reformatio Perennis: Essays on Calvin and the Reformation in Honour of Ford Lewis Battles*, edited by B. A. Gerrish and R. Benedetto. Pittsburgh: Pickwick, 1981.

Pearse, Meic. *The Great Restoration*. Carlisle: Paternoster, 1998.

Pelikan, Jaroslav. " 'Council or Father or Scripture': The Concept of Authority in the Theology of Maximus the Confessor." In *The Heritage of the Early Church: Essays in Honour of the Very Reverend George Vasilievich Florovsky*, edited by David Neiman and Margaret Schatkin. Orientalia Christiana Analecta 195. Rome: Pontificale Institutum Studiorum Orientalium, 1973.

Percival, Henry R. *The Seven Ecumenical Councils of the Undivided Church*. Edited by Philip Schaff and Henry Wace. Vol. 14 of *Nicene and Post-Nicene Fathers*. Peabody, MA: Hendrickson, 2004.

Perkins, William. *The Art of Prophesying*. Edinburgh: Banner of Truth, 1592. Reprinted in 1996.

Peters, Ted. *God as Trinity: Relationality and Temporality in Divine Life*. Louisville: Westminster John Knox, 1993.

Peterson, Erik. "Der Monotheismus als poltitisches Problem." In *Theologische Traktate*. Munich: Kösel, 1951.

Pieper, Josef. *Über die Liebe*. Munich: Kösel-Verlag, 1972.

Pinnock, Clark. "Systematic Theology." In *The Openness of God: A Biblical Challenge to the Traditional Understanding of God*. Carlisle: Paternoster, 1994.

Plantinga Pauw, Amy. "Personhood, Divine and Human." *Perspectives* 8, no. 2 (1993), cited in *Exclusion and Embrace: A Theological Exploration of Identity, Otherness and Reconciliation*, by Miroslav Volf. Nashville: Abingdon, 1996.

Prestige, G. L. *God in Patristic Thought*. London: SPCK, 1956.

Rahner, Karl. *The Trinity*. Translated by Joseph Donceel. New York: Crossroad, 2003.

Ranson, Guy H. "The Trinity and Society: A Unique Dimension of F. D. Maurice's Theology." *Religion in Life* 29, no. 1 (1959) 64-74.

Ratzinger, Joseph. *Called to Communion: Understanding the Church Today*. Translated by Aidan Walker. San Francisco: Ignatius, 1996.

———. *Church, Ecumenism and Politics: New Endeavours in Ecclesiology*. Translated by Michael J. Miller et al. San Francisco: Ignatius, 2008.

———. *Das neue Volk Gottes: Entwürfe zur Ekklesiologie*. Düsseldorf: Patmos, 1969.
———. "Demokratisierrung der Kirche?" In *Demokratie in der Kirche: Möglichkeiten, Grenzen, Gefahren*, edited by Joseph Ratzinger and Hans Maier. Limburg: Lahn, 1970.
———. *Die Geschtichtstheologie des Heiligen Bonaventura*. Munich: Schnell and Steiner, 1959.
———. *Eschatology, Death and Eternal Life*. Washington, DC: Catholic University of America Press, 1988.
———. *The Feast of Faith: Approaches to a Theology of the Liturgy*. San Francisco: Ignatius, 1986.
———. *Introduction to Christianity*. Translated by J. R. Foster. London: Search Press, 1971.
———. *Jesus of Nazareth: From the Baptism in the Jordan to the Transfiguration*. Translated by Adrian J. Walker. London: Bloomsbury, 2007.
———. "Kirche II, III." *Lexikon für Theologie und Kirche*, 6 (1957–67) 172–83.
———. *Offenbarung und Überlieferung*. Freiburg: Herder, 1965.
———. Preface to *Synthèse dogmatique: De la Trinité à la Trinité*, by Jean-Hervé Nicolas. Fribourg: Éditions Universitaires, 1985.
———. *Principles of Catholic Theology: Building Stones for a Fundamental Theology*. Translated by Mary Frances McCarthy. San Francisco: Ignatius, 1989.
———. *The Spirit of the Liturgy*. Translated by John Saward. Ignatius: San Francisco, 2000.
———. *Theologische Prinzipienlehre: Bausteine zur Fundamentaltheologie*. Munich: Erich Wewel, 1982.
———. *Volk und Haus Gottes in Augustins Lehre von der Kirche*. Münchener theologische Studien 2/7. Munich: Zink, 1954.
———. "Warum ich noch in der Kirche bin." In *Zwei Plädoyers*, edited by Hans Urs von Balthasar and Joseph Ratzinger. Munich: Kösel, 1970.
———. *Zur Gemeinschaft gerufen: Kirche heute verstehen*. Freiburg: Herder, 1991.
Ratzinger, Joseph, and Messori, Vittorio. *The Ratzinger Report: An Exclusive Interview on the State of the Church*. Translated by Salvator Attanasio and Graham Harrison. San Francisco: Ignatius, 1985.
Reid, J. K. S. "The Ratzinger Report." *Scottish Journal of Theology* 40 (1987) 125–33.
Reymond, Robert L. *A New Systematic Theology of the Christian Faith*. 2nd edition. Nashville: Thomas Nelson, 1998.
———. *What about Continuing Revelations and Miracles in the Presbyterian Church Today?* Phillipsburg, PA: P&R, 1977.
Robertson, O. Palmer. *The Final Word: A Biblical Response to the Case for Tongues and Prophecy Today*. Edinburgh: Banner of Truth, 1993. Reprinted in 2004.
Robinson, John. *The Works of John Robinson*. 3 vols. Edited by Robert Ashton. London: John Snow, 1851.
Roman Catholic Church. *Catechism of the Catholic Church*. London: Burns and Oates, 2000. Reprinted in 2010.
Russell, Letty M. *Church in the Round: Feminist Interpretation of the Church*. Louisville: Westminster John Knox, 1993.
Salmond, S. D. F. Prologue for *Hilary of Poitiers, John of Damascus*. Edited by Philip Schaff and Henry Wace. Vol. 9 of *Nicene and Post-Nicene Fathers*. Peabody, MA: Hendrickson, 1995.

Schaff, Philip. *Nicene and Post-Nicene Fathers*. Peabody, MA: Hendrickson, 1995.

———. Prolegomena to vol. 3 of *Nicene and Post-Nicene Fathers*. Edited by Philip Schaff and Henry Wace. Peabody, MA: Hendrickson, 1995.

Scholz, Heinrich. *Eros and Caritas: Die platonische Liebe und die Liebe im sinne des Christentums*. Halle, 1929.

Schleiermacher, Friedrich. *The Christian Faith*. Edinburgh: T&T Clark, 1928.

Schneider, A. Michael, III. "Prayer Regulated by God's Word." In *Worship in the Presence of God*, edited Frank J. Smith and David C. Lachman. Greenville: Greenville Presbyterian Theological Seminary, 1992.

Scholion. "Ecclesiastical Hierarchy." In *A Thirteenth Century Textbook of Mystical Theology at the University of Paris*, edited by Anastasius (the librarian). Paris: University of Paris.

Scholz, Heinrich. *Eros and Caritas: Die platonische Liebe und die Liebe im sinne des Christentums*. Halle, 1929.

Schüssler-Fiorenza, Elisabeth. *Bread Not Stone: The Challenge of Feminist Biblical Interpretation*. Boston: Beacon, 1984.

———. *Jesus: Miriam's Child, Sophia's Prophet*. London: SCM, 1995.

———. "Women in the Pre-Pauline and Pauline Churches." *Union Seminary Quarterly Review* 33 (1978) 153–66.

Schwandt, Thomas A. *Dictionary of Qualitative Inquiry*. 2nd edition. London: Sage, 2001.

Schwartz, Regina M. *The Curse of Cain: The Violent Legacy of Monotheism*. Chicago: University of Chicago Press, 1997.

Schweizer, Eduard. *The Good News according to Matthew*. Translated by David E. Green. London: SPCK, 1982.

Schwöbel, Christoph. "Die Suche nach Gemeinschaft Gründe, Überlegungen und Empfehlungen." In *Die Kirche Als Gemeinschaft: Lutherische Beiträge Zur Ekklesiologie*, by Heinrich Holze. Stuttgart: Verlag, 1998.

———. "The Quest for Communion: Reasons, Reflections and Recommendations." In *The Church as Communion: Lutheran Contributions to Ecclesiology (LWF Documentation No. 42)*, edited by H. Holze. Geneva: Lutheran World Foundation, 1997.

———. "Radical Monotheism and the Trinity." *Neue Zeitschrift fur systematische Theologie und Religionsphilosophie* 43 (2001) 54–74.

———. *Trinitarian Theology Today: Essays in Divine Being and Act*. Edinburgh: T&T Clark, 1995.

Shantz, Douglas. "The Place of the Resurrected Christ in the Writings of John Smyth." *Baptist Quarterly* 30 (April 1984) 199–203.

Siebel, Wiegand. *Der Heilige Geist als Relation: Eine soziale Trinitätslehre*. Münster: Aschendorff, 1986.

Siefrid, Mark A. "Romans." In *Commentary on the New Testament Use of the Old Testament*, edited by G. K. Beale and D. A. Carson. Grand Rapids, MI: Baker, 2007.

Skinner, Quentin. *Regarding Method*. Vol. 1 of *Visions of Politics*. Cambridge: Cambridge University Press, 2002.

Smyth, John. *The Works of John Smyth*, vol. 1 and 2. Edited by W. T. Whitely. Cambridge: Cambridge University Press, 1915.

Sobrino, Jon. *Christology at the Crossroads*. New York: Orbis, 1978.

———. *Jesus the Liberator: A Historical-Theological Reading of Jesus of Nazareth*. Translated by P. Burns and F. McDonagh. Maryknoll, NY: Orbis, 1993.

Sprunger, Keith. "English Puritans and Anabaptists." *Mennonite Quarterly Review* 46 (1972) 113–28.
Stallsworth, Paul T. "The Story of an Encounter." In *Biblical Interpretation in Crisis: The Ratzinger Conference on the Bible and the Church*, edited by Richard John Neuhaus. Grand Rapids, MI: Eerdmans, 1989.
Staniloae, Dumitru. *Orthodox Dogmatic Theology: The Experience of God*, vol. 1. Translated by Robert Barringer and Iona Ionita. Edinburgh: T&T Clark, 2000.
———. *Orthodoxe Dogmatik*. Translated by H. Pitters. Vol. 12 and 15 of *Ökumenische Theologie*. Einsiedeln: Benziger, 1984.
———. "Trinitarian Relations and the Life of the Church." In *Theology and the Church*, translated by Robert Barringer, pp. 11–44. Crestwood, NY: St. Vladimir's Seminary, 1980.
Steinfels, Peter. "Beliefs." *New York Times*, June 13, 1998. http://query.nytimes.com/gst/fullpage.html?res=9D05E7DD163DF930A25755C0A96E958260&sec=&spon=&pagewanted=1.
Stott, John. *Calling Christian Leaders: Biblical Models of Church, Gospel and Ministry*. Leicester: IVP, 2002.
———. *The Living Church: Convictions of a Lifelong Pastor*. Nottingham: IVP, 2007.
Studer, Basil. "Der Person-Begriff in der frühen kirchenamtlichen Trinitätslehre." In *Theologie und Philosophie* 57 (1982) 161–77.
Taylor, Charles. "The Politics of Recognition." In *Multiculturalism: Examining the Politics of Recognition*, edited by Amy Gutmann. Princeton, NJ: Princeton University Press, 1994.
Tertullian. *Latin Christianity: Its Founder, Tertullian*. Edited by Alexander Roberts and James Donaldson. Vol. 3 of *Ante-Nicene Fathers*. Peabody, MA: Hendrickson, 1995.
———. "De pudicitia" [On Modesty]. An unfinished work of Tertullian. Translated by Gösta Claesson. Tertullian Project. http://www.tertullian.org/articles/claesson_pudicitia_translation.htm
Thiselton, Anthony C. *1 Corinthians: A Shorter Exegetical and Pastoral Commentary*. Grand Rapids, MI: Eerdmans, 2006.
Thunberg, Lars. *Man and the Cosmos: The Vision of St. Maximus the Confessor*. New York: St. Vladimir's, 1985.
Törönen, Melchisedec. *Union and Distinction in the Thought of St. Maximus the Confessor*. Oxford: Oxford University Press, 2007.
Torrance, Thomas F. *The Christian Doctrine of God: One Being Three Persons*. London: T&T Clark, 1996. Reprinted in 2006.
———. *The Trinitarian Faith*. Edinburgh: T&T Clark, 1993.
———. *Trinitarian Perspectives: Toward Doctrinal Agreement*. Edinburgh: T&T Clark, 1994.
Troeltsch, Ernst. *The Social Teaching of Christian Churches*. Translated by Olive Wyon. London: George Allen and Unwin, 1931.
Turescu, Lucian. " 'Person' Versus 'Individual' and Other Modern Misreadings of Gregory of Nyssa." In *Re-thinking Gregory of Nyssa*, edited by Sarah Coakley. Oxford: Blackwell, 2003.
Turner, Nigel. *A Grammar of New Testament Greek*. Vol. 3, *Syntax*. Edinburgh: T&T Clark, 1963.
Van Dixhoorn, Chad. "The Making of the Westminster Larger Catechism." Highway. http://www.the-highway.com/larger-catechism_Dixhoorn.html.

Van Leeuwen, Mary Stewart. *Gender and Grace: Love, Work, and Parenting in a Changing World*. Downers Grove, IL: IVP, 1991.

Volf, Miroslav. "After Moltmann: Reflections on Future Eschatology." In *God Will Be All in All: The Eschatology of Jürgen Moltmann*, edited by Richard Bauckham. Edinburgh: T&T Clark, 1999.

———. *After Our Likeness: The Church as the Image of the Trinity*. Grand Rapids, MI: Eerdmans, 1998.

———. "Being as God Is: Trinity and Generosity." In *God's Life in Trinity*, edited by Miroslav Volf and Michael Welker. Minneapolis: Fortress, 2006.

———. "Catholicity of 'Two or Three': Free Church Reflections on the Catholicity of the Local Church." *Jurist* 52 (1992) 525–46.

———. "Christian Identity and Difference: About the Character of a Christian Presence in Modern Societies." Translated by Frank Dominik for K. J. Bidwell. "Christliche Identität und Differenz: Zur Eigenhart der christlichen Präsenz in den modernen Gesellschaften." *Zeitschrift für Theologie und Kirche* 3 (1995) 356–74.

———. Christliche Identität und Differenz: Zur Eigenhart der christlichen Präsenz in den modernen Gesellschaften." *Zeitschrift für Theologie und Kirche* 3 (1995) 357–75.

———. "The Church as a Prophetic Community and Sign of Hope." In *Worship, Adoration and Action*, edited by D. A. Carson. Grand Rapids, MI: Baker, 1993. Also published in *European Journal of Theology* 2, no. 1 (1993) 9–30.

———. "Church, State and Society: Reflections on the Life of the Church in Contemporary Yugoslavia." *Transformation* 6, no. 1 (1989) 24–31.

———. "Community Formation as an Image of the Triune God: A Congregational Model of Church Order and Life." In *Community Formation in the Early Church and in the Church Today*, edited by Richard Longenecker. Peabody, MA: Hendrickson, 2002.

———. "Doing and Interpreting: An Examination of the Relationship between Theory and Practice in Latin American Liberation Theology." *Themelios* 8, no. 3 (1983) 11–19.

———. *The End of Memory: Remembering Rightly in a Violent World*. Grand Rapids, MI: Eerdmans, 2006.

———. *Exclusion and Embrace: A Theological Exploration of Identity, Otherness and Reconciliation*. Nashville: Abingdon, 1996.

———. *Free of Charge: Giving and Receiving in a Culture Stripped of Grace*. Grand Rapids, MI: Zondervan, 2005.

———. "Introduction: A Queen and Beggar; Challenges and Prospects of Theology." In *The Future of Theology: Essays in Honour of Jürgen Moltmann*, edited by Miroslav Volf, Carmen Krieg, and Thomas Kucharz. Grand Rapids, MI: Eerdmans, 1996.

———. "The Nature of the Church." *Evangelical Review of Theology* 26, no. 1 (2002) 68–75.

———. "On Loving with Hope: Eschatology and Social Responsibility." *Transformation* 7, no. 3 (1990) 28–31.

———. Personal Profile. Yale Divinity School. http://www.yale.edu/divinity/faculty/Fac.MVolf.shtml.

———. "A Response to Robert Goudzwaard: Market, Central Planning and Participatory Economy." *Transformation* 4, no. 3 (1987) 60–63.

———. "Responses to Democracy: A Christian Imperative." *Transformation* 7, no. 4 (1990) 166–77.
———. "The Social Meaning of Reconciliation." *Transformation* 16, no. 1 (1999) 158–72.
———. "Soft Difference: Theological Reflections on the Relation between Church and Culture in 1 Peter." *Ex Auditu: Journal of the North Park Symposium on the Theological Interpretation of Scripture* 10 (1994) 15–30.
———. "Theology for a Way of Life." In *Practicing Theology: Beliefs and Practices in Christian Life*, edited by Miroslav Volf and Dorothy C. Bass. Grand Rapids, MI: Eerdmans, 2002.
———. "Theology, Meaning and Power." In *The Future of Theology: Essays in Honour of Jürgen Moltmann*, edited by Miroslav Volf, Carmen Krieg, and Thomas Kucharz. Grand Rapids, MI: Eerdmans, 1996.
———. *Trinität und Gemeinschaft: Eine ökumenische Ekklesiologie*. Mainz: Verlag, 1996.
———. "Trinity, Unity, Primacy on the Trinitarian Nature of Unity and Its Implications for the Question of Primacy." In *Petrine Ministry and the Unity of the Church "Toward a Patient and Fraternal Dialogue,"* edited by James F. Puglisi. Collegeville, MN: Liturgical Press, 1999.
———. "The Trinity Is Our Social Program: The Doctrine of the Trinity and the Shape of Social Engagement." *Modern Theology* 14 (July 1998) 403–423.
———. "When Gospel and Culture Intersect: Notes on the Nature of Christian Difference." *Evangelical Review of Theology* 22, no. 3(1998) 96–207.
———. "When the Unclean Spirit Leaves: The Tasks of the Eastern European Churches After the 1989 Revolution." *European Journal of Theology* 1, no. 1 (1992) 13–24.
———. *Work in the Spirit: Toward a Theology of Work*. Eugene, OR: Wipf and Stock, 2001.
———. "Worship as Adoration and Action: Reflections on a Christian Way of Being in the World." In *Worship, Adoration and Action*, edited by D. A. Carson. Grand Rapids, MI: Baker, 1993.
Volf, Miroslav, and Katerberg, William, eds. *The Future of Hope: Christian Tradition Amid Modernity and Postmodernity*. Grand Rapids, MI: Eerdmans, 2004.
Volf, Miroslav, Krieg, Carmen, and Kucharz, Thomas, eds. *The Future of Theology: Essays in Honour of Jürgen Moltmann*. Grand Rapids, MI: Eerdmans, 1996.
Volf, Miroslav, and Welker, Michael, eds. *God's Life in Trinity*. Minneapolis: Fortress, 2006.
Vos, Geerhardus. *Biblical Theology: Old and New Testaments*. Edinburgh: Banner of Truth, 1948. Reprinted in 2004.
Wainwright, Arthur W. *The Trinity in the New Testament*. London: SPCK, 1962. Reprinted in 1975.
Walls, Andrew F. *The Missionary Movement in Christian History: Studies in the Transmission of Faith*. Maryknoll, NY: Orbis, 1996.
Ware, Timothy. *The Orthodox Church*. London: Penguin, 1963.
Weber, Max. "Die protestantischen Sekten und der Geist des Kapitalismus." In *Gesam—melte Aufsätze zur Religionssoziologie I*. Tübingen: Mohr, 1963.
Weber, Otto. *Versammelte Gemeinde: Beiträge zum Gespräch über die Kirche und Gottesdienst*. Neukirchen: Buchhandlung des Erziehungsvereins, 1949.
Weinandy, Thomas G. *Does God Change? The Word's Becoming in the Incarnation*. Still River, MA: St. Bede's, 1985.

———. *Does God Suffer?* Edinburgh: T&T Clark, 2000.

Welker, Michael. *Gottes Geist: Theologie des Heiligen Geistes.* Neukirchen-Vluyn: Neukirchener Verlag, 1992.

Wendelbourg, Dorothea. "Person und Hypostase: Zur Trinitätslehre der neueren orthodoxen Theologie," cited in *Vernunft des Glaubens: Wissenschaftliche Theologie und kirchliche Lehre, Festschrift zum, 60. Geburstag von Wolfhart Pannenberg*, edited by J. Rohls and G. Wenz. Göttingen: Vandenhoeck and Ruprecht, 1988.

Westminster Assembly. *The Westminster Confession of Faith: The Larger and Shorter Catechisms of the Westminster Assembly with Scripture References.* Glasgow: Free Presbyterian Publications, 2001.

White, B. R. "The Development of the Doctrine of the Church among the English Separatists with Especial Reference to Robert Browne and John Smyth." PhD thesis, Oxford University, 1960.

———. *The English Baptists of the Seventeenth Century.* Didcot: Baptist Historical Society, 1996.

———. *The English Separatist Tradition: From the Marian Martyrs to the Pilgrim Fathers.* Oxford: Oxford University Press, 1971.

———. "The English Separatists and John Smyth Revisited." *Baptist Quarterly* 30 (October 1984) 344–47.

Whitely, W. T. *The Works of John Smyth*, vol. 1 and 2. Cambridge: Cambridge University Press, 1915.

Wilks, John G. F. "The Trinitarian Ontology of John Zizioulas." *Vox Evangelicala* 25 (1995) 63–88.

Williams, Rowan D. "Barth on the Triune God." In *Karl Barth: Studies of His Theological Method*, edited by S. W. Sykes. Oxford: Clarendon, 1979.

———. Foreword to *Communion and Otherness: Further Studies in Personhood and the Church*, by John D. Zizioulas. London: T&T Clark, 2006.

———. "Interiority and Epiphany: A Reading in the New Testament Ethics." *Modern Theology* 13, no. 1 (1997) 29–52.

———. *On Christian Theology: Challenges in Contemporary Theology.* Oxford: Blackwell, 2000.

Young, William Paul. *The Shack: Where Tragedy Confronts Eternity.* London: Hodder and Stoughton, 2008.

Zizioulas, John D. *Being as Communion: Studies in Personhood and the Church.* London: Darton, Longman and Todd, 1985.

———. "The Bishop in the Theological Doctrine of the Orthodox Church." *Kanon* 7 (1985) 23–35.

———. "Christologie et existence: La Dialectique créé-incréé et la dogme de Chalcédoine." *Contacts* 36 (1984) 154–72.

———. *Communion and Otherness: Further Studies in Personhood and the Church.* Edinburgh: T&T Clark, 2006.

———. "The Contribution of Cappadocia to Christian Thought." In *Sinasos in Cappadocia*, edited by Frosso Pimenides and Stelios Roïdes. London: Ekdoseis Agra, 1985.

———. "Die pneumatologische Dimension der Kirche." *Internationale Katholische Zeitschrift "Communio"* 2 (1973) 133–47.

———. "Die Welt in eucharistischer Schau und der Mensch von heute." *Una Sancta* 25 (1970) 342–49.

———. "The Early Christian Community." In *Christian Spirituality: Origins to the Twelfth Century*, edited by B. McGinn and John Meyendorff. New York: Crossroad, 1985.

———. "The Ecclesiological Presuppositions of the Holy Eucharist." *Nicolaus* 10 (1982) 333–49.

———. "Episkope and Episkopos in the Early Church: A Brief Survey of the Evidence." In *Episcopé and Episcopate in Ecumenical Perspective: Faith and Order Papers 102*. Geneva: World Council of Churches, 1980.

———. "Human Capacity and Incapacity: A Theological Exploration of Personhood." *Scottish Journal of Theology* 28 (1985) 401–448.

———. "La Mystére de l'Église dans la tradition orthodoxe." *Irénikon* 60 (1987) 171–212.

———. "La Relation de l'hellenisme et du christianisme et le problem de la mort: La réponse de Jean Zizioulas." *Contacts* 37 (1985) 60–72.

———. "L'Eucharistie: Quelques bibliques." In *L'eucharistie, Églises en Dialogue*, edited by John D. Zizioulas, J. M. R. Tillard, and J. J. Von Allmen. Paris: Mame, 1970.

———. "Some Reflections on Baptism, Confirmation and Eucharist." *Sobornost* 5 (1969) 644–52.

———. "The Teaching of the Second Ecumenical Council on the Holy Spirit in Historical and Ecumenical Perspective." In *Credo in Spiritum Sanctum: Atti del congresso teologico international di pneumatologiia*, edited by José Saraiva Martins. Vatican: Libreria Editrice Vaticana, 1983.

———. *Eucharist, Bishop, Church: The Unity of the Church in the Divine Eucharist and the Bishop during the First Three Centuries*. Translated by Elizabeth Theokritoff. Brookline, MA: Holy Cross Orthodox Press, 2001.

Scripture Index

Genesis
1–2   54, 203
17:10–12   71

Matthew
5:48   48
7:21–3   178
16:13–20   31, 120, 180
18:15–20   51, 59–60, 66, 76, 81, 180
18:20   65–67, 75–76, 173–74, 176, 179–84, 194, 233, 238
28:19   91, 193, 209, 239

John
1:14–18   172
5:19   94
10:30   94
10:38   48, 196
14:10–11   48, 196
15:5   94
17:11   94
17:21   48, 196
17:22   94

Acts
2:17–21   214
2:39   71

Romans
8:32   18N35
10:8–10   189, 191
10:14–17   190
12:6   214
14:1—15:13   48
15:19   191

1 Corinthians
3:9–17   171
10:17   97
11:2–16   54, 218
11:20   136
12:12–13   135, 139
12:27   114
12–14   186, 214, 219–24

2 Corinthians
1:3–4   211
8:1—9:15   211
10:1   211
13:14   211

Galatians
2:20	191
3:28	37–38, 54, 218

Philippians
4:15	214

Ephesians
1:22	114
5:21–33	38, 54, 175

Colossians
1:15	170
1:18	175

Thessalonians
1:5	191

1 Peter
4:10	214

Revelation
11:15	49
21–22	193

Index of Names

Afanasiev (Afanassieff), Nicholas, 124
Anglican Consultative Council, 9, 165
Athanasius, 2, 125, 206, 245
Augustine, 2, 67, 79, 93, 95, 97, 104, 106, 110–11, 115–18, 120, 122, 132, 148, 150–53, 156, 201, 206
Ayres, Lewis, 151
Balthasar, Hans Urs von, 93, 120, 144, 149, 169
Barnes, Michel René, 150
Barrett, C. K., 186, 190–91
Basil of Caesarea, 2, 28, 127, 129, 131, 151, 206
Bauckham, Richard, 204, 232
Bavinck, Herman, 164
Beale, G. K., 190–91
Brachlow, Stephen, 6, 62–64, 70, 80, 82, 84–85
Burgess, Walter H., 63, 66, 68–69, 71–72
Burrage, Champlin, 67–70, 84
Calvin, John, 59–61, 72, 149, 156, 159, 170–71, 176–77, 180, 182–83, 222
Carson, D. A., 180, 190, 220–22

Clement of Rome, 223–28
Coakley, Sarah, 150–52
Cyprian, 97, 173–74, 186–87, 193
Davies, W. D., and Allison, Dale C., 65, 71, 181–82
de Lubac, Henri, 98, 120
de Régnon, Theodore, 150, 153–54
Dexter, Henry Martyn, 58, 63, 69–70, 83
Eusebius, 224
Giles, Kevin, 243
Gregory of Nazianzus, 2, 28, 131, 151–53, 167, 206, 239
Gregory of Nyssa, 2, 28, 150–51, 206
Guardini, Romano, 97, 106, 120
Gundry, Robert, H., 37, 173–75
Gundry-Volf, Judith M., 8, 24, 36–40
Gunton, Colin E., 2–3, 48, 143, 145, 149, 151–52, 161, 200, 206
Hilary of Poitiers, 206
Hunsinger, George, 205
Ignatius, 128, 173–74, 177, 179, 223
Irenaeus, 120, 173, 179
Jenson, Robert W., 1, 29, 46, 143, 145, 161

John of Damascus, 2, 48, 54, 206–207
Kärkkäinen, Velli-Matti, 3, 148, 163, 204
Kasper, Walter, 29, 234
Keller, Timothy, 210
Kilby, Karen, 130, 151, 199
LaCugna, Catherine Mowry, 8, 12, 24, 35–6, 40
Lane, A. N. S., 155–56, 207
Lee, Jason K., 53, 57, 61, 63, 71–72, 82, 87, 88, 226–27
Letham, Robert, vii–viii, 3, 24, 29, 33, 46, 79, 133, 148, 150, 153–54, 156, 204, 206–7, 209, 239, 249, 253
Lossky, Vladimir, 148, 152, 170
Louth, Andrew, 153, 167–68, 207
Luther, Martin, 30, 44, 104, 159, 164, 177, 216, 176, 229
Maximus the Confessor, 124–25, 129, 167–71
McGrath, Alistair E., 156, 158
Meyendorff, John, 90, 152
Minear, Paul S., 114, 163
Molnar, Paul D., 201, 240
Moltmann, Jürgen.
    Charismatic Ecclesiology, 186, 188, 216, 220, 222
    Differences with Wolfhart Pannenberg, 25, 32–34, 40
    Differences with John D. Zizioulas, 131–32, 144, 202, 237
    Eshatology, 232
    General Theology, 16, 18, 35–36

Hermeneutic, vii, 158–59, 161, 204, 207
Influence Upon Miroslav Volf's Paradigm, 4–5, 8–9, 12–15, 17, 19, 29, 55, 194–95, 203, 209, 215, 235
Liberation, 55, 89
Social Trinity, 16, 20–23, 53–55, 130, 147, 154, 157, 198, 201, 205
Theological Paradigm, 22
Müller, Christoph Gregor, 166
Nichols, Aidan, 45, 97–100, 119–121
O'Donnell, John, 26, 202
Olson, Roger, 33, 209, 255
Origen, 18, 27–28, 167, 171, 193
Owen, John, 77, 79, 149, 211
Pannenberg, Wolfhart,
    Agreement with John D. Zizioulas, 143
    Ecclesiology, 27, 30–31
    Differences with Moltmann, 32–33, 145
    Differences with Volf, 34–35, 40, 145, 161
    Trinity, 27–30, 145, 212
    Volf's References, 8, 12, 25–6, 29, 194, 197, 202
Peters, Ted, 35, 45, 108, 130, 192, 204
Peterson, Erik, 108, 130, 192
Rahner, Karl, 1, 29, 35, 103, 132
Ratzinger, Joseph.
    Anti-Free Church, 98, 106
    Apostles' Creed, 91, 95, 121, 149, 155

Augustine, 93–95, 115–19
Christology, 139, 161
Church as an Image of the
    Trinity, 121, 237
Eucharist, 99–101
Faith, 99
Petrine Office, 103–104, 114
Sacramental, 96, 100, 109,
Trinity, 91–95, 107, 115,
    117–19, 122, 152, 23
Unity, 120, 145, 199
Ratzinger, Joseph, and Messori,
    Vittorio, 90, 103–4, 121
Reid, J. K. S., 90, 102
Robinson, John, 62, 64–66, 71–72,
    83, 85
Schaff, Philip, 167
Schleiermacher, Friedrich, 184
Schüssler-Fiorenza, 24, 39–40, 221
Schwartz, Regina M., 47–48,
    202–203
Schweizer, Eduard, 181–82
Schwöbel, Christoph, 130, 143, 145,
    161, 164, 205
Siefrid, Mark A., 190
Skinner, Quentin, 85
Smyth, John.
    Baptism, 69–72
    Changing Theology, 63–64,
        67, 71, 82–83, 88, 182,
        236
    Congregational, 66, 80, 86,
        173, 233
    Hermeneutic, 81, 159, 183,
        233
    Historical Context, 57
    Separatist, viii, 8, 58, 61, 70
    Trinity, 77–79

Staniloae, Dumitru, 29, 173 179,
    193, 197, 205
Tertullian, 174, 180, 194
Thiselton, Anthony C., 219, 222
Törönen, Melchisedec, 169
Torrance, Thomas F., 2–3, 79, 149,
    201
Volf, Miroslav.
    Anti-Hierarchical, 53, 112,
        98–99, 218
    Charismatic Ecclesiology, 222
    Hermeneutic, 159, 217–18
    Liberation, 50, 208
    Moltmann's Influence, 13–14
    Theological Paradigm, viii,
        55–56, 86–88, 159
    Tritheistic Tendencies, 205,
        212
Welker, Michael, 1, 187
Ware, Timothy, 77, 108, 152–53
    146–48, 165, 155, 198, 219,
    222
Weinandy, Thomas G., 201
Westminster Assembly, 63, 156, 155
White, B. R., 57, 60–69, 71–72, 77,
    83–84
Whitely, W. T., 63–69, 71, 77, 8
Williams, Rowan D., 49, 55, 90
Zizioulas, John D.
    Apostolic Succession, 127
    Baptism, 124
    Bishop and the Church, 126,
        137
    Church as an Image of the
        Trinity, 3, 7, 48, 166
    Disagreement with Volf, 129,
        131, 140, 145–47, 160,
        236

Eucharist, 136, 237
Incarnation, 135
Trinity, 130, 132–34, 141–46,
    151, 161, 216, 237
Zizioulas School, 143–45, 161

www.ingramcontent.com/pod-product-compliance
Lightning Source LLC
Chambersburg PA
CBHW070338230426

43663CB00011B/2369